MERRILL JENSEN
Vilas Research Professor of History
University of Wisconsin
ADVISORY EDITOR TO DODD, MEAD & COMPANY

THE DISUNITED STATES

The Era of Civil War and Reconstruction

THE
DISUNITED
STATES

The Era of Civil War
and Reconstruction

THOMAS H. O'CONNOR

Boston College

Dodd, Mead & Company

New York   1973   Toronto

LIBRARY OF CONGRESS CATALOG CARD NUMBER: 76–184193
ISBN: 0–396–06547–3

SECOND PRINTING

PRINTED IN THE UNITED STATES OF AMERICA

ILLUSTRATION CREDITS

CHAPTER
1. The New York Historical Society, New York City
2. Harry T. Peters Collection, The Museum of the City of New York
3. The New York Public Library
4. Brown Brothers
5. Boatmen's National Bank of St. Louis
6. The Museum of the City of New York
7. Brown Brothers
8. The New York Public Library
9. The New York Public Library
10. The New York Public Library
11. Brown Brothers
12. Library of Congress
13. The New York Public Library
14. The Bettmann Archive
15. The New York Public Library

To Mary

CONTENTS

MAPS

FOREWORD

In the United States the second half of the nineteenth century opened against the background of an unpopular war in a foreign land (the Mexican War), brought about by an unpopular President (James K. Polk), according to what some considered unconstitutional procedures, and conducted for what many believed to be immoral purposes. It was a time of rapid change: factories were replacing fields, towns were growing into cities, intellectuals were becoming alienated from their government and their society, and foreign-born immigrants were experiencing bigotry and persecution. Clergymen led humanitarian crusades, liberated women fought for their rights, bearded youths clamored for universal reform, and agitators demanded freedom for the black man.

It was a time when Presidents were selected because of their availability rather than for brilliance of mind or integrity of spirit, and when young political radicals tried in vain to wrest control of their parties from the withered hands of older leaders. In less than a decade after 1850 the issues dividing the nation became so intense that when it came time to elect a President of the United States in 1860 hardly any American could stay out of the controversy. The failure of compromise, the polarization of politics, and the all-consuming issue of race led directly to the disruption of the Union and the coming of the Civil War.

This war touched every village and family, ravaged the land, and transformed the economy of the nation. It sparked widespread riots over the injustices of conscription, and it touched off heated debates about the role of the black American in the democratic process. It raised searching questions concerning the powers of the President in time of war, and it posed serious problems about the authority of government in peacetime. It set the stage for large-scale industrial expansion; it paved the way for new political alliances between the North and the South; and it led the black man to expect a level of social and political equality that the nation was not willing to concede.

The Civil War period has long held a prominent place in American-history scholarship, and a distinguished list of teachers and historians have helped to insure that this time-honored prominence will never be disturbed. In recent years, however, many students have become skeptical about the relevance of this particular phase of history to the contemporary scene. They are often hostile to studying the conflict, which they regard as a glorification of war. There are historians, too, who raise their eyebrows at the unusual popular interest in this period and who question the professional integrity of many writers in the field. Some of their reservations are based upon assumptions that Civil War history is a romantic enterprise engaged in by devoted antiquarians or amateur military buffs who pay little attention to professional methods and procedures.

As a result, whether they view it as romantic nonsense in a world of urgent crisis, or as unprofessional trivia in the hallowed realm of scholarship, students may reluctantly concede the entrenched position of Civil War history but fail to see either its relationship to contemporary issues or its contribution to their own educational experience. One reason, perhaps, why the Civil War period has failed to sustain interest among students is that many historians have focused on highly specialized topics that obscure the War's relationship with the past and its meaning for the present. Research in specialized areas is essential to historical scholarship, but it is also necessary to maintain historical perspective by viewing individual topics in the light of their broader implications.

It is my hope that this brief volume can provide for the college and university instructor a general, overall summary of the major events of this controversial period. In favoring a very broad approach which encompasses the causes of the Civil War, the out-standing developments of the War itself, and the most significant consequences of the Reconstruction period, instead of concen-trating on any one of these particular phases, the work may serve as a useful supplement for introductory courses in American his-tory as well as a convenient text for more advanced courses.

I believe that by using a wider lens on the panorama of the Civil War period it can be demonstrated that although this was, indeed, our greatest national trauma—complete with startling contrasts of tragedy and comedy, bravery and cowardice, strengths and weaknesses—it should not be brushed aside or hidden away. The period should be examined slowly and care-fully to understand what it meant *then* and what it might have to say for *now.*

It is impossible and unreasonable to consider the course of American history without taking into account the Civil War. It *did* happen. There were reasons why it happened, and there were consequences of the crisis that have affected the life and thought of successive generations. This volume will attempt to analyze why the crisis occurred when it did and how it did, and to de-scribe the way the tragic events ran their course, so that one may speculate on the long-range consequences the Civil War trauma continues to have on American life and society.

THOMAS H. O'CONNOR

*On February 5, 1850, Henry Clay followed up his compromise pro-
posals of a week earlier with a two-day speech in which he appealed
to the North for concession and to the South for peace. For several
days it was known that Clay would speak, and the Senate floor and
galleries were crowded with men and women who came from great
distances to hear the famous seventy-three-year-old statesman. This
was the last time that the celebrated triumvirate of the Senate—
Clay, Calhoun, and Webster—would appear together to debate a
national issue. Calhoun died within the month; and Clay and Webster
were among the pallbearers at his funeral in the Senate chamber.*

→

A S THE nineteenth century neared the halfway point, it was apparent that the United States had grown from a small, rural, seacoast republic into a large and impressive nation whose cultural horizons had expanded tremendously and whose physical growth had been matched by technological achievements.

By the late 1840's Ralph Waldo Emerson was publishing his "Poems," and his close friend Henry David Thoreau was writing his impressions about the week he spent on the banks of the Concord and Merrimack Rivers and reflecting upon the nature of civil disobedience. In 1847 Nathaniel Hawthorne completed *The Scarlet Letter,* Henry Wadsworth Longfellow published *Evangeline,* John Greenleaf Whittier became corresponding editor for the *National Era,* and James Russell Lowell sent off the first of his "Biglow Papers" to the *Boston Courier.* Herman Melville had just finished his writings about the South Pacific and was starting out in search of his great white whale, Walt Whitman was working on his *Leaves of Grass,* and Edgar Allan Poe was making his way through a tragic labyrinth of poetry, loneliness, and destruction. William Hickling Prescott produced his famous work on the conquest of Peru in 1847, and that same year he persuaded his friend, John Motley, to turn his talents from state department diplomacy to the study of history. Young Francis Parkman entertained readers of the *Knickerbocker* magazine with tales of his adventures in California and along the Oregon Trail, and the following year began what was to become a lifetime's labor on the French and Indian wars.

Mechanical invention kept pace with intellectual creativity during the late 1840's and clearly stepped up the tempo of American life. In 1846 Elias Howe patented his sewing machine, and the following year Cyrus McCormick opened up a factory in Chicago for the production of his mechanical reapers. George Page produced the revolving disc harrow which helped to reduce the burden of plowing, and John Heath finished his work on the automatic binder which mechanized the harvesting of grain. John Roebling spanned the Monongahela River with the most daring suspension bridge yet built, and Richard Hoe invented the rotary printing press which revolutionized the printing industry. Telegraph communications were established between New York and Chicago in 1848, the Associated Press was organized by a group of New York newspapers, and A. T. Stewart put up the first department store on Broadway. On October 16, 1846, Dr. William Morton performed the first public surgical operation using ether at the Massachusetts General Hospital, and in 1847 the American Medical Association was founded at Philadelphia.

The Woman's Rights movement was nearing its climax in the East, while Brigham Young and his Mormon followers were reaching the end of their famous trek across the Western plains and mountains to the Great Salt Lake. In November of 1847 American newspapers carried accounts of the massacre of Marcus Whitman and his party by Oregon Indians; and the next month an Illinois Whig named Abraham Lincoln took his seat as a member of the Thirtieth Congress.

The closing years of the 1840's also marked the end of the war between the United States and Mexico and the fulfillment of the dreams of those who had prophesied that America's future lay in the West. In Washington, the pro-administration newspaper, the *Daily Union,* loudly hailed the outcome of the war as a glorious victory for the Democratic President, for the nation, and for the entire civilized world. "It is true that the war has cost us millions of money, and what is more precious, the lives of some of our noblest citizens," it admitted. "But what great advantages has it not obtained for us? It has covered us with glory. It has extended our fame to the remotest corners of the earth!" As he prepared to leave office after his single term, President James K. Polk could take pride in the warm and comforting reflection that in that single term he had added more territory to the United States of America than any President before that time.

The war with Mexico had proven to be unexpectedly short as American military forces displayed unusual strength and flexibility. With Zachary Taylor strongly entrenched in northern

Mexico, with Winfield Scott in possession of Mexico City, and with Stephen Kearny in control of California, Mexico had no alternative but to sue for peace. Deftly the northern republic deprived its unfortunate neighbor to the south of about two-fifths of the Mexican lands lying south and west of the United States border. Under the terms of the treaty signed at Guadalupe Hidalgo on February 2, 1848, the United States came into possession of the territories of California and New Mexico—a vast area of more than one-half million square miles stretching all the way to the Pacific Ocean.

Even as the Treaty of Guadalupe Hidalgo was being signed, in California an obscure carpenter named James Marshall was finding gold at John Sutter's sawmill in the Sacramento Valley. News of the discovery spread rapidly and produced one of the greatest gold rushes of all time. Not only did adventurers rush to California from all over the United States, but also from Canada, Europe, China, and Australia as well. Although most of the "forty-niners" made their way to the West Coast in covered wagons in an overland journey that usually took about five or six months, many relied upon sea routes—either traveling completely around Cape Horn or making the shorter but more hazardous land portage across the Isthmus of Panama. By 1850, the population of California had grown to more than 100,000 people—a tenfold increase in only two years—and there was no sign of its leveling off.

In 1850 the United States stretched from "sea to shining sea," and the future seemed brighter than ever before. The nation had won a stunning military victory and had acquired a vast expanse of valuable land which assured the logical completion of Manifest Destiny. The simultaneous discovery of gold in the new territory promised an inevitable influx of population which would make these new lands an integral and viable part of the nation. To many Americans, the acquisition of gold and territory in California was no mere coincidence; it was inescapable proof that Divine Providence still guided the destiny of the American Republic.

But what first appeared to be a windfall in the acquisition of the new lands in the Southwest soon divided the nation into two

Wilmot Proviso

disparate factions warring over how the new lands should be organized and what kind of people should be allowed to live there.

The excitement over the war and the Treaty of Guadalupe Hidalgo had barely declined when the nation began to prepare for the elections of 1848. Even before Polk left office it was obvious that the Mexican War had created more problems than it had solved. Congress and the nation were already engaged in bitter debate over whether slavery should be allowed to expand into the sprawling lands taken from Mexico. Evidence that the slavery question would be a troublesome issue had appeared early in August, 1846, less than three months after war was declared against Mexico, when Representative David Wilmot, a Democrat from Pennsylvania, proposed an amendment to an administration bill for a $2 million appropriation. The Wilmot Proviso proposed that "neither slavery nor involuntary servitude" should ever exist in any lands the United States might acquire from Mexico as a result of the war. Although the Wilmot Proviso was twice defeated in the Senate, the bitter debate it created in both houses of Congress foreshadowed more trouble to come. In 1848, neither California nor New Mexico had yet been provided with a territorial government, and the organization of the Oregon Territory, although it was clearly unsuited to slavery and therefore outside the current controversy, was delayed because of the unrelieved violence of the congressional debates. Oregon was finally organized as a territory, but the question of what was to be done with California and New Mexico was still unresolved.

As the elections of 1848 drew near both major political parties tried to quiet the more extremist members and pushed the explosive features of the slavery question into the background to avoid alienating either their Northern or Southern wings. When the Democrats met in Baltimore in May, 1848, they quickly voted down the platform advanced by some liberal New York delegates, known popularly as "Barnburners," opposing the extension of slavery into the territories. Choosing to follow the more conservative "Hunker" point of view, the Democrats once again adopted their 1840 platform, which denied the right of the Federal Congress to interfere with the domestic institutions of any

" barnburners "
" Hunker "

sovereign state. Because of his well-known views favoring "squatter sovereignty"—the concept that the people of a territory should decide for themselves whether they wished their territory to be admitted as a slave or a free state—Lewis Cass of Michigan was chosen as the Democratic standard-bearer.

The bothersome slavery issue also created problems for the Whig party. The "Cotton Whigs," men like Abbott Lawrence, Nathan Appleton, and Robert C. Winthrop of Massachusetts, still controlled the party and refused to brook any interference. Although these conservative business leaders were criticized for ignoring the slavery issue because of their own heavy investments in cotton, they doggedly insisted that the Whig party was obliged to maintain its time-honored stand of keeping the slavery issue out of the political arena completely. They were challenged by a group of young, liberal "Conscience Whigs" including Charles Francis Adams, Henry Wilson, and Charles Allen, who emphasized the immoral character of slavery and demanded that the Whig party take a stand against it. However, the conservative Whig leadership was able to keep the young Conscience Whigs in check at convention time. Bypassing such old party war-horses as Henry Clay and Daniel Webster, they staked their hopes for victory in November on the colorful hero of the Battle of Buena Vista—General Zachary Taylor. The Conscience rebels still had enough muscle left, however, to prevent the nomination of Abbott Lawrence, a New England textile manufacturer, as the old general's running mate. Insisting that cotton should not appear on both ends of the ticket (a reference to the fact that Taylor owned slaves), they forced the convention to fall back upon the lackluster but acceptable Millard T. Fillmore of New York as a compromise candidate for the vice-presidential nomination. The Whigs made little effort to frame a meaningful platform in 1848, choosing to rely on "Old Rough and Ready's" personal popularity as a military hero, his vague campaign speeches, and his appeal to Southern voters as a Louisiana slaveholder.

Effectively cut off from their own party and disappointed at the failure of the Whigs to take up the challenge of slavery, disgruntled New York Barnburners held a meeting of their own at

"Cotton Whigs"
Conservative > Conscience Whigs"

Utica where they founded the Free-Soil party—the first third party of serious consequence in American political history. Before adjourning, they nominated former President Martin Van Buren, a Democrat, for the presidency and issued a call for a national convention at Buffalo in August.

When the members of the newly formed party gathered at Buffalo, they were joined by dissident antislavery groups from other parties and factions—more liberal Barnburners from New York, free-soil Conscience Whigs from Massachusetts, former members of the old Liberty party, and dissatisfied Democrats. Selecting Charles Francis Adams, a Massachusetts Conscience Whig, as their vice-presidential candidate, they drew up a platform opposing the extension of slavery into the territories and called for free lands for bona fide settlers under the slogan of "Free Soil, Free Speech, Free Labor, and Free Men."

Although it was apparent even to themselves that they did not have a chance of victory, the Free-Soilers cut so deeply into the New York vote that the balance of power tipped in the direction of the Whigs. Zachary Taylor, their military-hero candidate, became President-elect in 1848 with Fillmore his second in command. Despite their loss of the highest office, the Democrats were able to maintain sufficient power to remain in control of the Senate, although their power in the House of Representatives (112 Democrats to 105 Whigs) was seriously threatened by a coterie of thirteen Free-Soilers who promised to hold the balance of power in the House.

Often when a legislative body falls into inactivity because of conflicting forces within its structure, the personal dynamism and expertise of a strong executive can mean the difference between stagnation and motion. This was a factor lacking in 1849. Although Zachary Taylor was a capable military commander, he was devoid of any kind of political insight, national perception, or social consciousness. As a result, when the Thirty-first Congress met in December, 1849, the political situation facing the nation was disastrous.

Without competent executive leadership the many complex problems facing the Congress could not receive swift and expert decisions. California, for example, had gone ahead and organized a state government, and was sending its officials eastward to demand recognition from Washington. Utah, too, had formed a state government and was submitting its constitution for congressional approval. Trouble was reported in Texas where there was talk of American settlers taking over additional lands belonging to Mexico. Slaveholders from the Southern states were loudly demanding positive congressional action to stop fugitive slaves from fleeing northward. And representatives from the Northern states were denouncing in equally loud terms the right of slaveholders to get back their runaway slaves. From all parts of the country, angry, vocal, and determined constituents were converging on Washington, bearing their demands and insisting upon positive action.

Considering the violent tempers and extreme agitation that prevailed in the Thirty-first Congress, and the lack of a stabilizing force in the White House, there seemed to be no way to deal effectively with the urgent problems at hand. Northerners insisted that slavery be kept out of the new territories altogether. They frowned upon the slave trade in the District of Columbia, and they were opposed to the return of fugitive slaves. Southerners were equally adamant in their insistence that slavery in the District of Columbia was permissible, and that the Northern attitude toward fugitive slaves was constitutionally indefensible. Taunts, jeers, catcalls, and threats of violence reverberated through the halls of the legislature, leading one Congressman to complain: "On the whole, a seat in Congress is a most undesirable possession." By the end of 1849, the machinery of government had wound down almost to a halt.

It was against this background of debate and recrimination that, late in January, 1850, the elderly Henry Clay rose in the Senate to offer a solution that he hoped might restore some measure of sectional harmony. Although Clay's personal influence was an important factor in obtaining a reasonable hearing for the proposals, the ideas themselves had been worked out behind the scenes by a number of Senators and especially by Stephen A. Douglas of Illinois. "If any man had a right to be proud of the success of these measures," said Jefferson Davis afterward, "it is the Senator from Illinois."

Clay's plan was a compromise designed to appeal to the moderate sentiment in both sections. To appease the North, he proposed to abolish the slave trade in the District of Columbia. To appease both sides—and to postpone the whole question of slavery indefinitely—Clay proposed that the new territories acquired from Mexico be organized without any mention at all of slavery. In keeping with Cass's theory of squatter sovereignty, the settlers would decide for themselves whether or not they wanted slavery when the time came to form their own governments. Peace and conciliation were the basic ingredients of Clay's compromise proposals. The question was: How would the other Senators react to this compromise arrangement?

From the South came a definite "No!" Too ill to read his own speech, the dying John C. Calhoun sat bundled up, his dark eyes blazing, while Senator Mason of Virginia read his defiant reply to Clay. The South, wrote Calhoun, would yield no more. "She has already surrendered so much that she has little left to surrender. . . ." There was only one way the specter of secession could be avoided and the union of the states be preserved, insisted the South Carolina Senator, and that was by adopting measures that would permit the Southern states to remain in the Union "consistently with their honor and safety." "The South asks for justice, simple justice," he wrote, "and less she ought not to take!"

In the deadlock there was still one more Senator with the same national stature as Henry Clay and John C. Calhoun whose influence might help to carry the compromise proposals into law: Daniel Webster. On March 7, 1850, the Senator from Massachusetts rose to speak. In the last great speech of his long career he held the galleries spellbound with an eloquent defense of Clay's proposals. Saying of the extreme Abolitionists of his own state that they had "produced nothing good or valuable" in the whole twenty years of their existence and had "actually served to bind faster the slave population of the South," Webster went on to denounce with equal vigor those extremists of the South who preached the dangerous doctrine of "peaceable secession," which could only end in civil war. The Union, said Webster in his stirring climax, *cannot* be broken. Instead of groping in the darkness with "horrid and horrible" ideas, he called upon the American people to come out into the light of day and enjoy the "fresh air of Liberty and Union."

Antislavery elements in the Northeast attacked Webster in outraged indignation, and in newspapers, magazines, speeches, and sermons the New England literati condemned him as a self-seeking traitor and an opportunist rascal. Theodore Parker called him another Benedict Arnold, Horace Mann likened him to a fallen Lucifer, and James Russell Lowell characterized the "godlike" Daniel as a politician "whose soul had been absorbed in tariff, banks, and the Constitution, instead of devoting himself to the freedom of the future." Emerson accused Webster of believing that "government exists for the protection of property"; and John Greenleaf Whittier sadly lamented "the light withdrawn which once he wore!"

But to the business community of the Northeast, to a majority of the men of wealth and property and standing, Webster was the man of the hour. The Compromise of 1850 might not be the best solution, most of them agreed, but it was far better than disunion and war. "Mr. Webster's views have opened to us a new and cheering prospect," the influential *Journal of Commerce* reported to its readers. "The position of Northern conservatives is gloriously vindicated by Mr. Webster. A conservative may breathe freely in the North after this."

Although Webster's oratorical appeal was passionate and popular, the compromise proposals continued to be the subject of heated debate. Southern supporters of Calhoun opposed compromise in any form, and advocates of a separatist movement in the South took immediate steps to demonstrate their opposition to Clay's compromise measures and to bolster general support for the states'-rights cause. In the House, Representative Robert Toombs threatened that "if by your legislation you seek to drive us from the territories of California and New Mexico . . . and to abolish slavery in this District . . . I am for disunion." Another spokesman for the South warned that if the Congress were to pass any bill abolishing slavery in the District of Columbia or tried to enact the Wilmot Proviso, he would "introduce a resolution in this House declaring . . . that this Union ought to be dissolved."

Early in March, 1850, the Mississippi state legislature adopted resolutions calling for a convention of slave states to meet in June at Nashville, Tennessee. Although the convention met as scheduled, with members representing nine states, the death of Calhoun on March 31 undoubtedly helped the moderates control the proceedings and steer the conference in a conservative direction. To the disgust of the "ultraists," Robert Barnwell Rhett, Edmund Ruffin, and Beverly Tucker, who hoped to stimulate support for a secession movement, the convention adopted a relatively mild resolution calling for the extension of the Missouri Compromise line westward to the Pacific.

Even though Calhoun was gone, the compromise measures continued to meet stiff and stubborn opposition from the White House. Indicating his own preference for dealing with each of the territorial problems separately, Zachary Taylor held out against the package arrangement proposed by Clay and came to an open break with the Whig leader over the issue. Yet, in his Annual Message to Congress in December, 1850, Taylor recommended the immediate admission of California as a free state in spite of the opposition of many of his Southern supporters.

The following June, however, "Old Zack" suddenly died, and this development changed the political complexion of things dramatically because so little was known about the colorless Millard T. Fillmore. Although he had a reputation as a free-soiler at the time of his nomination for the vice-presidency, Fillmore was impressed by the compromise arguments he had heard as presiding officer of the Senate. As a result, almost as soon as he assumed the Presidency he came out publicly in support of the Compromise and began making his moderate Whig position evident in his Cabinet appointments.

Supported by President Fillmore, and carefully shepherded by Senator Douglas, the five compromise bills were guided through

Fugitive Slave Act of 1850

both houses of Congress and signed into law in September, 1850. As a result, California was admitted to the Union as a free state —the preference of its own voters. Territorial government for New Mexico and Utah was to be provided without reference to slavery at all until the time came for the inhabitants to form their state constitutions and seek admission to the Union. Since it seemed obvious that the topography of these Western lands would most likely prevent slavery from spreading into the area, most Congressmen were persuaded that in supporting these measures they were only confirming a physical fact of life.

At the same time, it was agreed that the slave trade (but not slavery itself) would henceforth be prohibited in the District of Columbia, and a new fugitive slave act was passed. Amending the original law of 1793 which had not proved effective in forcing Northern states to return runaway slaves, the new Fugitive Slave Act of 1850 placed all such cases under exclusive federal jurisdiction. Special United States Commissioners were given much broader powers, and were paid larger fees, if fugitive slaves were returned than if they were set free. An affidavit by the claimant was accepted as sufficient proof of ownership, alleged fugitives were denied the right of trial by jury, and their testimony was not accepted as evidence at any hearings or proceedings. Private citizens could be pressed into service in the pursuit and apprehension of a fugitive slave, and any citizen aiding in the concealment or rescue of a fugitive slave was subject to fine, imprisonment, and charges for damages.

Slaves/

The terms of the Compromise of 1850 were not acceptable to Northern Free-Soilers such as William H. Seward of New York or Salmon P. Chase of Ohio—and certainly not to Abolitionists who railed against cooperating with the moral evil of slavery at all and particularly against the Fugitive Slave Act. Nor was the Compromise acceptable to Southern states'-righters Rhett of South Carolina, William L. Yancey of Alabama, or Jefferson Davis of Mississippi, who resented the fact that the South had been forced to barter away the time-honored Constitutional right, in their view, to take slave property anywhere in the United

States. But the support provided by such moderates as Clay of Kentucky, Webster of Massachusetts, Douglas of Illinois, Cass of Michigan, Henry Foote of Mississippi, and Howell Cobb of Georgia was sufficient to establish a solid political basis for the Compromise and to mirror the sentiments of those who would accept the arrangements as the only alternative to disunion.

When the New York Whigs met at Syracuse in September, for example, and adopted resolutions which endorsed the critical position taken by Senator William Seward, forty conservative delegates of the Fillmore wing of the party walked out of the convention hall, led by the silver-haired Francis Granger, a personal friend of Fillmore and a strong advocate of compromise. The "Silver Grays," as the conservatives came to be called, held their own convention the following month at Utica, and there they condemned the policies of Seward and supported those of President Fillmore.

In Georgia a similar demonstration of conservative sentiment was to be found in the Georgia Platform adopted by a state convention at Milledgeville in December, which indicated that while Georgia did not wholly approve of the Compromise she would abide by it on the assumption that it constituted a "permanent adjustment of this sectional controversy." The delegates warned, however, that any further attempts by Congress to modify the Fugitive Slave Act, to suppress the interstate slave trade, or to abolish slavery in the District of Columbia would be resisted violently by Georgia—"even to the disruption of every tie which binds her to the Union."

With the passage of the Compromise of 1850, the lines were clearly drawn as to where the institution of Negro slavery could and could not go in the United States. And since it was unlikely that there would soon be any further major territorial acquisitions, it appeared that the compromise arrangements were final. Many persons, even those who had strong personal feelings about doing away with slavery completely, had to conclude that the slavery question, as a concrete political issue, was beyond recall. Although citizens everywhere would undoubtedly continue to debate the moral, social, and economic aspects of slavery in the United States, as long as the territorial compromise between the slave states and the free states remained in force there was no way the slavery issue could be brought back into the arena of political debate.

Although it was made after the Civil War, this Currier and Ives lithograph was a very popular and nostalgic image of an ante-bellum Mississippi cotton plantation. A highly romanticized version of the single-crop basis of the Southern economy, it painted a picture of the peace, prosperity, and industry that was supposed to have characterized the plantation system of the Old South. By 1835, after the effects of the cotton gin had been felt, more than 1,000,000 bales of cotton were produced annually in the South. By that time cotton had become the South's principal crop and the largest single item of export from the United States.

IN REVIEWING the controversy touched off by the question of slavery in the Southwest, it is interesting to compare the situation in 1850 with that of thirty years earlier, at the time of the Missouri Compromise. When the Territory of Missouri requested admission to the Union as a slave state in 1819, the matter sparked such a fierce congressional debate that a substantial compromise finally had to be worked out balancing the admission of Missouri as a slave state with the admission of Maine as a free state and guaranteeing that in the future slavery would be excluded in the Louisiana Territory north of the 36°30′ line.

In 1819–20, however, most of the arguments centered on the threat Missouri would pose to the political balance of power in the nation—not the morality of the institution itself. To be sure, there were elements of moral consciousness lurking in the background—especially after Representative James Tallmadge of New York introduced his amendment calling for the limitation of slavery in the Louisiana region—but the accent of the controversy was essentially political.

In 1850, by contrast, the considerations were decidedly moral ones, since the question of political balances of power was no longer relevant. In 1820 there had been eleven free states and eleven slave states, with twenty-two Senators representing the interests of each section. The population of the North that year was a little over five million, while the population of the South was not very far behind with a total of nearly 4½ million. In 1850, however, there were seventeen free states and fifteen slave states. The contrast between the sections was even more noticeable in terms of overall population as the free states had already recorded nearly 13½ million people to the slave states' 9½ million—a figure that included over three million Negro slaves.

Obviously something had occurred during the thirty years between 1820 and 1850 that transformed the subject of slavery from a matter of political balance of power into a major question of morality. Something had converted the institution of slavery from a "peculiar institution" of largely local interest into a critical dilemma of national concern, precipitating a serious crisis between the two sections of the country.

In the first place, slavery was neither a static nor a dying institution. On the contrary, in the years between 1820 and 1850 the institution had grown in numbers, in geographical distribution, and in total economic worth. Despite the fact that the slave trade itself was officially ended in 1808, the number of slaves had grown steadily from 1½ million in 1820 to over three million in 1850 when the Federal Census reported that one-third of those persons residing in the states of the South were black. The advent of technical innovations like the cotton gin and the wider use of steam power raised both the productivity and the profits that derived from slave power, and the new lands thrown open to settlement during the westward movement of the 1820's and 1830's greatly increased the demand for black workers. Generations of planting and replanting of staple crops like tobacco and cotton had slowly worn out the soil of Virginia, the Carolinas, and Georgia. Without scientific methods of farming, without proper fertilizing methods and adequate crop rotation, a state of soil exhaustion was the result. With plenty of fine land available in the Gulf region, however, Southerners began a steady migration into the new states of Alabama, Mississippi, and Louisiana where the climate was warm and moist, the rainfall heavy, the soil black and rich, and where convenient seaports were at hand for profitable export to all parts of the world.

Until 1790, cotton production had been chiefly confined to a small area of South Carolina, and from 1790 to 1810 it moved only slowly beyond that point. Between 1810 and 1840, however, cotton suddenly spread throughout the entire South. As cotton cultivation spread, it took slavery with it. Nothing shows more clearly the path of the new plantation economy than the southwesterly movement of slavery during the decades that followed. In 1820, for example, there were only 75,000 Negro slaves in Alabama and Mississippi; by 1840 there were 500,000; by 1850 there were over 650,000; and by 1860 there were over 850,000.

disposition of slaves

The states of the Old South, with their crop productivity declining and their need for income growing, were forced to ship out slaves to the labor-hungry sugar and cotton plantations of the Gulf region at a rate of some 25,000 a year between 1830 and 1860.

Price of a slave

As the demand for slaves increased in the new areas of the plantation country, so did their market value. The price of a good field hand, for example, rose from $300 or $400 to $1,000 or $1,500 between 1820 and 1860, demonstrating that the institution of slavery had not only expanded in numbers and in geographical distribution but also had become an integral part of the economy of the Southland worth hundreds of millions of dollars.

Legally, the black slave was at the complete disposal of his master. His status was that of chattel; he was the personal property of the owner. Actually, there were many types and varieties of slaves. The majority were field hands who worked on the plantations in gangs, picking cotton or cutting sugarcane under the constant supervision of foremen or drivers who were themselves slaves. There were others who were skilled workers and craftsmen, such as blacksmiths, carpenters, and mechanics; and still others occupied a relatively high social status as maids, butlers, footmen, and personal servants in and around the master's house.

Ripped away from his African home and heritage, torn from his family and his friends, the black man was placed in the stifling confines of an institution that controlled him with absolute power and distorted his personality. Education was forbidden the blacks, their religious instruction was carefully supervised, and their daily activities were thoroughly regimented. Every Southern state had a slave code prescribing the rules and penalties that kept the black population under constant and rigid control. Whipping, branding, marking, and other kinds of mutilation were permissible at the discretion of the master for infractions of the codes, and the death penalty was enforced for more serious breaches of the rules. Perhaps the thing that white Southerners feared most was the possibility of a slave insurrection. The historic example of the black uprising on Haiti (1794–1804) was a frightening specter that haunted every plantation and made the

slave codes

slave codes an absolute necessity in the eyes of every white planter.

Contrary to popular opinion, the antebellum South was not a place where every white man was the owner of a sprawling plantation with thousands of slaves doing the work while he lounged on the veranda of a gracious mansion and sipped mint juleps. Actual ownership of slave property in the South was confined to a relatively small number of whites. On the eve of the Civil War it is estimated that only one family out of four held any slaves at all. Further, at least two out of three of these slaveholders owned fewer than ten slaves each. This means that out of a total white population of about six million in the antebellum South, the number of "great" planters, men who owned over fifty slaves, was probably not more than seven thousand—roughly one per cent.

Between the slaveholding patrician class at the top of the social ladder, and the lowly "poor whites" who eked out a miserable existence at the lower levels, the South was populated in large part by small-propertied, independent, yeoman farmers. These men raised a variety of crops such as grain, cereals, and sweet potatoes, and for the most part they either did not own any slaves or else worked side by side in the fields with one or two of them.

The statistics of slaveholding in the antebellum South are apt to be very misleading, though, if political conclusions are drawn only in terms of economic factors. Despite the fact that 23 per cent of white Southerners owned fewer than twenty slaves, and 76 per cent owned no slaves at all, many small slaveholders and nonslaveholders were committed to preserving the institution of slavery without change and without exception. Indeed, it seemed at times that those who were the loudest in their insistence that the black man be kept in strict bondage were those whites who had never owned a slave in their lives. The heavy concentration of blacks in the South—in some regions amounting to two-thirds of the population—created a serious and ominous problem in race relations. Southern whites, rich and poor alike, believed that the only way to preserve their culture and society was to maintain the institution of slavery on an inflexible basis. Even if it could have been proved that slavery was economically unsound, socially unacceptable, and politically unstable, it is still extremely doubtful that the white population of the South would have altered its view that slavery was the only practical and effective method of maintaining white supremacy.

Then, too, many a small planter and yeoman farmer dreamed of the day when they would be great planters, masters of white-pillared plantation houses, and owners of a large parcel of slaves. This was a hope which the society of the South held out for all of its white members. Any plans to abolish the "peculiar institution" would have destroyed what many regarded as their only chance of rising to prominence and prosperity in this world. Even that small number of impoverished "white trash"—shiftless, listless, diseased, and deficient—refused to consider the possibility of setting the blacks free. The "poor whites" were almost fanatic in their determination to preserve their only claim to status, to preserve the only social system that would allow them to hold a superior position to another group of human beings. They were able to lord it over the black men whom they hated and despised, and who, in turn, held these "crackers" in ill-disguised contempt.

As slavery grew and expanded, so did the dangers of a slave uprising. White Southerners became more apprehensive about rapidly increasing numbers of slaves, and they showed themselves to be extremely sensitive to the words and actions of those who would promote dissension among the ranks of the blacks. Despite the long-established myth that the Negro slave was content with his lot in life and resigned to his condition of servitude, recent scholarship has produced numerous examples of slave uprisings and insurrections in the antebellum South. In 1800, for example, more than a thousand slaves under the leadership of Gabriel Prosser and Jack Bowler planned an attack on Richmond. Betrayed by two of their fellow slaves, the insurrectionists encountered a force of six hundred troops who executed more than thirty of the ringleaders. Over the course of the next twenty years, there were several slave uprisings along the Atlantic seaboard, in Kentucky, and in Louisiana; and in 1822 a free Negro named Denmark Vesey planned an uprising in Charleston, South Carolina. Once again, however, the plans of the slaves were betrayed, and the authorities crushed the insurrection and executed nearly fifty of the black leaders.

Perhaps the most frightening slave insurrection in the ante-bellum South was led by a slave named Nat Turner in South-ampton, Virginia, in August of 1831. Erupting in violence that took the lives of some sixty whites, the rebellion was swiftly met by forces of the state and federal governments. More than a hundred slaves were killed during the ensuing fight, and a score of the leaders were executed after the uprising was finally suppressed. Although all the slave uprisings eventually ended in failure, the number of them testifies not only to the desperate desire of the Negro to achieve freedom in his own right, but to the determination of the white society to maintain the institution of slavery by force of arms.

Almost from the very start of slavery in America there had been some prominent white men, too, who protested against the institution and who engaged in efforts for its gradual removal. For this purpose numerous organizations were formed, many of them located below the Mason-Dixon line and with impressive Southern memberships. These early antislavery societies were largely apologetic in their attitude toward slavery, admitting that they regarded it as an undesirable institution inherited from their forebears that should slowly be done away with. Although the organizations differed widely as to just how emancipation could be achieved, for the most part they were similar in their general attitude and approach. First, emancipation was to be a gradual process—slavery would not be abolished immediately but over the course of many years and generations. Second, it was to be a partial process—a small percentage of Negro slaves would be set free at regular intervals over a long period of time. And third, it would be a compensatory process—slavery represented a major capital investment running into hundreds of millions of dollars, and the slaveholders would have to be compensated for the grave economic loss they would endure.

A prominent example of this early type of antislavery organization was the American Colonization Society, which proposed to reduce the problem of slavery in the United States by purchasing

Turner revolt

plans for emancipation

Liberia > American Colonization Society

Liberia

the freedom of a number of slaves every year and sending them
back to Africa. Founded at Washington during the winter of
1816–17, this association acquired a territory in West Africa as
the place to which their freed slaves would be sent; the ex-slaves
sent there named their new nation Liberia. Boasting a membership that included such prominent Southern statesmen as Judge
Bushrod Washington, Henry Clay, and John Randolph of Roa-
noke, the Colonization Society is only one example of the many
attempts to whittle away at the slavery problem in a conservative,
reasonable, and moderate manner.

There were other Americans, however, who regarded the institution of human slavery with the utmost horror and disgust, who
regarded any gradual attempts to solve this problem as temporary
and hypocritical, and who demanded its immediate abolition. The
attitude of such people was translated into action on January 1,
1831, when William Lloyd Garrison ran off the first issue of a
newspaper called *The Liberator* from a small hand press in a little
office in Boston.

"the
"Liberator"

Although Garrison was by no means the first Abolitionist, he
was certainly the most articulate spokesman for a militant approach to the problem. The traditional strategy of quiet reason
and gentlemanly moderation was rudely thrust aside by this outspoken man who declared publicly that he would not use moderation "in a cause like the present," and who insisted that he would
be as "harsh as truth" and as "uncompromising as justice." But the
external and obvious differences between the new Abolitionist
movement and the earlier antislavery organizations went far beyond their external differences in character, attitudes, and approach. To understand the passionate thrust of the Abolitionist
movement and the fanatical zeal of its leaders, one must appreciate that its opposition to slavery was based solidly upon moral
grounds. Garrison and his followers took the unequivocal position
that slavery was a sin and a crime against humanity that went
against all the basic moral and religious principles of decent society. Seen in this light, the Abolitionists viewed every slaveholder as a sinner and a criminal according to the moral law, dis-
regarded statutory or constitutional sanctions of every kind, and

refused to accept any solution to the slavery question that did not call for the immediate and total emancipation of every Negro slave.

Garrison gathered a small band of followers about him and formed the New England Anti-Slavery Society in 1831. Leaders in other states and sections, like Arthur Tappan, a wealthy New York merchant, Theodore Weld of Ohio, James G. Birney of Kentucky, and Samuel May, a Unitarian minister from Connecticut, joined with Garrison to form the American Anti-Slavery Society in Philadelphia in 1833. In the face of open hostility in many parts of the North from those who regarded them as crackpots, agitators, anarchists, and troublemakers, the Abolitionists drew up a publicity program, organized local lectures, distributed pamphlets, sent out lecturers, and raised funds to further the cause of total and immediate abolition.

In one sense, the Abolition movement was a symbol of the times. It was one in a long list of social and humanitarian reforms that sprang up during the 1830's and '40's in the heady atmosphere of Jacksonian Democracy. Sparked by a religious idealism that regarded the nature of man and man's relation to God in definitely sympathetic terms, and further inspired by the lofty philosophy of Transcendentalism which emphasized individual freedom, the reform movements took on the aspect of religious crusades. Indeed, as the eminent historian Henry Steele Commager has pointed out, these were the only major reform movements in American history in which the clergy took an active and physical part, at least until the civil rights and peace movements of the 1960's.

In an effort to elevate intellectual standards, promote education, improve morals, broaden culture, and expand the best features of American life, reformers sought new ways for all to share in the opportunities of a democratic society. Horace Mann introduced major reforms in American education and helped to create the nation's public school system. Enthusiastic supporters of the temperance movement attacked the evils of "demon rum," and dedicated leaders of the pacifist movement worked strenuously to remove the scourge of war. Women like Elizabeth Cady

Other reform movements:

Stanton, Lucretia Mott, and Margaret Fuller inaugurated an active campaign to achieve equal social, educational, and political rights for women at the same time that the first major reforms were being made in reducing punishments for crime and improving conditions in American prisons. The heroic Dorothea Lynde Dix sparked the first significant advancement in the treatment of the insane and the mentally ill, and Dr. Samuel Gridley Howe and the Reverend Thomas H. Gallaudet brought new hope to the handicapped with their care and treatment of the deaf, the dumb, and the blind.

Like the other reform movements, Abolitionism was an effort to cleanse the nation of one more unsightly curse. It was one more attempt to raise the level of human dignity a notch higher. But the Abolition movement became so powerful in its influence, so wide and all-encompassing in its scope, and so compelling in its appeal to moral principles, that it gradually absorbed the drive and energies of the other movements. Despite the opposition of those who felt that Garrison and his followers were using intemperate language and provocative tactics, the Abolition movement grew larger and stronger every month.

If Garrison and his movement met opposition in the North, the reaction was relatively mild compared to the response of the South. Already angered at Northern politics, Yankee tariffs (the "Tariff of Abominations" was only three years old), and Federal centralism (John C. Calhoun was working out his doctrine of nullification at almost the same time that Garrison was turning out his *Liberator*), the section prepared to defend the cornerstone of Southern life and society against the attacks of the Yankee Abolitionists. After 1831, the tone of Southern writers became decidedly less apologetic and more forthright in presenting the institution of slavery, not as a political liability or an economic problem, but as a positive moral good. No one saw more quickly than the Southerner that the basis of the Abolitionist attack was a moral one, and he immediately accepted the challenge on these terms. If Garrison condemned slavery as a moral evil, then the Southerner had no alternative but to present the counterargument —that slavery was a moral good.

In order to support their position, Southern writers used a variety of arguments starting with the source of Christian moral principles, the *Holy Bible,* to demonstrate that there was nothing sinful about the institution of slavery. Claiming that the black race was the descendant of Chanaan, whom Noah had cursed and condemned to be "a servant of servants . . . unto his brethren," Southerners went on to show that many of the patriarchs in the Old Testament, like Abraham and Isaac, had held slaves, proving, in their eyes, that God had not delivered any strictures against the institution. It was pointed out that in the New Testament St. Paul had explicitly admonished the slaves to be obedient to their masters, and writers challenged Northerners to point out where Christ had ever spoken out against the institution.

Closely following the Scriptural argument came the assertion that slavery was an essential part of the natural law and an inevitable feature of human society. Reading from the tracts of universal history it was observed that at all times, in all ages, among all peoples, in all parts of the world, the institution of slavery could be found as a matter of historical record. For this reason, concluded the Southern writers, slavery was natural, traditional, and universal. To alter the institution was to deny historical evidence and deprive mankind of something obviously natural and normal.

The proslavery propagandists relied heavily on the preconceived assumption that the black race was biologically inferior to the white race. Arguments varied widely as to the exact scientific status of the black—whether he was a separate species, a subhuman species, an inferior strain—but most whites, even some in the North, were agreed that it was a fundamental, indisputable, scientific fact that the black man belonged to a different biological category. Further, the defenders of slavery explained that a separate institution had to be created for the benefit of this separate category of human beings. For this reason, they argued, the institution of slavery not only benefited the slave but served the best interests of society as a whole. Because of this institution, George Fitzhugh pointed out in his *Sociology for the South,* the black was no longer cannibalized in Africa, nor was he allowed

Fitzhugh — Sociology for the South.

to freeze or to starve in the slums of the industrial North. In the South, the black was provided with an institution peculiar to his wants, his intelligence, and his moral capacities, wherein the master occupied the place of his parent or guardian. He received food, clothing, medical care, religious instruction, and the kind of personal care and sympathy one would give to a child ("he is but a grown up child"). "The Southerner is the negro's friend, his only friend," wrote Fitzhugh. "Let no inter-meddling abolitionist, no refined philosophy, dissolve this friendship."

And finally, proslavery writers pointed out that without this vital institution the states of the South faced economic bankruptcy and financial ruin. Modern historians and economists, working from hindsight, may marshal statistics and draw elaborate graphs to demonstrate the inefficiency of the system of slave labor, or to predict the inevitable collapse of the system in the face of growing industrialization; but the preponderance of Southern opinion in the mid-nineteenth century insisted that slavery was essential to both the economic prosperity and the cultural superiority of their region. A sample of Southern opinion in this regard may be seen in the violent reaction that greeted the famous book by Hinton R. Helper, a Southerner, *The Impending Crisis of the South: How to Meet It*, published less than five years before the outbreak of the Civil War. Relying heavily on statistics drawn from the Census of 1850, Helper concluded that slavery was the main cause of the South's inferior economic position and urged the end of the slave system as the economic base of life there. Throughout the South, Helper's book was burned and banned (it had to be published in New York), and anyone who supported its conclusions ran the serious risk of mob violence and public fury. Southerners insisted that the work of cultivating tobacco, producing rice, cutting sugar cane, and picking cotton in the tropic temperatures could only be accomplished by black slaves. If slavery were abolished, the economy of the South would be destroyed; and if this happened, the life, the culture, and the whole society of the Southland would be gone forever.

The early days of the Abolitionist movement were far from peaceful and the results anything but encouraging. Members of

Abolitionist organizations were socially ostracized from "respectable" circles, and contempt quickly turned to violence in many parts of the North when the antislavery impulse showed no signs of subsiding. Outbursts of mob violence became more frequent and physical attacks almost commonplace. In October of 1835, a "broadcloth mob" in Boston broke up a meeting of the Boston Female Anti-Slavery Society, took Garrison prisoner, and threatened to lynch him until he was clapped in jail under protective custody. Lecturers were constantly the object of mob attacks, speakers were pelted with rocks and eggs, and in 1837 violence reached a dramatic climax when Elijah P. Lovejoy, an antislavery editor, was shot and killed at Alton, Illinois, while trying to prevent the destruction of his printing press.

The "terror" of 1835–37 not only failed to halt the Abolition movement, however, but it also acted as a fatal boomerang by providing more sympathy and more converts than the organization itself had ever been able to gain through its own efforts. The list grew swiftly, as men of wealth, background, and position joined Garrison's cause. Membership increased every day, and by 1838 there were more than two hundred antislavery societies in Massachusetts alone, with enough funds to send out propagandists and literature to all parts of the country.

The remarkable growth and expansion of the Abolition movement throughout the North caused increased tensions in the South—especially when the same year that produced the *Liberator* in Boston (1831) also saw the outbreak of Nat Turner's rebellion in Virginia. In addition to tightening their slave codes, restricting the movements of their slaves, establishing rigid curfews, and looking to their local military defenses, the Southern states took immediate action to stem the flow of Abolitionist reading matter below the Mason-Dixon Line. In 1835, a mob broke into a Charleston post office and destroyed mail sacks containing "inflammatory" literature from the North, and from that point on there were few Southern postmasters who dared to deliver antislavery mail. Legislatures throughout the South passed resolutions demanding that the Northern states put an end to the "incendiary" activities of the Abolitionists and threatening economic reprisals if this were not done. In the United States Congress, Southern Representatives secured passage of the "gag rule" in 1836, according to which all antislavery petitions were to be automatically laid on the table without being read.

Despite these repressive measures, the Abolition movement continued to grow in membership and in influence, and the slavery question was fast becoming an important issue on the political scene. For a time, both major political parties, the Democrats and the Whigs, had uniformly sidestepped the issue of slavery and refused to acknowledge either Garrison or his unpopular program. This was perfectly agreeable to Garrison himself, since he resisted all attempts to involve his Abolition program in party politics. The ballot box, he charged in the columns of his *Liberator,* was on the side of slavery as long as it was surrounded by a Constitution which he classified as a "covenant with death and an agreement with hell." Wendell Phillips, his close friend and collaborator, also agreed that one of the "primary objects" of the Abolitionists should be to "dissolve the American Union." Any compact which embraced slavery was essentially evil, claimed many of the leading Abolitionists, and any such union must necessarily be dissolved in accordance with the principles of a "higher law."

But it was virtually impossible for an issue as explosive as slavery to be kept for long out of the turbulent arena of American politics. Western Abolitionists, headed by James G. Birney and Theodore Weld, had already swung into political action; and the New York group, led by William Jay and the Tappan brothers, was beginning to ignore Garrison's "no-government" order as impractical and ineffective. Passive Abolitionism was quickly becoming a thing of the past, as more and more Abolitionists became convinced that their only hope for success lay in the size and the effectiveness of the political pressure that they could bring to bear. By the end of the 1830's the issue of slavery was raising questions in political elections that had never before been seriously considered: What about the morality of slavery? What about the extension of slavery? What about slavery in Texas? What about the slave trade in the District of Columbia? What about runaway slaves? Candidates of both leading parties were amazed at the number of complicated questions about slavery with which they were suddenly confronted. Party leaders were shocked into the realization that slavery had already become a full-fledged campaign issue.

It was in 1840 that the Liberty party was first launched, with James G. Birney of Michigan (formerly a Kentucky slaveholder) as its presidential candidate. Although the new party did not actually call for outright abolition—maintaining that slavery in the states could not be touched—it did call for "free soil" in the territories. Lacking any real structure or cohesion, and gaining little support from the "pure" Abolitionists (Garrison contemptuously dismissed free-soilism as merely "white-manism"), the Liberty party polled only about 7,000 votes in the election of 1840. Nevertheless, it was a prophetic signal that slavery would no longer be divorced from politics—and the coupling of the two became more evident as national events during the 1840's forced the issue of slavery into the forefront of political debate.

Liberal Party / free soilers

These were the years of "Manifest Destiny"—years when American settlers moved into the Western territories and then gradually infiltrated the lands to the south belonging to Mexico. Once the frontiersmen in Texas made good their independence from Mexico after the Battle of San Jacinto in April, 1836, there was strong sentiment in favor of adding this new piece of territory to the Union. Almost immediately, however, the issue of slavery, with all the moral overtones that had recently been raised by the Abolitionists, made the Texas question a political controversy of major proportions.

Texas

In the North, there were many who flatly opposed the admission of Texas, convinced that the addition of this Southern territory would upset the precarious balance of sectional power and would permit the institution of slavery to spread beyond the point where it could no longer be circumscribed or controlled. Abolitionists immediately condemned the Texas movement as part of an overall conspiracy by the new leaders of the South to build greater "slave pens" in the new territory. But moderate and conservative members of the Northern community, too, reacted un-

Texas annexation question

favorably to the acquisition of new lands in the Southwest. Many businessmen, for example, opposed the annexation movement on the grounds that it would bring into the Union an alien population ("vagrants, runaways, and cutthroats") who could not be assimilated into Anglo-Saxon society; and there were also many who objected to the fundamental idea of slavery's being expanded beyond its current limits. This point of view was given open expression by Daniel Webster in March, 1837, in his address at Niblo's Theater in New York, in which he condemned the extension of an institution that he denounced as "a great moral, social, and political evil."

As a result of the growing antislavery spirit in the Northeast, therefore, the question of Texas hung fire as politicians hesitated to commit themselves on the issue. Martin Van Buren adroitly sidestepped all attempts to force a decision on the question during his four-year term of office, and although John Tyler was an ardent expansionist his lively dispute with the Whig Congressional leaders quashed any possibility that Texas might come into the Union through treaty arrangements. The election of the announced annexation candidate, James K. Polk, in November, 1844, made the acquisition of Texas a foregone conclusion. Just before he went out of office, Tyler demanded that Congress annex Texas by joint resolution, an action that required only a simple majority. Since the voters had just elected Polk, who had campaigned on this very platform, Congress could hardly refuse Tyler's demand; and on March 1, 1845, they passed the resolution formally admitting Texas to the Union.

With the annexation of the Lone Star State, as many contemporary observers had warned, war with Mexico was only a matter of time. On May 11, 1846, President Polk sent his war message to Congress, while Mexican and American forces were already skirmishing along the disputed borders. Once again, Northerners—especially in the New England region—voiced their objections against what they charged to be a further demonstration of the "Slavocracy's" plot to enlarge the slaveholding regions of the South. The record shows that many prominent Southern leaders such as Calhoun of South Carolina and Alexander H. Stephens of

Georgia opposed a war they viewed as imperialistic and feared would have tragic consequences in long-range terms—("Mexico is forbidden fruit," warned Calhoun; "the penalty of eating it would be to subject our institutions to political death"). Yet, it was almost impossible to convince citizens of the Northeast that the war was not the direct outgrowth of the South's insatiable greed for empire.

It was this constant and unremitting background of bitterness, hostility, and mutual suspicion—spread over nearly twenty years—that made the crisis of 1849–50 such a dangerous one ("the future historian will pause with astonishment and terror when he comes to record it," prophesied Rufus Choate of Boston) and made some kind of workable compromise a vital necessity. It was this intensity of moral feeling that caused moderates on both sides to stretch out their hands eagerly, even desperately, to grasp at the proposals Henry Clay offered in 1850. Once the compromise measures were passed into law, the moderates convinced themselves that the new legislation would pave the way for a more peaceful relationship between the North and the South in the years to come.

CHAPTER 3
THE SLEEPING
TIGER

THE WHIGS were overjoyed at having passed the Compromise of 1850, and they were delighted that President Fillmore had named Daniel Webster to the post of Secretary of State and had placed a significant number of "safe," "solid," "compromise," "Union" men in positions of power in the administration. They looked forward to following up these successes with another Whig victory in the elections of 1852.

These hopes proved to be vain, however, for when the Whigs had chosen General Zachary Taylor as their standard-bearer in 1848 they were setting the stage for their own destruction. The election of 1848 was a Pyrrhic victory, for although the old-line Cotton Whigs preserved the traditional party structure and won with a popular candidate who knew nothing about politics and even less about the slavery issue, they drove the young Conscience Whigs out of the Whig party forever. Without young blood in its veins, it was only a matter of time before the Whig body suffered political rigor mortis—and the election of 1852 showed that the day of the Whigs had passed. At their convention that year, it was easy enough to bypass such party stalwarts as President Fillmore and Daniel Webster, but it took fifty-three ballots to decide upon another hero of the Mexican War, sixty-six-year-old Winfield Scott, as the presidential nominee. The

Although the Constitution forbade the importation of slaves after 1808, the number of slaves grew steadily from less than one million in 1800 to over four million in 1860. They constituted an enormous capital investment of the South. Planters relied heavily upon slave auctions in major ports and commercial centers of the South for the acquisition of new slaves. This sketch by Theodore Davis shows slaves being sold at an auction like other articles of merchandise and property. One newspaper editor in 1823 reported that most Southern towns had slave markets, auction blocks, and slave pens "strongly built and well supplied with thumbscrews and gags and ornamented with cowskins and other whips oftentimes bloody."

Whigs expected that the military glamor of "Old Fuss and Feathers" would more than compensate for the party's lack of a substantial political platform.

But the Democratic party, too, took account of the nation's anxieties, and they looked around for someone new who could calm fears and continue the apparently peaceful relations of North and South that came about with the Compromise of 1850. Having pushed aside the seventy-year-old Lewis Cass, who was regarded as having outworn his political usefulness, the party leaders faced a deadlock among the logical front-runners—William L. Marcy, the three-time governor of New York; James Buchanan of Pennsylvania, a well-known Jacksonian Democrat; and thirty-nine-year-old Stephen A. Douglas of Illinois, whose political star was so obviously on the rise. After forty-nine ballots had failed to resolve the deadlock at the convention, the party leaders found an acceptable dark horse candidate. Franklin Pierce of New Hampshire, who had served as a brigadier general under Winfield Scott during the Mexican War, was now supported by several prominent military men who were openly hostile to Scott himself. To round out the ticket and to provide evidence that the North and the South could indeed work together, the party nominated Senator William R. King of Alabama as Pierce's running mate.

With something like a national sigh of relief, the bulk of the American people voted for the Democratic party, hoping to push the explosive slavery controversy into the background. Southern Unionists like Robert Toombs and Alexander H. Stephens of Georgia, fearing that the Northern Whigs might all be converted to the Conscience cause if they got too much power, threw their support to the Democratic ticket. The radical New York Barnburners broke off their connections with the Free-Soilers and returned to their native Democratic party; and in Massachusetts these developments caused the almost immediate dissolution of a temporary alliance between antislavery Democrats and Conscience Whigs. The local Democrats could hardly take a stand different from that of their national party, and so they had no alternative but to campaign for Pierce and the Compromise.

The Democrats were right in asserting that the voters were ready for a compromise President and a quiet four years. Pierce defeated Scott by the overwhelming margin of 254 electoral votes to 42, leaving "Old Fuss and Feathers" with only the four states of Massachusetts, Vermont, Kentucky, and Tennessee. For the most part, however, Northern Whigs took their defeat with good grace. They dismissed the one-sided defeat of their presidential candidate as inconsequential and looked upon the election of the placid New Hampshire Democrat as the start of a new era of national accord. Assuming that the quiet and conservative Pierce would mend political fences between the North and the South and would avoid measures that might create further antagonism, the Whigs were confident that they had secured enough time for the entire nation to become adjusted to the prospects of inter-sectional harmony. They hoped that by the end of Pierce's four-year term, the American people would be ready to return to a real "National" party, a conservative "American" party, a party that stood above sectionalism and localism—a party "knowing no North and no South."

"We expect Mr. Pierce will give us a quiet, moderate, conservative, unexceptionable, good-for-nothing kind of Administration, to which nobody will think of making any especial objection or opposition," wrote James Pike, the *New York Tribune's* Washington correspondent, who predicted that "by the close of his term there will be a pretty general fusion of all parties." And the opening years of the new administration did, indeed, exceed the fondest hopes of conservatives as President Pierce, smiling, confident, looking younger than his fifty years, assured the nation in his Inaugural Address that he personally considered the Compromise of 1850 to be the final settlement of the issue of slavery. "I fervently hope that the question is at rest," he concluded, "and that no sectional or ambitious or fanatical excitement may again threaten the durability of our institutions or obscure the light of our prosperity." And at the close of the year, in his first Annual Message, the President again promised that "this repose is to suffer no shock during my official term, if I have the power to avert it."

Crystal Palace Exhibition's

Some folks called it another "Era of Good Feelings." The nation was at peace, the administration had the support of both houses of Congress, the Treasury was full, foreign relations were relatively peaceful, and business was getting better every day. The great Compromise of 1850 had obviously solved all the political disputes that had brought the country close to violence. Conservative gentlemen in the North and South congratulated one another on the future prospects for peace between the sections, and the nation as a whole plunged into a round of building and spending.

In London, at the fabulous Crystal Palace Exhibition in 1851, Yankee inventions were the talk of the town, from such prosaic products as picks, hoes, shovels, scythes, road-scrapers, posthole augers, and ice-cream freezers to the more complicated intricacies of American sewing machines, mechanical reapers, automatic binders, revolving disc harrows, and padlocks with revolving cylinders. Not to be outdone, America held its own industrial exhibition at New York's version of the Crystal Palace during the summer and fall of 1853. To thousands of interested spectators, displays from all over Western Europe provided a glittering backdrop against which America proudly and self-consciously attempted to compete with the Europeans in luxury items and exotic wares. Although the garish furniture, ornate statuary, and grotesquely elaborate metalwork failed to match the real ingenuity of the more humble products produced by the nation's inventors, most Americans regarded this World's Fair as one more evidence that the United States was passing out of its adolescence of sectionalism and parochialism and moving into an era of greater national unity and international maturity.

Restricted markets rapidly gave way to nationwide selling as Northern manufacturers sought out customers throughout the Middle West and down into the Gulf states. McCormick reapers, Seth Thomas clocks, and Colt revolvers soon became household words. Newspapers everywhere testified to the increasing size and wealth of the nation. Capital invested in manufacturing rose to new heights, and cotton growers were enjoying an unaccustomed prosperity as the price of cotton pushed upwards from its

1845 low of six cents a pound to over twelve cents during the early 1850's. Day by day, America was becoming more national in its transportation, communication, and business markets. The 1850's witnessed a tremendous expansion of the railroad system that was now extending its network from the Atlantic seaboard into the interior sections. The stretch of the Pennsylvania Railroad between Philadelphia and Pittsburgh was completed in 1852, and the following year the New York Central Railroad was formed by a merger of ten short lines between Albany and Buffalo. On February 20, 1852, the first through train from the East pulled into Chicago by way of the Michigan Southern, and in 1853 the Baltimore and Ohio reached Wheeling on the Ohio. One unfortunate by-product of all this railroad expansion was the list of 65 railroad accidents recorded during 1853 and the first half of 1854.

Every morning an avid American reading public followed the attempts of Cyrus Field to lay a cable across the Atlantic Ocean. The newspapers also contained the latest records being set by the new Yankee Clipper ships. These contributed to the total tonnage of American ocean traffic, which exceeded British tonnage by 15 per cent in 1853. The same year Donald McKay set a new world's record of 89 days 8 hours sailing his *Flying Cloud* from New York to San Francisco, and the American yacht *America* defeated the British *Aurora* in the international yacht race and brought the Royal Cup to the United States. Some readers followed the sensational tour of P. T. Barnum's latest discovery, Jenny Lind, the "Swedish Nightingale"; they were astounded to learn that she received $1,000 for each of her 150 concerts. Others were fascinated by the series of public receptions given to the Hungarian hero of liberation, Louis Kossuth, during his successful tour of the United States. The ill-fated filibustering expeditions of General Narciso Lopez and his men in Cuba absorbed America's attention during the early 1850's, as did the demands of groups called "Young Americans" who agitated for aggressive nationalism, southward expansion, and aid to democratic elements in other countries. It was on July 8, 1853, that Commodore Matthew Calbraith Perry arrived at Japan with a letter from President

Pierce to the Emperor, and Americans were intrigued by the descriptions of the two men-of-war, belching smoke, steaming into Yedo Bay to open up Japan to American commerce and influence.

During the middle decades of the century, Americans were becoming increasingly conscious, even alarmed, about the wave of European immigration that was already changing the population patterns of the nation and threatening to alter its traditional habits and customs. During the 1840's and 1850's, a total of nearly four and a half million immigrants—three-fifths of them from Germany and Ireland—came to the United States seeking refuge from political purges, incessant warfare, or outright starvation. While most of the Germans were able to move away from the port cities and into the farmlands of the West, the Irish remained where they landed at the various East Coast cities—too poor to move on, and too desperate to care. These impoverished and often illiterate settlers created serious social, economic, and political problems for their communities, and soon became a disturbing element absorbing the attention of many so-called "Native Americans" during the early 1850's.

Preoccupied with domestic prosperity, national expansion, and mechanical progress, and now shifting their political attention to the newer and hopefully more all-consuming crusade against foreign immigrants, many Americans hoped that this cluster of new interests would help make everyone forget all about the issue of slavery while they worked together toward achieving a more united and peaceful nation.

"Men spoke softly not to rouse the sleeping tiger," the historian Allan Nevins wrote, "but in his sleep he stirred and growled." It would be absurd, of course, to suggest that every vestige of the extreme bitterness that the slavery question had engendered during the past twenty years completely died out overnight. On the contrary, there were many incidents that continued to force the troublesome issue of slavery back into the spotlight of public attention and make the nation fear that the tiger would awaken.

One thing that kept the slavery question alive during the 1850's, after the Compromise of 1850 was supposed to have settled the issue forever, was the attempt to enforce the new

Fugitive Slave Law in the Northern states. It had seemed reasonable—back in the troubled days of 1850—for Northern congressmen to agree to a set of compromise proposals including a guarantee that fugitive slaves would be returned. This was not too drastic a concession to make when the peace and security of the nation were at stake—and besides, in all probability there would be no attempt to enforce such a law.

But during the 1850's the South *did* attempt to enforce the new law in an effort to see just how far the Federal Government was prepared to go in supporting the Compromise measures and to make sure that citizen-slaveholders were guaranteed ownership to their rightful property. The South was prepared to push this issue even if it meant going into the North itself and bringing back fugitives who had been living there as free men for years.

The great manhunt was on, and when Northerners actually heard the sounds of the human chase in their own streets and saw helpless blacks being dragged back to the horrors of slavery, it was a different story. In cities like Boston, New York, and Syracuse, when slave-catchers began making their arrests and shipping their victims back to the South, even old-time conservatives were shaken out of their routine complacency. Mass meetings were held to safeguard the black inhabitants of Northern cities and warnings were posted informing Negroes of the presence of slave-catchers and advising them to stay out of sight. Local citizens' committees were formed to defend blacks against arrest, and in several instances groups of citizens actually broke into courthouses and effected the release of Negroes accused of being fugitive slaves. In 1851, for example, a Negro named Shadrach was rescued by some Boston blacks who spirited him away from the United States Marshal; and in Syracuse, members of the Liberty party, headed by Gerrit Smith and William Seward, rescued a captive named Jerry McHenry and helped him to slip away to freedom.

One reaction to the application of the new federal Fugitive Slave Law was to enact "Personal Liberty Laws." These were state measures guaranteeing to the alleged fugitive (contrary to the federal law) the writ of habeas corpus and trial by jury. In

Personal Liberty Laws

addition to prohibiting the use of any state and county jail for the detention of fugitives, these laws actually imposed heavy fines upon all citizens and public officials who assisted in the enforcement of the federal act. These Personal Liberty Laws came close to nullifying the United States Constitution in that they were in direct contravention of a federal statute, and they demonstrated to the South the degree to which antislavery sentiment had expanded and solidified throughout the Northern states since the Compromise of 1850.

In spite of strong antislavery opposition, the Fugitive Slave Act really ruled out the possibility of safety for runaway blacks, even in the free states of the North. Thousands of slaves, with the help of the "Underground Railroad," now headed for the borders of Canada as their only sanctuary. The so-called railroad was actually a highly secret group of blacks and dedicated white Abolitionists who lived in various states north of the Mason-Dixon Line and helped fugitive slaves reach the "Promised Land" of freedom in Canada. Whites like Quaker Levi Coffin of Indiana, who was called the President of the Underground Railroad; Calvin Fairbanks, a dedicated antislavery worker, and John Fairfield, a skillful and inventive underground agent, worked together with blacks such as John Parker, a former fugitive slave who returned to help others; Jane Lewis, who rowed fugitives across the Ohio River; Elijah Anderson, a major figure in the underground network; and Harriet Tubman, the heroic woman who is said to have traveled into the South on nineteen occasions and brought out more than three hundred slaves.

The fugitives had only the North Star to guide them, since all travel took place in the darkness of night. Slaves would be hidden in a friendly house ("station") by day and then sent along to the next station where they would be met by a friendly "conductor" and quickly tucked away until dark. One major route north ran through Ohio and Indiana; the other went through Maryland, Delaware, and Pennsylvania. Over these uncharted pathways, the operators of the Underground Railroad were able to rescue thousands of slaves (at least 50,000) and thereby create a constant source of annoyance to Southern slaveholders who complained of the illegal abduction of their rightful property. They also provided a corps of eloquent blacks for the antislavery crusade who could bear dramatic and first-hand witness to the evils of human slavery.

One person who did much to break through the silence that enveloped the slavery question after 1850 was Harriet Beecher Stowe, who wrote *Uncle Tom's Cabin,* which started out as a serial in June, 1851, and was finally published as a book in 1852. Although some twentieth-century students are inclined to dismiss this work as an exaggerated example of Victorian prose and raise questions about Mrs. Stowe's accuracy regarding the statistical data of slavery, *Uncle Tom's Cabin* had a profound emotional effect upon those who read the book and who attended the plays based upon it.

Instead of speaking in broad and general terms about "the slavery issue," "the Negro problem," or "the slavery question," Mrs. Stowe *personalized* the issue of human bondage by presenting specific men, women, and children, both black and white, with whom readers and audiences could relate immediately and emotionally. The issue of slavery was certainly not a new one in the United States, and it had been a growing subject of controversy for at least twenty years. There had been no lack of speakers, lecturers, preachers, and writers to denounce the institution as a moral evil and to castigate slaveowners as minions of the devil. But *Uncle Tom's Cabin* took slavery out of the lecture halls, the speakers' circuits, and the Senate chambers, and brought it for the first time into the living rooms, the dining rooms, and the kitchens of almost every home in the North. Now men, women, and children could relate directly to those who were victimized by the evil of human slavery and could visualize the horrible consequences in personal terms. When audiences cheered Eliza crossing the ice with her baby, when they hissed and jeered at Simon Legree, and when they wept openly at the tragic plight of Uncle Tom, they had crossed the line separating intellectual acknowledgment of an evil from the moral determination to bring that evil to an end. In the tradition of the dedicated social novelist, Harriet Beecher Stowe seized upon an issue which had long been recognized, studied, and debated, and created a new emotional upheaval by translating a great and universal issue into personal and individual terms.

Another approach Mrs. Stowe took, marking her book off from the flood of invective that had poured out of Abolitionist presses since 1831, was to present the institution of slavery in its *best* form, rather than its absolute worst. With a subtle irony that has often been overlooked by many of her critics, Mrs. Stowe emphasized the fact that the real evil of slavery did not result from the fact that sadistic masters brutalized their slaves, but that even under the kindest of owners (like St. Clare) the institution was so intrinsically evil that families could be bought, sold, separated, and subjected to the cruelties of such slave-traders as Simon Legree. More effectively than any previous writer, Mrs. Stowe demonstrated that the institution of slavery did not depend upon the personal morality of the slaveowner but was an evil that transcended the intentions and the motivations of any individuals involved.

Uncle Tom's Cabin sold 300,000 copies during the first year of its publication, and millions of Americans not only read the book but were also deeply moved by the numerous stage performances presented throughout the North. It was certainly difficult to convince most of these people that slavery was no longer an important issue, that the Compromise of 1850 solved the controversy —that everything had been "settled." And yet, despite the outbursts of sympathy for the plight of the black man, the local reactions against the Fugitive Slave Law, and all the tears that were shed for Uncle Tom, the Compromise of 1850 still held firm. The lines formally dividing slave territory from free territory were just as clearly established as ever, and it was evident that the leaders of both the Whig and Democratic parties were perfectly content to maintain the status quo.

Conservative political leaders in the North refused to be stampeded into another serious breach with the South like the one that had occurred after the Mexican War. Although they made it clear that they were not happy about the Fugitive Slave Law and the way in which it was being enforced in the North, they made it equally clear that they considered themselves honor-bound under the Constitution to obey it to the letter until it was officially repealed. They were willing to accept the unpalatable features of the Fugitive Slave Law as part of their gentleman's agreement to accept the Compromise of 1850 as establishing precisely and permanently the limitations of slavery in the United States. Unless something completely unforeseen took place, there was no way in which the issue could be brought back into the national political scene.

CHAPTER 4
BIBLES ON
THE PLAINS

THE BLOW that slammed down upon the rickety political house of cards and sent the peace and security of the nation flying in all directions came from the beefy fist of the "Little Giant" —Senator Stephen A. Douglas of Illinois. On January 4, 1854, acting in his capacity as Chairman of the Senate Committee on Territories, the young politician reported a bill into the Senate calling for the formation of two new territorial governments, to be called Kansas and Nebraska, in the unorganized lands north of the 36°30′ line. He then went on to propose that these new territories be allowed to enter the Union "with or without slavery" as determined by their constitutions at the time of their formal application for statehood. This proposal would "leave the people, under the Constitution, to do as they may see proper in respect to their own internal affairs," he insisted, and it would be accepted throughout the country as a progressive piece of national legislation. "I say frankly," he concluded, "that, in my opinion, this measure will be as popular at the North as at the South, when its provisions and principles shall have been fully developed and become well understood." Douglas was more sadly mistaken than he ever could have imagined.

Whatever Douglas's motives may have been in sponsoring this provocative piece of legislation—whether it was an unselfish act

A nineteenth-century engraving by Felix Darley showing a group of hard-bitten "border ruffians" from Missouri on their way to Kansas Territory to keep the region from falling into the hands of Yankee Abolitionists. In the spring of 1855 thousands of Missourians crossed into Kansas and took part in the elections for a territorial legislature. Although there were probably only about 1,500 legal voters in the territory, over 6,000 votes were counted in the election. Clashes between proslavery elements from Missouri and antislavery settlers in Kansas led to the outbreak of violence and bloodshed there that continued all through the Civil War years.

◄

of statesmanship, an ambitious grab for political power, or a crass attempt to organize the lands through which a transcontinental railroad would make its way from Chicago to the West Coast— one thing is certain: Douglas had made slavery an explosive political issue once again. The ground rules had been broken, the dividing line between free soil and slave soil had been erased— the fight was on! The passage of the Kansas-Nebraska Act would nullify the effects of the 36°30′ line in the Missouri Compromise, forbidding slavery in new states to the north of that boundary. The very fact that the Act had been proposed was enough to destroy the uneasy truce established by the Compromise of 1850.

Throughout the South, but particularly in the border states, Douglas was highly acclaimed. Now regarded by many as a Northern man with a true Southern outlook, he strengthened his already prominent position as a leading Democratic candidate for the presidency. Although there were many in the Northwest who bitterly opposed the opening of new lands to a flood of slaveholders, Douglas received strong backing from his constituents and from all of those, nationwide, who believed that geography alone would keep slavery well below the 36°30′ line. Applauding the fact that Douglas had established the principle of letting territories manage their own affairs, the *Detroit Free Press* called the Kansas-Nebraska bill "the greatest advance movement in the direction of human freedom that has been made since the adoption of the Constitution." "Never before," it stated, "has the right of all American Communities to self-government been fully recognized." With solid support in the South, and with a devoted following in the West, Douglas had little doubt that his bill would receive strong endorsement from both sections when it came up for a vote.

In the Northeast, however, the Kansas-Nebraska bill touched off a wave of indignation that was as violent as it was unexpected. As anyone would guess, militant Abolitionists and radical anti-slavery leaders leaped to the attack, denouncing the measure as additional proof that the South was engaged in an insidious conspiracy with congressional leaders to extend their "Slave Empire" into new territories. But among the groups in the Northeast that set themselves firmly against the "Nebraska infamy" none were more forceful and resentful than the conservative gentlemen of business, commerce, and banking. For over twenty years this particular group had gone out of their way to contain the slavery agitation and to placate their friends and associates in the South. To make matters worse, they had swallowed all of the unpalatable features of the Compromise of 1850 for the sake of establishing permanent guidelines that would restore peaceful relations between the North and South and put an end to the slavery issue. They had even gone so far as to demonstrate their good intentions by supporting the distasteful features of the Fugitive Slave Law in principle and by actually cooperating with federal authorities in returning fugitive slaves to the South.

And now—without prior discussion or consultation—Douglas ripped the lid off Pandora's box and let loose the terrible spectre of slavery to plague the nation! Shocked, hurt, and embarrassed—especially after they had pledged their word (the businessman's bond) to keep their part of the bargain—Northern businessmen were determined to strike back at the Little Giant and his preposterous proposal to throw open the free lands of the West to indiscriminate settlement. In New York, Horace Greeley reported that the merchants of that city were the first to protest, and his *Tribune* accused Douglas of "great perfidy" in overturning the Missouri Compromise. "We regard the Nebraska movement of Douglas and his backers as one of measureless treachery and infamy," he wrote. "The City of New York is awake at last," declared the *New York Post* as great numbers of bankers and businessmen held mass meetings throughout the city and adopted resolutions calling for the defeat of the bill. And in Boston, some three thousand "solid men" of the city gathered at Faneuil Hall on February 3 to protest the Nebraska bill and to demand that the nation return to the spirit of 1850. "The commercial class have taken a new position on the great question of the day," reported the *Boston Times,* observing that a number of prominent merchants, "who had never before given their influence on the anti-slavery side," had just signed a public petition calling for the repeal of the Fugitive Slave Act.

The Kansas-Nebraska bill had indeed made strange political bed-fellows. Conservative businessmen, who had remained aloof from the whole unsavory slavery controversy for twenty years and had led the fight against Abolitionism, now found themselves on the same side as the radical Abolitionists in opposing the proposed legislation. In his desire to bring organization to the land west of Missouri and Iowa, Douglas had unwittingly caused conservative economic interests in the Northeast, for the first time, to unite and to range themselves against the further expansion of slavery into the territories—a major shift in the traditional balance of political power in the North.

The consummate political skill of Senator Douglas, however, proved more than a match for the irate protests of his Northern opponents. Borne along by the furious energies of this "steam engine in breeches," supported by approval from the White House, and sustained by jubilant Southerners, Whigs, and Democrats alike, the Nebraska Act swept through the Senate and managed to overcome stiff Northern opposition in the House. The bill was signed into law by President Pierce on May 30, 1854. It provided for the two new territories of Kansas and Nebraska, called for the outright repeal of the Missouri Compromise, and presented a clear-cut defense of the doctrine of popular sovereignty.

With the final passage of the Douglas bill, the whole question of the extension of slavery broke wide open once again. Abolitionists and those already committed to an antislavery position denounced Douglas and the hated slavocracy and called upon all their own adherents to renew the all-out assault against the evil of slavery wherever it existed. The conservative business interests of the North, however, found themselves in a frustrating dilemma. As realistic men of business, they appreciated only too well the fact that it was essential to their own best interests to retain the faith and good will of the Southern plantation economy whose production of cotton fed the hungry textile mills of New England, formed an integral part of New York capital-credit operations, and supplied the nation's shipping industry with one of its most valuable export commodities.

On the other hand, as men of honor and integrity, they felt

consumed by a righteous wrath at the selfish designs of unscrupulous politicians who were gambling with the stakes of national unity for the sake of railroad ties and caucus votes. They had always assured their Southern friends that they would never interfere with the institution of slavery where it was formally sanctioned by the Constitution. But they had come to believe that the "peculiar institution" should not be allowed to expand beyond its present limits. They were willing to live with slavery and work with it where it already existed, but now that Douglas's cheap political trick had destroyed the essence of compromise and provoked a new crisis, they were ready to take action. Although the Kansas-Nebraska Act had been passed despite their objections, they made up their minds to use the provisions of the Act itself to defeat Douglas and establish permanent boundary lines between free territory and slave territory. They reasoned that if population was to be the determining factor in deciding the fate of Kansas Territory, then they would see to it that a veritable flood of free citizens went west. This was a new and highly significant segment of the Northern population which had the money, the power, the influence—and now the motivation—to see that free settlers made Kansas a free state.

The earliest organized response to the Kansas challenge centered about the Massachusetts Emigrant Aid Society, created early in the spring of 1854 by Eli Thayer of Worcester, a member of the Massachusetts legislature, as a means of aiding the cause of free men and also making a sound profit in land speculation. The company was quickly taken over by a group of Bay State businessmen under the leadership of Amos A. Lawrence, the textile magnate, who reorganized it as the New England Emigrant Aid Company and stressed the humanitarian goals of the organization. Lawrence insisted that the company stock would never pay dividends and doubted that the stockholders would ever see their money again. Determined to maintain a middle course between the rights of the Southerners and the demands of the Abolitionists, these Cotton Whigs set out to stop the expansion of slavery within the letter of the law. They employed the Emigrant Aid Company as a means of providing Eastern volunteers with free transportation to Kansas and with enough funds to take care of their basic needs until they had accommodated themselves to their new environment.

This Massachusetts organization became a model that other states soon followed and other businessmen hastened to sponsor. There were similar emigrant aid societies established in New York City, Providence, Rhode Island, New Haven, Connecticut, Cincinnati, Ohio, and numerous other cities throughout the North; and there was even a Union Emigrating Company formed in Washington, D. C., to which thirty Congressmen subscribed the sum of $50 each.

In July of 1854, the first group of thirty emigrants, loaded down with tents, bedding, cooking utensils, and even a printing press, traveled by train to Buffalo, and headed from there to St. Louis and Kansas. Following the Santa Fe Trail for about fifty miles west from what is now Kansas City they came to an elevation of land, just south of the Kaw or Kansas River, from which they could look out for miles in all directions. Here, at a settlement they called Lawrence, they pitched their tents and became the vanguard of a small but dedicated group of Free-Soilers. "The crusaders are already on their way," Edward Everett Hale boasted to his brother Charles, "and they will pass into the valleys of the Nebraska and the Kansas, as the waters of the mountain stream pass into the lake in the valley."

In September, a second party of 66 settlers left Boston and were joined by 25 New Yorkers at Albany; before reaching Kansas their ranks had been swelled to 114 members. On they came, and before the winter of 1854–55 closed in, there were 600 Free-Soil emigrants settled on the banks of the Kaw, clustered in tents, grass-thatched huts, and mud-plastered log cabins, at the settlements of Lawrence, Manhattan, Topeka, and Osawatomie. All were under the general direction of Dr. Charles Robinson, an experienced colonist, a practicing physician, and an ardent Free-Soiler who had been selected by the Massachusetts Emigrant Aid Company as its official agent in Kansas. With even more settlers arriving in the spring of 1855, the Eastern backers felt confident that the future of the Kansas Territory had been settled and that Douglas's plan to bring slavery into the territories had been nipped in the bud. Assuming that there was no question as to the legitimate status of the Free-Soil emigrants in Kansas, Lawrence formally requested President Pierce to recognize the free settlers as the legally constituted government of the Kansas Territory.

The Easterners, however, reckoned without the hostile attitude of the proslavery settlers who lived just across the border in western Missouri. Angered at what they considered to be unwarranted interference by outsiders in the normal course of Western pioneer settlement, Missouri border-men—bull-whackers, buffalo hunters, and Indian fighters—prepared to take whatever steps were necessary to prevent free-soil Yankee imports from creating an artificial, moralistic free state right next door.

The Missourians had already taken action to forestall the "Abolitionizing" of Kansas in November, 1854, when the territorial governor, Andrew Reeder, called for the election of a territorial delegate. Into Kansas swarmed a horde of Missouri "ruffians" to stuff the ballot boxes in favor of slavery and elect John W. Whitfield the proslavery delegate. When Reeder called for the election of a territorial legislature in March, 1855, the Missourians once again carried the day for proslavery candidates. Disregarding the ineffectual protests of Reeder and set upon their own course of action, the new legislature proceeded to enact proslavery statutes providing severe penalties for any kind of antislavery agitation and establishing a test oath for all office-holders.

Neither the Free-Soil settlers nor their backers in the East were ready to accept this turn of events without a fight. The emigrants held their own antislavery convention at Big Springs early in September, 1855, where they denounced the proslavery territorial legislature as illegal and demanded admission of Kansas to the Union as a free state. The next month, they held a Free State convention at Topeka and drew up a formal constitution that specifically outlawed slavery. After submitting this constitution to the electorate for ratification, the Free-Soilers named Charles Robinson as their own governor and elected an exclusively Free State legislature. At this point Kansas had two governors and two legislatures.

Back East, supporters of the Free-Soil cause not only sent letters of encouragement and additional sums of money but also decided that more drastic steps would have to be taken so that the settlers could defend themselves against the onslaughts of the proslavery ruffians. In the middle of May, 1855, the first of a series of shipments of wooden crates arrived at Lawrence, Kansas, and when the emigrants tore open the crates variously stamped "hardware," "machinery," "books," and even "Bibles," they found themselves in possession of a hundred of the most advanced type of breech-loading weapon—the Sharps rifle. With increased firepower, the Free-Soil settlers were, for the first time, in a position to offset the numerical superiority of the hostile Missourians across the border, most of whom were still armed with antiquated muzzle-loaders and buffalo guns. At this point the situation had resolved itself into a deadlock that proved impossible to break.

The questions raised were now thrown back on official Washington. Which was the lawful government of Kansas? Who was the legal governor? Which was the legitimate legislature? Which votes were valid? Which were fraudulent? Who would make the final decision?

In the hope of providing new leadership and a more positive approach to the Kansas impasse, President Pierce removed Reeder from office and sent in William Shannon, a proslavery man from Ohio, as the new Governor. The President denounced the action of the Free-Soil settlers as "treason" and declared that the Government of the United States would support the proslavery territorial government as the only lawful government of Kansas. Interpreting the administration's position as a direct violation of his cherished principle of popular sovereignty, Stephen Douglas came out in opposition to Pierce's statements and argued that this was not a question for Congress to decide at all. The issue of slavery would have to be resolved by the settlers in the territories themselves.

Soon it was clear that the Kansas crisis had provoked as much division and dissension in Washington as it had in the Territory itself. Unable to arrive at any clear consensus of its own, in March, 1856, Congress tried to clarify matters by appointing a three-man committee to investigate conditions in Kansas and report back to the Congress. In midsummer, this committee only further confused the issue by returning a majority and a minority report, which renewed the controversy and brought congressional tempers to a white-hot pitch.

As the debate on the Kansas issue reached its climax in the Senate in May of 1856, Senator Charles Sumner of Massachusetts rose to give his famous two-day philippic entitled "The Crime Against Kansas." In rolling Ciceronian periods, he denounced the attempts of the South to seize Kansas for slavery as the "crime of crimes," the "rape of virgin territory," and he went out of his way deliberately to insult and outrage those in the Senate who disagreed with his Abolitionist views. The whole Kansas affair, he charged, was the result of a national conspiracy in which Senator David Atchison of Missouri, a modern-day Catiline, was engaged in insidious plots with Stephen A. Douglas, whom he described as a "noisome, squat and nameless animal."

Condemning the entire slaveholding South for its insatiable greed for more slave pens in which to hold their human chattels, Sumner directed his sharpest barbs at the state of South Carolina, with its "shameful imbecility" of slavery—and he singled out that state's elderly and well-liked senior Senator, Andrew Pickens Butler. The tall, handsome Senator from Massachusetts not only mocked the old Southerner outrageously (calling him "Heroic Knight!" and "Exalted Senator!"), but accused him of being a liar, a blunderer, and a reprobate who had taken the "harlot slavery" as his "mistress." He even went so far as to ridicule a physical disability of the old man by referring to the "loose expectoration of his speech" which occurred whenever he spoke.

Southern Congressmen were aghast at the viciousness of Sumner's verbal assault, and their pent-up emotions found a violent outlet when Congressman Preston S. Brooks of South Carolina, a relative of Senator Butler, took it upon himself to avenge the honor of his family and his native state. Coming to the Senate chamber on the afternoon of May 21, as the session adjourned and as members were making their way home, the young Southerner came down behind Sumner as he sat at his desk writing. In a blind rage, he brought his heavy gutta-percha cane crashing down on the Senator's head, neck, and shoulders, and continued to lash him unmercifully until he was pulled away by other Senators while Sumner sank to the floor of the Senate, unconscious and bleeding.

Some measure of how quickly relations between the North and the South had deteriorated since 1854 can be seen in the contradictory reactions of the two sections to this shocking event. Although some Southern newspapers did express regret that the incident had taken place in the hallowed halls of the Senate, most Southerners let it be clearly known that they felt it was about time that some red-blooded American gave the arrogant Yankee Abolitionist the horsewhipping he deserved. "We repeat," said one Alabama newspaper, "let our Representative in Congress use the cowhide and hickory stick (and, if need be, the bowie knife and revolver) more frequently, and we'll bet our old hat that it will soon come to pass that our Southern institutions and Southern men will be respected." Although Brooks resigned his seat in the House, he was unanimously reelected by his constituents, and he received gifts of ornate and suitably inscribed canes from all over the South to replace the one he had broken over Sumner's head.

In the North, on the other hand, Charles Sumner was hailed as a hero and a martyr—the innocent victim of an unprovoked assault, the defenseless target of a bully's club. Even many of those who had regularly opposed his Abolitionist principles and who had tried their utmost to prevent his election to the Senate now joined in the triumphant celebrations that greeted the bandaged statesman upon his return to New England.

Violence begat violence; for even while blood began to flow in the nation's capital, the conflict between the political factors in the Kansas Territory had degenerated from the opposition of legislatures and constitutions to the crash of rifle fire and the thud of bowie knives. At almost the same time that Charles Sumner went crashing to the floor of the Senate, a proslavery posse of about a thousand men came riding into the "Boston Abolitionist town" of Lawrence, Kansas, and touched off a chain of events that set the prairies ablaze.

On May 2, 1856, armed with warrants calling for the arrest of "treasonous" Free-Soil leaders, a United States Marshal led his thousand-man posse into Lawrence. After taking a number of Free-Soilers into custody, the Marshal turned the posse over to the local proslavery sheriff—at which point the posse became an avenging mob set upon the destruction of Lawrence's anti-slavery newspapers and large hotel. Smashing the shops of the *Kansas Free State* and the *Herald of Freedom*, destroying the type and throwing the forms into the river, the posse drew up the five artillery pieces it had brought with it and blasted away at the Free State Hotel. After five volleys, the torch was applied to the big hotel, and then the Missourians proceeded to ransack a number of homes before riding out of the town in high glee.

The sack of Lawrence provided the trigger for action by a self-appointed defender of the Free-Soilers, a fanatical Abolitionist named John Brown. Already disgusted at the Free-Soilers for being too timid and defensive in their reactions to the proslavery groups, Brown looked upon the attack on Lawrence as final proof that someone would have to fight back and show the relentless power of Almighty God in punishing those who supported the evil of slavery. In the dead of night on May 24, only three days after the sack of Lawrence, Brown with four of his sons and two other followers, went down into the proslavery district near Pottawatomie Creek. There they brutally hacked to death five proslavery settlers in retaliation for the Missourians' attack, in a gruesome demonstration of what Brown regarded as Divine retribution.

It was now an eye for an eye and a tooth for a tooth, as the plains of Kansas became the battleground for one of the bloodiest and most vicious confrontations in American history. Guerrilla bands roamed the countryside spoiling for a fight, and savage marauders were apt to descend upon the homes of innocent set-tlers at any time. Men went out to farm their lands only in groups of five or ten, all heavily armed, and passing strangers were quickly challenged at gunpoint with the blunt question: "Free-state or proslave?" And there were some people who saw in the tragic struggle that was taking place in "Bleeding Kansas" the prelude to an even larger conflict which could soon engulf the entire nation.

George Caleb Bingham, the noted American painter, moved from Virginia to Missouri where he became active in politics. Although he returned East to study at Peale's Academy in Philadelphia, he never lost his fascination for the colorful life of the frontier West. He specialized in recording the everyday activities of fur-trappers, river-boatmen, backwoodsmen, and farmers. In this painting, Bingham obviously has caught the enthusiastic spirit of Jacksonian Democracy on the frontier and the vigorous deliveries of those engaged in stump speaking. It shows a typical scene of a Missouri crowd listening to the speaker, attired in the long white alpaca coat and black silk tie of the frontier statesman, while his opponent in the background takes notes.

➤

THE Kansas-Nebraska Act not only broke the Compromise of 1850 and brought violence to Kansas Territory, it also disrupted the traditional balance in the nation's political structure. As many outraged Northerners sought to express their opposition to the extension of slavery into the territories, they were confronted with the frustrating fact that there was no practical way in which this could be done. The Democratic party had traditionally held that slavery was a question for the states to decide. The Whig party, on the other hand, had consistently refused to take any official stand on the question, insisting that slavery was a moral question each individual had to decide for himself. It was definitely not a political issue, they felt, and had no place in party platforms. Reaction to the Kansas-Nebraska Act, however, made it impossible to maintain the Whig "conspiracy of silence" any longer. Northern voters were demanding a political party that would express public opposition to slavery just as the Democratic party gave it sanction and support.

The Kansas-Nebraska Act, therefore, sparked the rise of a new political organization which soon presented a serious challenge to the Democrats. The name "Republican" was first applied to this new party when a large convention was held under the oaks in Jackson, Michigan, in July, 1854, and within the next few months the old Jeffersonian label was making its appearance in many localities throughout the Western states. At the outset, the new grouping was a random fusion of those Northern Whigs, Free-Soilers, and Northern Democrats who opposed the territorial policies of the Pierce administration and the principles of Stephen A. Douglas. It was frequently referred to as the "Anti-Nebraska" party. Adopting a platform that called for the repeal of the Kansas-Nebraska Act and the Fugitive Slave Act, it attracted all those who felt that the time had come at last to end the expansion of slavery through direct political action. Despite its strong opposition to slavery, however, it was soon clear that the new Republican party was not an Abolitionist party in the strict sense of the term. Republican leaders admitted that there was nothing they could do about the institution of slavery in those states of the South where it already existed under constitutional safeguards. But they did pledge themselves to do all in their power to prevent slavery from spreading into the territories. This explains why the new Republican party was not only despised by proslavery Southerners, but also rejected by extreme no-government Abolitionists like William Lloyd Garrison and Wendell Phillips who insisted that the American political system was still compromising with the evil of slavery. One example of just how swiftly the new party grew could be seen in the state of Illinois where, in the congressional elections of November, 1854, Anti-Nebraska candidates captured five out of nine districts and seriously reduced Democratic majorities in all of the other districts.

Outside the Northwest, however, the new Republican party was slow in gaining political momentum. Many Anti-Nebraska Democrats were reluctant to sever their connections with their old Jacksonian party; Free-Soilers were annoyed to have their program taken over by another group and could not see why a new party was needed at all; and old-line Whigs made a desperate effort to hold their organization together and fight against what appeared to be total extinction. Of all the political parties that had seen their organizations torn and twisted as a result of Douglas's bill, the Whigs had been the most badly damaged. The Southern branch of the Whig party had already leaned dangerously in the direction of the Democrats in 1852 when party leaders insisted upon General Winfield Scott as the Whig candidate. Now it went over completely in 1854 by siding with Douglas in his plans to overthrow the Missouri Compromise and dispense with the Compromise of 1850. When it became known that the Southern Whigs were throwing their support to the Kansas-Nebraska Act, Horace Greeley concluded: "It was clear enough to all discerning vision that old party distinctions were suspended and meaningless."

The disappearance of the Southern wing of the party left Northern Whigs uncertain about their future. Occupying a position midway between the extreme proslavery forces of the South and the militant antislavery forces of the North, the conservative

Whigs had stood firm for over twenty years, remaining apart from the violent sectional controversies and refusing to permit their organization to become embroiled in the politics of the slavery issue. Despite their relatively small numbers these Northern conservatives, because of their social status and political influence, were able to maintain their strategic center position between the feuding forces as a respected element of calm and neutral detachment.

Once the Whigs had thrown themselves into the Kansas fray, however, and once they had gone so far as to give money, moral support, and even guns to the free settlers in the Kansas Territory, their theoretical principles and practical politics were no longer as clear as they used to be. They had by no means become Abolitionists—that was perfectly clear, and they insisted upon it—and they were not really antislavery people in the accepted use of the term. Although they had come close to going over to the side of the Conscience Whigs in their attempts to defeat Douglas and prevent the expansion of slavery into Kansas Territory, they still could not bring themselves to make common cause with those young party rebels whom they regarded as reckless agitators and radical troublemakers.

For all practical purposes, then, the dreaded "firebell in the night" that Thomas Jefferson professed to hear at the time of the Missouri Compromise had sounded the death-knell of the old Whig party. Split asunder, their program repudiated, their principles ridiculed, and their influential leadership dying off, the old Whigs did not know where to go or what to do. Upon what terms could they justify a separate existence now that they had come out so openly in the struggle for Kansas? Could they preserve any longer their own independence? Where could they go? With whom could they ally themselves? Certainly not with the Democrats! As far as the Whigs were concerned, the Democrats lost any claim to integrity when they supported Douglas and his nefarious bill.

For some distraught Whigs, the only apparent and practical alternative to political oblivion was to align themselves with the new Anti-Nebraska party which was now rising out of the rubble of the Kansas debacle. Already there was an alarming movement

of former Whigs into the ranks of the new Republican organization, and a series of "union" and "fusion" conventions took place
throughout the Northern states as early as 1854 in an effort to
establish vigorous party tickets; these new groups won a surprising number of local victories. In Michigan, Whigs had already
begun moving into Republican ranks; and in New York, Thurlow
Weed was hard at work during 1854 pulling the disparate antislavery elements together under a single banner. The Whig party
and the Republican party decided to hold separate conventions at
Syracuse in September, 1855. But the reports of the invasion of
Kansas by Missouri ruffians produced such an emotional reaction
throughout the North that at convention time Weed marched his
Whig followers over to the Republican hall where they all agreed
to the appointment of a single central committee, settled on a
joint Republican ticket, and formed a single political party. A
number of conservative mercantile Whigs from New York City
condemned this surrender of the Whig party to the forces of
sectionalism and angrily voted to hold a separate Whig convention the following month. But it was no use. Most of the Whigs,
especially those from upstate New York, supported the idea of
fusing with the Republicans as the only effective means of stopping the expansion of slavery and checking the power of the
Democrats.

In Massachusetts, the Nebraska bill had hardly passed into
law in 1854 when Conscience Whigs like Charles Sumner, in the
high emotion of the moment, tried to form a brand new party out
of the antislavery elements in the state. Now was the time to
forget about tariff disputes, internal improvement conflicts, and
all those other controversies that had kept the Northern parties
divided. Now was the time to form "A Grand Junction Party" in
the North, he argued, a party that could "take control of the
Government."

Sumner lacked the finesse and the political base of a Thurlow
Weed, however, and there were also certain specific reasons why
his fervent appeals for fusion went unheeded and why the Republican party took such a long time to develop solid roots in Massachusetts, the home of the Abolitionist crusade. Influential Cotton Whig leaders simply refused to accept the principle of fusion

or to admit that the traditional ideals of Whiggery were no longer viable or relevant. Compared with the "ultra" Southern views of the Democrats, the radical sectional principles of the Republicans, and the "reckless" ideals of the Conscience Whigs and Free-Soilers who were rushing from one party to another, many old-time conservatives clung stubbornly to the tattered banner of the Whig party. This represented something "more pure, more patriotic, more faithful to the principles of the Country and the true principles of the Constitution" than the alternatives.

Sumner's great expectation, too, that all the antislavery forces would instantly and harmoniously join the ranks of the new Republican party, proved premature. Antislavery Democrats, for example, stood fast, and remained true to their traditional party loyalties. Even more significant was the fact that many Free-Soilers could not be persuaded to accept the Republican party as the only road to political salvation. Under the leadership of Henry Wilson, a number of them were already experimenting with the political possibilities offered by the appearance of the newly created "American" party.

For some time there had been a growing concern about the rapid growth of foreign immigration to the United States. Americans of the old English, Scotch-Irish, and German stocks were appalled at the way the immigrants' illiteracy, intemperance, and propensity for crime endangered the traditional institutions of American life. Many persons of Anglo-Saxon-Puritan background charged that the unprecedented wave of immigration was really a subversive plot masking a new Roman Catholic threat to the peace and security of the Western world. Pledging themselves to the task of exposing and suppressing these threatening groups, especially those of Irish extraction, local societies with elaborate titles sprang up throughout the country in the late 1840's and early 1850's. In 1852 and 1853, various local Nativist groups combined into a single national political party, known officially as the "American" party—and unofficially as the "Know-Nothing" party because its members refused to give out any information about its organization or its membership.

Seeing a ready-made political organization with a highly emotional content and considerable national appeal, many factions sought to take over the new structure. They felt that they could move into the political vacuum created by the collapse of the Whig party and the temporary eclipse of Democratic power in the North. In New York City, a number of influential mercantile Whigs, still burning over their party's fusion with the Republicans, gave their support to the Know-Nothing ticket as the only practical way to preserve "a great Union party" as opposed to the other two parties which offered either Abolition or sectionalism. In Massachusetts, many Free-Soilers, under the leadership of Henry Wilson, took the opportunity to join the Know-Nothing organization and contributed greatly to its dramatic growth. Hoping to win enough political support to send him to Washington as Sumner's antislavery colleague in the Senate, Wilson came out in support of the Know-Nothing candidate for governor of Massachusetts.

Northern Whigs, too, fighting for their political existence could see distinct tactical possibilities in a newly built political structure as a practical alternative to dismantling their own party and meekly surrendering to the new Republican principles. In many instances, there is no doubt that the strong antiforeign and anti-Catholic planks of the American party platform were decidedly popular among the commercial and industrial classes of the Northeast. But for many people who were attracted to the American party at this particular time, nationalistic and religious prejudices were essentially a secondary (though highly acceptable) issue when compared with the political potential of the made-to-order party. Many conservatives saw no reason why they could not move into control of the new party, deprive it of some of its more obnoxious social characteristics, and use it as a political wedge to splinter and destroy the existing parties. As Henry Wilson explained, there were "hundreds of thousands" who did not believe in the principles or purposes of the American party, but were "willing to use its machinery to disrupt the Whig and Democratic parties." Time was crucially short, and absorbing the American party was one practical way of bypassing the necessity of organizing and developing an entirely new political party.

In addition to its organization, the American party offered the
possibility of a national appeal that might push the divisive elements of sectionalism and slavery back into obscurity. Conjuring
up a national platform of peace, prosperity, Protestantism, and
No-Popery, many Whigs felt that they could easily develop a new
basis of understanding with their friends in the South. With a
united North-South crusade to fight the terrifying spectre of for-
eign-bred Catholicism, possibly the immediate menace of the
slave problem might be lost in the scuffle.

The Whig power in such urban centers as Boston, New York,
Philadelphia, Baltimore, and St. Louis, took a sudden and decided
swing toward the policies and the politics of the American party.
The spring of 1854 saw a Know-Nothing sweep in Pennsylvania;
New York was estimated to have more than 70,000 registered
American voters by the fall of the same year; and in Massachusetts
the newly formed American party ran away with the state by an
overwhelming margin. In less than a year, the party absorbed
enough power to poll over 80,000 votes—putting it 50,000 votes
ahead of its nearest rival in the Bay State.

The following year, Know-Nothing forces and their conservative Whig allies were able to hold back the growing threat of Republicanism. In New York, the businessmen of the city polled
enough votes to bring about the defeat of the Republican candidate, and they expressed the hope that the following year would
see a revival of the old Whig party in the national elections. And
in Massachusetts, thanks to the encouragement and support of
prominent Cotton Whigs (the "Rip Van Winkles of our politics,"
Charles Sumner called them), the Know-Nothings were able to
sweep to victory again in the state elections. At this point Sumner
and his friends were ready to give up all hopes for the success of
Republicanism in Massachusetts.

But the triumph of the Know-Nothing party, although swift
and substantial, was remarkably short-lived. The cause was nebu-
lous, the issues were artificially contrived, and the attempt to establish a broad base of political power on religious prejudice
collapsed of its own weight. In the South, the cause of Nativism
sputtered violently for a moment and then died out quickly because the total number of foreign immigrants below the Mason-

Dixon Line was comparatively small and their political influence trifling. Representative William T. S. Barry of Mississippi defended Catholics against Know-Nothings, and Alexander H. Stephens of Georgia maintained that "Thousands of Catholics are as true patriots as ever breathed American air." In Tennessee Andrew Johnson spoke out sharply and fiercely against their attempts to organize the state. "Show me a know-nothing," he once declared, "and I will show you a loathsome reptile on whose neck every man should set his heel!" And in Illinois an aspiring politician, Abraham Lincoln, rejected an offer of support by Know-Nothing representatives, stating that if they got into power and reworded the Constitution to read: "All men are created equal except Negroes, foreigners, and Catholics," then he might as well move to Russia where they enjoyed their despotism in a "pure" state. The terrors the spectre of Irish politicking and papal machinations could arouse in the South and in the West were nothing compared with the immediate and all-consuming preoccupation of the white population with the institution of slavery and its prospects for the future.

Throughout the Northern states, too, the American party steadily lost adherents after a brief and gaudy triumph. For one thing, religious bigotry proved a poor cement for the foundations of a truly national political organization. In Massachusetts, especially, a farcical series of investigations of Catholic schools and colleges by a Nunnery Committee brought such discredit upon the Nativist movement that its political underpinnings collapsed in ridicule and laughter. It was bad enough that the committee went about its work with heavy-footed boorishness, poking into closets, searching cellars, embarrassing nuns, and frightening children—things were even worse when the members charged their frequent liquor bills to the state. But when the committee tried to have the state pay for their entertaining a lady of uncertain virtue, the legislature put an abrupt end to the group's activities.

Then, too, violence in Kansas and the United States Senate during the early part of 1856 brought the controversial issue of slavery back into prominence with such dramatic impact that other activities were practically forgotten, and political forces became more widely polarized than ever before. Any hopes that conservative elements in New York and Boston may have had that the national elections of 1856 would see a revival of the old Whig party were crushed with appalling finality. The reports of the sack of Lawrence by proslavery forces and the tales of John Brown's bloody massacre at Pottawatomie Creek created a political chasm that was almost impossible to bridge, and the news of the beating of Charles Sumner in the halls of the Senate a few days later provided the final blow. "It looks as if Brooks's bludgeon has given a sort of *coup de grâce* to the Whig Party," Robert C. Winthrop of Massachusetts acknowledged sadly as the last bastions of conservatism collapsed and most of the Whigs went off to the Republican fold.

Against the immediate background of Bleeding Kansas, the sack of Lawrence, John Brown, and the beating of Charles Sumner, the national conventions took place in anticipation of the presidential elections of 1856. Still hoping to build a national structure on the local successes of the past two years, the American party held their convention early, in February, 1856. Passing a noncommittal resolution on the slavery issue that caused a number of Northern delegates to walk out in disgust, the Americans emphasized the virtues of "pure nationalism," called for a return to the principles of the Founding Fathers, and nominated Millard T. Fillmore as their presidential candidate. By dramatizing their position as a neutral, national, and essentially non-geographical third party, they hoped to appeal to those moderates in the nation who were becoming equally frightened by the belligerency of Southern proslavery Democrats and Northern antislavery Republicans.

Early in June, the Democrats met in Cincinnati, the first time they had ever met west of the Appalachians. Countering the Republican determination to stop the expansion of slavery into the territories, the Democrats set out to ensure the continued support of their powerful Southern wing, and to stigmatize the Republicans as irresponsible law-breakers who were endangering the foundations of the Union. Democratic leaders, recalling the Kentucky and Virginia Resolutions, rejected the right of Congress to interfere with the domestic institutions of the states and called for continued national support of the Compromise of 1850 and the Kansas-Nebraska Act. Bloodshed and violence, they charged, occurred only after antislavery forces refused to abide by normal constitutional procedures and resorted to "armed resistance to law." Sidestepping the delicate issue of whether settlers could act against slavery before the achievement of statehood (as the Douglas people insisted) or afterwards (as Southern Democrats claimed), the convention emphasized the broader principle of popular sovereignty and the right of self-determination.

As they sought to capitalize on their position as the party of law, order, and stability, the Democrats were careful to select a presidential candidate who would best represent these ideas and whose image would most effectively appeal to a disturbed and anxious nation. Lewis Cass was too old; Franklin Pierce was too weak; and Stephen A. Douglas was tainted with the unpopularity of his controversial Kansas-Nebraska Act. The most suitable candidate seemed to be James Buchanan of Pennsylvania, who had served in both the Senate and the Cabinet, and whose recent services as Minister to Great Britain had kept him out of the territorial turmoil. Tall, white-haired, and distinguished-looking, the sixty-five-year-old politician was acceptable to both the North and the South (especially after John C. Breckinridge of Kentucky was named his running-mate), and he could win the support of a voting public that was looking for tangible assurances of peace and security in the four years ahead.

About two weeks later the new Republican party held its first national convention in Philadelphia in a spirit of great optimism. The party's rapid growth throughout the Northern states during its brief two years of existence, and the recent defection of supporters from the ranks of the American party, raised the hopes of every Republican delegate. The new party left no doubt where it stood regarding the slavery issue. In their declaration of principles, the Republicans opposed the repeal of the Missouri Compromise and denounced the Kansas-Nebraska Act. Arguing from the spirit of the Declaration of Independence and the terms of the Northwest Ordinance of 1787, they insisted that Congress had both the right and the responsibility to prohibit the extension of slavery into the territories. Having thus solidified the support of

their antislavery supporters, Republican leaders sought to attract
former Whigs and Northern business interests with a plank favoring federal aid for a Pacific railroad and congressional appropriations for local improvements. Divorcing themselves from the
Know-Nothing movement and seeking greater immigrant support
for their growing party, they issued another plank promising
"liberty of conscience and equality of rights."

Although there was considerable discussion during the early
stages of the convention about the best presidential nominee—
conservatives tended to favor Salmon P. Chase of Ohio, while
more liberal members considered William Seward of New York
the logical candidate—John C. Frémont was nominated on the
first ballot. Young (forty-three), glamorous, and dashing, Frémont combined a colorful career as an explorer and a soldier
with a solid political base that included an attractive wife, Jessie
Benton Frémont, whose father, Thomas Hart Benton of Missouri,
had for many years been one of the most powerful figures in the
United States Senate.

Since the South's 120 electoral votes would almost certainly
go to Buchanan, the Republicans made little effort to campaign
south of the Mason-Dixon Line. Instead, they concentrated their
efforts on attempting to win the necessary majority of electoral
votes (149) from the 176 electoral votes of the Northern states.
In order to do this, they made as much as possible of the continued strife and bloodshed in Kansas and capitalized upon the
glamor of Frémont and the charm of his lovely wife. Their stunning upset victory in Maine's state elections in September clearly
indicated the speed with which Republican political power was
growing in the North.

The Democrats, meanwhile, secure in the knowledge that they
would sweep the South, concentrated their efforts and money in
the critical states of Pennsylvania, Indiana, and Illinois. Campaigning on the slogan that a Frémont victory would mean confrontation and secession, while the election of Buchanan would
ease tensions and preserve the Union, they went out of their way
to assure the voters that Buchanan would do nothing to harm the
interests of free-soil settlers moving into the Western territories.

The Republicans were beaten in their first attempt to capture the presidency. With their greater funds, better organization, and a calculated appeal to moderate voters, the Democrats won the election of 1856. Buchanan polled 1,838,169 popular votes and won 174 electoral votes in 14 slave states and 5 free states. Frémont polled 1,335,264 popular votes, and won 114 electoral votes, all of them in 11 free states. He carried every free state in the North except New Jersey, Pennsylvania, Illinois, Indiana, and California, and he could have won the election if he had carried Pennsylvania and *either* Illinois or Indiana.

Fillmore, the Know-Nothing candidate, also made a surprisingly strong showing in the election. Although he received only the eight electoral votes of the slave state of Maryland, he polled a total of 874,534 popular votes. Frémont and Fillmore, therefore, together polled more popular votes than Buchanan, whose victory was made possible by the narrow plurality he received by carrying Pennsylvania, Illinois, and Indiana. The election results clearly indicated the hardening of sectional lines, the rapid growth of Republican power on a national scale, and the importance of political developments in Pennsylvania, Illinois, and Indiana over the next four years. Perhaps more dramatic than anything else, however, the election of 1856 demonstrated that it was clearly possible for a candidate to win a national election without *any* Southern votes. This was a point that was by no means lost either upon Southern Democrats or Northern Republicans.

Even in defeat, Republican leaders had every right to congratulate themselves upon their party's excellent showing after less than two years' existence. Convinced that they had won a moral victory, they began making preparations for what they regarded as an inevitable and overwhelming victory in 1860.

Although the elections of 1856 settled the immediate question of who had the most political power, they really failed to settle any of the larger and more complicated questions that had plagued the candidates all through the campaign. The question of the Federal Government's right to prohibit slavery in the territories was certainly as vague as it had been before the elections, and each disputing faction was as firmly committed to its convictions after November as it had been before. The Republicans continued to assume that the Federal Government had the power to regulate slavery and could exercise it whenever it thought appropriate. Southern states'-righters continued to insist that slavery was a matter within the exclusive domain of each sovereign state and flatly denied the right of Congress to act in this area. Senator Douglas and his supporters continued to invoke the principle of popular sovereignty, which bypassed the whole question of institutional decision and gave into the hands of the settlers the ultimate right to determine their own destiny.

Some people felt that the air would be cleared and the tensions reduced if the highest constitutional authority in the land, the United States Supreme Court, would speak out clearly, distinctly, and authoritatively on this thorny question. If this could be done, people would know what was what, and then they could all get back to their normal pursuits.

Such a ruling did, in fact, come from the Supreme Court, in the case of Dred Scott, a decision handed down only three days after James Buchanan was inaugurated as the fifteenth President of the United States on March 4, 1857. The effects of this famous decision were, however, far different from what the conciliatory President had anticipated. Instead of deciding the issue once and for all and putting to rest the fears and anxieties of the nation, the Dred Scott decision rekindled the flames of sectional differences over the question of the expansion of slavery into the territories and made the peaceful resolution of differences between the North and the South more difficult than ever.

The prosperity of the early 1850's led to overexpansion of railroads, overproduction of industry, and overextension of credit. The collapse of the inflated economy started in the late summer of 1857 with the fall of a powerful financial house, the Ohio Life Insurance and Trust Company. The painting shows Wall Street on October 13, 1857, the day the banks of New York City suspended specie payments. In the foreground are several prominent men of the day, including Commodore Vanderbilt, Jacob Little, and Frederic Hudson, managing editor of the New York Herald. It was sixty days before the worst effects were over and the banks could resume payments.

➤

CHAPTER 6
THE SOUND OF
DISTANT THUNDER

DRED SCOTT was a Negro slave. As the property of an army surgeon named John Emerson he had been taken from the slave state of Missouri into the free state of Illinois where he stayed for a considerable period of time. Here the Northwest Ordinance of 1787 originally stipulated that neither slavery nor involuntary servitude could be extended into the regions north of the Ohio River. Later Scott moved with his master into the free territory of Wisconsin where slavery was prohibited by the terms of the Missouri Compromise. After Scott returned to Missouri, a suit was instituted on his behalf, asking that he be declared free by virtue of the fact that he had resided in a free state and a free territory. The appeal for Scott was denied by the Missouri courts on the grounds that he was a slave and therefore subject to the laws of that commonwealth. After Scott became the property of John A. Sandford of New York, the suit was renewed in 1854, and the case of *Dred Scott* v. *Sanford* finally reached the United States Supreme Court on appeal early in 1856.

Technically speaking, the Court might well have fallen back on precedent to avoid becoming embroiled in a major political controversy simply by declaring Scott to be a slave subject to the laws of Missouri and therefore not eligible to have his case heard in a federal court. Sufficient precedent existed in the case of *Strader* v. *Graham* (1850) to allow the Court to decide Scott's fate in this manner without going into broader and more abstract issues.

In 1856–57, however, circumstances were such that members of the Court found it impossible to deal with the issue of slavery without commenting upon some of the urgent constitutional questions of the day. Then, too, there were specific pressures at work that helped to shape the thinking of the justices as they weighed the relative merits of the case. For one thing, President-elect James Buchanan wanted a clear decision from the Supreme

Court on the question of slavery in the territories. The Kansas question was still red-hot, and a statement from the highest court in the land, especially if it were in harmony with the administration's position on the issue, might go a long way toward finally resolving that bothersome problem. It is now known that Buchanan corresponded with Justice John Catron of Tennessee on these matters prior to his inauguration and that he approached Justice Robert C. Grier, a Democrat from Pennsylvania, regarding the disposition of the case. Certainly this was pressure from the highest level.

Another consideration that undoubtedly influenced the five Southern-born justices of the Court to explore the delicate questions of constitutional rights and political power was their fear that Justices Benjamin Robbins Curtis of Massachusetts and John McLean of Ohio were preparing decisions giving Northern and essentially antislavery views on the Dred Scott Case. Spokesmen throughout the South had been demanding for some time that Southern members of the Court speak out boldly and publicly on such matters. Justice James M. Wayne of Georgia was known to be particularly eager to do so, and the Dred Scott decision seemed like the most appropriate and strategic occasion for airing the Southern point of view. In addition to Wayne and Catron, Peter V. Daniel was from Virginia, John A. Campbell was from Alabama, and the eighty-year-old Chief Justice, Roger B. Taney, came from Maryland. The free-state justices included Samuel Nelson of New York who, along with Grier was known to be a loyal Democrat; and Grier had strongly upheld the Fugitive Slave Law in his home state. The two non-Democrats were McLean of Ohio, a Republican, and Curtis of Massachusetts, who remained a Whig. The prospect of having two Northern justices use the Bench as a sounding board for their Free-Soil views without giving the Southern constitutional point of view the same chance to be heard seemed unthinkable.

And finally, there was the general atmosphere in the country; no one would be pleased if the Court were to hand down a decision affecting the future of only one single slave. The Justices would have to take a stand and use the force of their prestige to place the whole subject of slavery and territorial expansion in proper perspective. It might have been possible for the Court to deal with procedural matters and avoid becoming involved in the substantive issues of national concern in 1850, but in 1857 the Court could no longer evade what the new administration and much of the general public had come to regard as its duty and responsibility. The time had come for the Supreme Court of the United States to speak out on the issue of slavery and the question of territorial expansion.

Although each of the Justices handed down separate opinions, that of Taney is viewed as the majority opinion of the Court which went against Scott's claim by a vote of six to three. The majority held that Scott was not a citizen of the United States nor of the state of Missouri and therefore was not entitled to bring suit in federal courts. The Court held that Scott's temporary residence in free territory had not made him free and that his status would have to be legally determined by the laws of the state of Missouri.

Technically, perhaps, having denied jurisdiction in the case and having remanded Scott to the custody of Missouri, the Court might have ended the case at this point. But it did not. In order to substantiate his position that Scott was not a citizen in any legal sense, Taney sought to establish the fact that no Negro, slave or free, could become a member of "the political community formed and brought into existence by the Constitution of the United States." Reviewing the 150-year history of the Negro in North America from colonial times through the development of the Declaration of Independence and the formulation of the Constitution, the Chief Justice ruled on the basis of the historical evidence that "neither the class of persons who had been imported as slaves, nor their descendants, whether they had become free or not" had ever been considered citizens either of a state or of the Federal Union. After refusing to consider the Negro a citizen, or "person" in legal sense, the Court then went on to define his status as being chattel property. This was the official designation approved by the Constitution of the United States, the Court argued, and it was with this understanding that all citizens were allowed to traffic in slavery "like an ordinary article of merchandise and property" for at least twenty years after that document had been written.

Once having established the constitutional status of the Negro, the Court proceeded to construct a philosophy for territorial expansion based upon that premise. First of all, since Congress could not deprive any citizen of his property anywhere in the United States or its territories, Congress could not legislate against the expansion of slavery into the territories. "No word can be found in the Constitution which gives Congress a greater power over slave property," wrote Taney, "or which entitles property of that kind to less protection, than property of any other description."

But the Court went one step further. Not only did it deny Congress the authority to prevent slavery from following the United States flag wherever it went, but it also insisted that Congress had the responsibility of giving active aid and positive protection to that property, just as it would ensure the right of every citizen to hold every other form of personal property in peace and security wherever he chose to live in the United States. The only power that Congress had over slavery in the territories, stated Taney, was the power "coupled with the duty of guarding and protecting the owner in his rights." In other words, Congress could not prevent slavery from going into the territories, and it must actually give slavery active encouragement and protection wherever it went.

President Buchanan was surely disappointed if he hoped that this decision of the Supreme Court would put the issue of slavery to rest, would reestablish peaceful relations between warring factions, and would usher in his new administration on a strong and harmonious basis. Throughout the North, the Dred Scott decision produced a storm of violent protest against what people saw as Taney's callous view of basic human rights in depicting Negroes as mere property, to be bought and sold like hunting dogs and racehorses.

Eagerly, Northerners referred to the dissenting decisions of Curtis and McLean, which took issue with Taney's interpretation of American history by showing that as a matter of fact Negroes had been recognized as citizens in several states even before the Constitution was adopted and that they had actually held suffrage rights equal to whites in those states. Early in its history, the United States agreed to give citizenship to persons of color in treaties covering Louisiana, Florida, and the Cherokee and Choctaw territories; and more recently, under the terms of the Treaty of Guadalupe Hidalgo, persons of color in the lands acquired from Mexico were also guaranteed citizenship. One of their most telling arguments, however, lay in their support of the extensive legislative powers of Congress itself. This was extremely important because legal aspects of the Dred Scott decision also had serious political implications. The decision that Congress had no power or authority to legislate against the expansion of slavery into the Western territories cut into the very heart of the Republican platform. The Republicans were promising that if their members were elected to national office they would use the power of the Federal Government to prevent the expansion of slavery into the territories. And now the Supreme Court of the United States stated that the Federal Government did not have the constitutional power to do so. If this decision went unanswered, the Republican party was dead. But Curtis argued that the Congress of the United States had the power to regulate affairs in the territories both in *theory* (according to Article IV, Section 3, which gives Congress the power to make "all needful rules and regulations respecting the territory or other property belonging to the United States"), and in actual *practice*. He pointed out that Congress had, as a matter of historical record, both permitted and excluded slavery in various territories (including those covered by the Missouri Compromise) in at least eight major instances without anyone's even questioning its constitutional right to legislate in such matters.

Furnished with such constitutional ammunition, Republicans everywhere stood ready to repel this assault on the fundamental basis of their party's existence. Press and pulpit denounced the Court as the willing tool of Southern slaveholders. State legislatures in Maine, Vermont, and Massachusetts, announced that no part of the Dred Scott decision would be binding upon their citizens except the portions specifically "necessary to the determination of the case." New York announced that any slave brought into that state would be immediately set free and that any individual even passing through the state with a slave in his possession could be subject to a prison term up to ten years. The Republicans were obviously not going to take the decision lying down, and had taken the offensive before the Court's action could be accepted by default.

Hostile Republicans were only one source of Buchanan's troubles, though, for well-placed factions within his own party were shortly to attack the administration's position on the slavery question.

In the first instance, however, most Democrats were jubilant over the Dred Scott decision, and Southerners were delighted beyond words that the highest tribunal in the land had ruled that Congress could not prohibit slavery from going into the territories and must protect and sustain slavery wherever it went. Armed with such a decision, Southern leaders of the Democratic party were prepared to settle for nothing less as the basic policy of the Democratic party.

Backers of Stephen A. Douglas and his theories of popular sovereignty, as well as supporters of Lewis Cass and his Free-Soil views, were far from satisfied with the way things were going with the Buchanan administration. For one thing, the Dred Scott decision could well mean that squatter sovereignty was as dead as the Missouri Compromise seemed to be as a result of Taney's decision. The voice of the people would have no effect at all in determining the tide of slavery. According to the Dred Scott decision settlers would have to swallow slavery whether they wanted it or not—and Federal bayonets would be standing by to see that they accepted it. Was this what Douglas understood by popular sovereignty?

Douglas and his followers were even further antagonized by the way the Illinois Senator was being cut out of administrative operations. Buchanan was hardly in office when veteran observers in both the Democratic and Republican parties noticed that the new President was avoiding giving Cabinet posts, federal offices, and other political favors to the friends of Douglas. This was true to such an extent that the Little Giant concluded that Buchanan wanted to crush the power of the Northwestern Democrats while cultivating favor among the Southern wing of the party and those who would pay court to the administration's wishes. This trend was evident early when the President placed in his Cabinet such Southerners as Howell Cobb, a vigorous young Georgian who took over the Treasury Department, and Jacob Thompson, a businessman-planter from Mississippi who headed the Department of the Interior. The trend was even clearer when the President brought in as Attorney General a close friend from Pennsylvania, Jeremiah Black, who was noted for his rigid and legalistic views on constitutional issues.

The gap between the Buchanan wing and the Douglas wing grew even wider as events in Kansas continued to plague the new administration. After the sack of Lawrence and John Brown's bloody retaliation in May of 1856, open warfare broke out between the free-staters and the proslavery forces. Early in June, Brown attacked and captured a small detachment of proslavery men, but late in August a force of several hundred angry proslavers marched into the Free-Soil territory to avenge the victims of the Pottawatomie massacre. One of Brown's sons was killed by the vanguard of this force, which then proceeded to overwhelm the small band of defenders and burn their settlement at Osawatomie to the ground.

In September, President Pierce sent in John W. Geary as the new territorial governor, and this blunt frontiersman managed to persuade both sides to cease their fighting and come to terms while he attempted to work out a long-range and equitable solution of the dilemma. Geary's recommendations, that both sides participate in free and open elections, were ignored by the proslavery faction whose legislative leaders met at Lecompton early in 1857 and called for a census count to be held in March. If there proved to be enough settlers, the census would be followed by an election in June for delegates to a constitutional conven-

tion. Disgusted at this blatant disregard for democratic procedures, and enraged that no provision was made for submitting
the final constitution to a popular vote, Geary resigned his post.
When Buchanan took office, he replaced Geary with Robert J.
Walker of Mississippi, a transplanted native of Pennsylvania,
who had acquired a national reputation as an entrepreneur and
promoter, and who had served with Buchanan in Polk's cabinet
as Secretary of State. Armed with a pledge that the President
would support his efforts to work out a fair and balanced decision in Kansas, Walker set out on his new assignment.

By the time Walker reached Kansas, however, the proslavery
faction had already arranged for elections for a constitutional
convention, and despite all of his persuasive efforts he could not
prevail upon the freestaters to take part in what they regarded
as an out-and-out fraud. In June, therefore, as a result of the
free-staters' staying away from the polls, the slaveholders elected
an all-proslavery convention whose delegates were determined
to construct a proslavery constitution for Kansas Territory. The
best concession Walker and the free-staters could exact from
their high-riding opponents was a promise that voters would be
given a chance to vote on whether slaves should be admitted to
Kansas *in the future*. Furious at what he regarded as a trumped-
up election, fraudulent procedures, and a one-sided constitution,
Walker stormed back to Washington and demanded that the
President keep his word and support his efforts to give all the
settlers in Kansas—free-state and proslave—a fair vote on the
slavery issue.

Buchanan, however, was fed up with the eternal bickering and
fighting which had marked the course of Kansas history since
Douglas first introduced his bill in 1854. Anxious to end the
confused situation once and for all, hard-pressed by his Southern
supporters, and conscious of the precarious position of the Democratic party, the President recommended to Congress that Kansas
be admitted under the proslavery Lecompton constitution.

This decision drove Douglas and many of his Northern supporters into revolt against the Buchanan administration. Like
Walker, Douglas had assumed that the President was anxious

for a fair and impartial vote in Kansas, with all factions honestly represented. Now he was aghast that the administration would accept a constitution that was endorsed at an election in which no free-staters had participated. This was a cruel mockery of popular sovereignty, and Douglas refused to accept the President's decision without a fight because it violated his cherished political principles and because it seriously endangered his own political future and that of his party. In getting Northern Democrats to accept the Kansas-Nebraska Act, Douglas had staked his political reputation on the assurance that popular sovereignty would prevail and that local self-government would determine the destiny of that Western territory. He was coming up for reelection as Senator from Illinois the next year, and if he went into those elections appearing to be either the ignorant dupe of the Lecompton crowd or the unwitting tool of Buchanan and his Southern cohorts, then he faced the possibility of losing the power base in his own home state. If he lost Illinois in 1858 (it had been a key state in 1856 and was sure to be crucial in 1860), he would have to give up hope of becoming a presidential candidate. And if the Democratic party could not hold Illinois in 1860, the Republican party might well sweep the entire North. Supported by Senator John J. Crittenden of Kentucky who condemned the Lecompton constitution a "gross violation of principle and good faith," Douglas demanded that an honest vote be taken on the issue.

Although Buchanan was able to secure the support of the Senate, Douglas helped to bring about the defeat of the Kansas Admission bill in the House; and the issue was deadlocked. A House-Senate compromise known as the English bill was finally adopted on May 4, 1858, as a means of fulfilling the technical requirements of popular sovereignty while at the same time assuring passage of the Lecompton constitution. The people of Kansas were asked to vote a third time on the constitution. If a majority accepted it, the state would be admitted to the Union immediately. If the constitution were voted down, then Kansas would have to wait until its population was large enough to justify admission through the usual processes. The obvious expectation was that voters in Kansas would be so anxious to have their territory become a full-fledged state that they would swallow the unpalatable features of the proslavery constitution. In this respect, however, the administration's plans were thwarted, as the Kansans overwhelmingly rejected the Lecompton constitution in August, 1858, and voted to remain a territory. Although slavery continued to remain legal in Kansas for the time being, the free-staters took control of the legislature, and it was apparent to all that slavery would be abolished as soon as Kansas achieved statehood on its own terms. For all practical purposes, the battle for Kansas had been won.

Reaction in the North to the Dred Scott decision and the Kansas crisis might well have reached even more extreme and violent proportions except for the severe financial disaster that suddenly paralyzed the entire nation—the Panic of 1857. Already, American economic development demonstrated a cyclical pattern, and the year 1857 brought a precarious downward swing in the cycle. American business had been growing and expanding at a phenomenal rate during the middle nineteenth century. Railroads were being built throughout the nation, European immigration was mushrooming, industrial production was on the rise, new lands were being thrown open to settlement, and the discovery of gold in California was bringing a flood of people to the Far West. New banks were established, facilities were expanded, deposits climbed, and loans were generously given out with little or no collateral. Speculation in land, agriculture, transportation, and stocks promised swift and profitable returns. By 1856–57, the economic spiral had reached dangerous heights, and the domestic situation was made even more critical by contemporary developments in Europe.

Events on the Continent during the mid-1850's speeded up the breakdown of the American economy. The involvement of Britain and France in the Crimean War, the French military operations in Algeria, the unexpected Sepoy rebellion in India, and the campaigns of the British in China and Persia all caused Europeans to pull specie out of the United States during the winter of 1856–57 in order to finance the heavy costs of their military adventures. To make matters worse for American industry, many European capitalists were convinced that it was more profitable to invest money in enterprises in their own countries. Either through fear, anxiety, greed, or patriotism, therefore, Europeans proceeded to sell off a good many of their American securities and dump them on the American exchange, thus forcing prices down at the same time that gold was being shipped back to Europe.

American stocks and bonds quickly dropped in value, and American bank notes lost their standing as gold reserves were drained off. As the demand for American raw materials also went into a sharp decline, farmers were unable to meet their mortgage payments, factories were forced to shut down, laborers were thrown out of work, and banks discovered that they had loaned out so much cash that they were in no position to meet the growing demands of their depositors. One after another the banks began to fail, and by the middle of October, 1857, most of them had closed their doors. Business was at a standstill, firms of all sorts were going into bankruptcy, and masses of unemployed were left without work and without food.

The Panic of 1857 was particularly severe in the commercial areas of the Northeast. By the end of September all the banks in Philadelphia had failed, and by mid-October the New York City banks had shut down too. Boston suffered greatly as the crisis grew to larger proportions than the Panic of 1837. "The financial derangement in the country now absorbs everything," complained one leading Massachusetts industrialist. "Our manufacturing interest is for the present completely broken down and discredited."

The West, too, felt the impact of the depression, and Cleveland, Chicago, Milwaukee, and St. Louis experienced widespread distress. Prices of wheat, grain, dairy products, and livestock dropped disastrously. Western farmers found themselves without money to pay their mortgages, and enthusiastic land speculators no longer made enough to cover their debts.

The South, however, did not experience the excess speculation and runaway prices that marked the course of the other two sections during the early 1850's. Cotton prices did not go up like food prices, there was no speculative boom in cotton lands, and cotton production progressed in a steady rather than a spectacular fashion. As a result, the plantation South was hardly touched by the extreme hardships of financial depression and economic dislocation. Cotton production continued at its steady pace, domestic sales were lively, and overseas shipments of cotton regularly met the demands of European nations. The money brought in from the sale of cotton helped to rescue commission merchants from financial disaster and kept the small number of Southern banks from closing their doors.

The South concluded that the economy of their section was more prosperous, stable, and secure than that of the North. They were convinced that the hard-pressed manufacturers could stay alive only by depending on the markets of the plantation kingdom and so they took advantage of their momentary position of power to force a substantial readjustment of economic relations with the North. Denouncing the money changers of Wall Street and State Street who were bleeding the honest planters of their profits, the South called for an end to the policy of financial subjugation. The North, the Southerners said, could not survive without Southern markets; and unless there were changes the South would boycott all articles and merchandise "purchased directly or indirectly in any of the Northern States." Furthermore, the North would be cut off from the precious bales of Southern cotton, unless the textile manufacturers were willing to come to satisfactory terms. "What would happen if no cotton was furnished for three years?" asked Senator James Hammond of South Carolina in a blistering speech on the floor of the Senate. Expanding on the awful possibilities of idle mills, empty spindles, and grass growing in the streets of industrial ghost towns, Hammond hurled defiance at the Northern states. "Cotton is King!" he cried, as the Southland applauded his battle cry and carried forward the banner of King Cotton.

The South's threats were not lost on the commercial and industrial interests of the North. Since the introduction of Douglas's Nebraska bill in 1854, Northern business interests, like other groups in the North, had grown more critical of the Southern states and hostile to the institution of slavery and its expansion into the territories. Business opposition to Senator Douglas, as well as the funding of emigrant aid societies, the outright support of the free-state settlers in Kansas, and the growing approval of antislavery members of the Congress, all indicated a more outspoken and critical attitude than the financial North had ever before dared to express. Now, in haste—indeed, in panic—the businessmen dependent on Southern cotton took immediate steps to disassociate themselves from the political connections that would be disapproved in the South. Northern conservatives began to reassure the South of their sympathy, their support, and their good intentions. The cry of the *New York Herald* that the North should forget about the slavery issue and the Kansas question was taken up in earnest by manufacturers throughout the Northeast. During February and March, 1858, New York merchants agreed to support the Buchanan administration and accept the Lecompton Constitution. The *Journal of Commerce* complained that Northern businessmen were displaying such positive "distaste for public affairs" that they had stopped voting and were no longer using their influence against "the sectionalism of the day."

The Panic of 1857 certainly produced financial dislocation and intersectional tensions for the Northern businessmen. But the Panic produced one more pressure that, acting contrary to the purely economic effects, nudged many hesitant conservatives much closer to the Republican party. Playing the Panic and depression as political instruments to lure the business and commercial interests into their own orbit, Republicans blamed the depression on the actions of a Southern-controlled Democratic administration in Washington. The financial welfare of the entire nation, they claimed, was being jeopardized and undermined by people like Franklin Pierce, James Buchanan, and their Dixie supporters, whom they accused of working against good business practices by refusing to make grants available to railroads, failing to pass effective tariff legislation, and neglecting to provide adequate bankruptcy laws. The only way the businessmen of the

North could ever secure a national government sympathetic to their needs, went the argument, would be by supporting the Republican party.

There were few Northern businessmen who had the temerity to alienate the Southland further during this period of financial dislocation. For the time being they withdrew from active political affairs and continued to soothe the anxieties of the Cotton Kingdom. But in the long run, they proved a most fertile field for the persuasive seeds of Republican logic. If the new party could truly offer national support for industrial growth and financial expansion, then it would be ridiculous to suffer the continued prospect of government indifference and neglect. Once the immediate crisis was over and business operations assumed a more normal pattern, the Northern businessman moved closer and closer to a permanent alliance with the Republican party.

CHAPTER 7
A HOUSE
DIVIDING

FAR FROM providing a final settlement for the slavery question and a quiet prelude to the Buchanan administration, the Dred Scott decision moved the contestants ever further apart and helped to provide a wholly new set of issues for the congressional elections of 1858. Nowhere were these issues debated more forcefully, more eloquently, and more dramatically than in exchanges between Abraham Lincoln and Stephen A. Douglas, the most prominent events of that year.

Republicans in Illinois, like members of their party everywhere in the North, were optimistic about their prospects for victory in 1858. The rapid growth of their own party in the four years since it was founded, the blunders and weaknesses displayed by the Buchanan administration, and the growing breach between Southern Democrats and the Douglas faction were all causes for rejoicing in the Northern ranks. Hoping to unseat Douglas, Illinois Republicans selected the man they viewed as the most capable and effective Republican spokesman in the state—Abraham Lincoln.

"Old Abe" was born in Kentucky in 1809, though his parents brought him to Illinois at an early age. He worked his way up from poverty and obscurity on the frontier to become a man of means and prominence in Springfield. After serving one term as

A scene from the Lincoln-Douglas debates of 1858. Lincoln, still beardless, is speaking to the crowd in the outdoor setting, with Douglas standing behind him waiting his turn. Anxious to capitalize upon Douglas' fame and popularity, Lincoln's campaign managers had badgered the Democrats into accepting a challenge to a series of joint debates in seven different Illinois towns. These debates were carefully reported and printed in two important Chicago newspapers, the Republican Press *and* Tribune *and the Democratic* Times. *Each paper assigned a team of reporters to accompany the debaters on their journeys and take down the speeches verbatim in shorthand.*

◄

a Whig Congressman in the House of Representatives (1847–49), he devoted himself to the practice of law and, although he was almost wholly self-educated, he soon was recognized as one of the ablest and most successful lawyers in the state. He was forty-nine years old in 1858, and his bony frame and his unusual height (6′4″) gave him a lanky and somewhat disjointed appearance that belied considerable strength. A deep, thoughtful, and often melancholy man, he could tell amusing anecdotes or boisterous tales to entertain his listeners or to prove a point. He possessed a keen and logical mind as well as a graceful style of writing; but his open-hearted sincerity and his abiding faith in the common people always served to keep his logic from becoming dogmatism or his eloquence from degenerating into pious platitudes. His fellow Republicans had no one with greater natural ability or shrewdness to put up against the Little Giant in his own home territory. Recognizing the importance of what was at hand, Lincoln worked on his acceptance speech with painstaking care, proposing to move his party out from local affairs and territorial issues into the broader field of national interests and moral concerns.

On a hot June night in the Capitol Hall in Springfield, the members of the Republican State Convention unanimously acclaimed Abraham Lincoln their candidate for the Senate seat held by Douglas. In accepting the nomination, Lincoln maintained that the controversy over the slavery issue would continue until a "crisis" had been reached and passed. "A house divided against itself cannot stand," he said. "I believe this government cannot endure permanently half slave and half free. I do not expect the Union to be dissolved—I do not expect the house to fall—but I do expect it will cease to be divided. It will become all one thing, or all the other. Either the opponents of slavery will arrest the further spread of it and place it . . . in the course of ultimate extinction; or it will push it forward until it shall become alike lawful in all the States, old as well as new, North as well as South." Insisting that Douglas had shown utter disregard for the moral issues involved in slavery, Lincoln accused the Democrats from the White House to the Supreme

Court of engaging in a conspiracy to expand slavery. He closed with an emotional appeal for Northerners everywhere to support the Republican party as the only effective opposition to the aggressive force of the slave power. This was the opening salvo in a battle between two political giants that brought the major issues of the day into sharper focus than ever before and set the stage for the elections of 1860.

As he left Washington to return to Illinois for the senatorial race, Stephen A. Douglas realized that he faced the political fight of his life. He knew that he confronted one of the shrewdest and toughest foes the Illinois Republicans could put up against him, and he was also aware that he faced the hostility of elements within his own party. Unwilling to forgive him for his opposition to the administration's position on the Kansas question, President Buchanan and such staunch Southerners as Howell Cobb, Jacob Thompson, John B. Floyd, and Jeremiah Black, were determined that the time had finally come to end the Little Giant's career for good.

But Douglas was always ready for a good scrap, and he had hardly returned to Springfield when he struck out at his Republican rival. Standing by his cherished principles of popular sovereignty and emphasizing the role he had played in beating down the Lecompton constitution and supporting the rights of the settlers of Kansas, Douglas accused Lincoln of trying to set one section of the country against another section with his highly praised "house-divided" speech. There would always have to be different regions and sections in the United States, Douglas insisted; and it was ridiculous to fight against the differences imposed by such things as customs, climate, and geography. Further, he denounced Lincoln for declaring that the Negro was the social equal of the white man. Like other natural differences, this racial difference, too, would always exist despite the efforts of people like Lincoln and his Republican backers. The issue had been joined, and the fight was on!

As the campaign got under way, Lincoln challenged Douglas to a series of debates at a prominent site in each congressional district in the state. Douglas reluctantly agreed to appear on the same platform, and arrangements were made for a total of seven debates running from the middle of August to the middle of October. The first meeting was held in northern Illinois at Ottawa—a three-hour debate in an open square under a hot summer sun. Claiming that Lincoln and the Republicans had thrown in their lot with the fanatic Abolitionists, Douglas started out by refuting Lincoln's theory that the nation could not survive half slave and half free. The nation *could* exist half slave and half free, Douglas insisted; it had already done so for seventy years, and would continue to do so unless such people as Lincoln succeeded in their plans to turn Northern states like Illinois into refuges for emancipated blacks who had been filled with the notion that they were the social equals of white men.

Lincoln responded by denying that the Republican party was an Abolitionist party as Douglas charged. "I have not proposed, either directly or indirectly," he said, "to interfere with the institution of slavery where it is." As for Douglas's assertion that the Union had already existed for seventy years, Lincoln maintained that this was despite slavery, not because of it. While it was true that the Founding Fathers accepted slavery, he argued, they had set in motion various ways (such as outlawing the slave trade and prohibiting slavery in the Northwest Territory) of seeing that the institution was placed in the course of "ultimate extinction." When this finally happened, the Union would be secure and peace would come to all parts of the nation.

While Lincoln denied outright Douglas's charge that he wanted political or social equality between the white and black races, he was quick to emphasize that the natural right of the Negro to life, liberty, and the pursuit of happiness must be recognized and respected. "The black man might not be the equal of the white man in very many respects," he admitted, but as to the right to eat the bread he has earned with his own hands, then "he is my equal, and the equal of Judge Douglas, and the equal of every living man."

After Ottawa, the debaters traveled north to Freeport, just below the Wisconsin border, where some 15,000 people gathered to witness the second round in the now-famous battle. This was the most important of the debates both from the point of view of the political futures of the two candidates and the historical significance of the issues they debated. Shrewdly maneuvering Douglas into reaffirming his belief in the principle of popular sovereignty in the face of the recent Dred Scott decision, Lincoln quickly made it obvious that the two positions could not be reconciled—that one actually negated the other. He asked Douglas whether or not the people of a territory could prohibit slavery even if the Supreme Court said that they could not. With ill-concealed anger, Douglas flared back at Lincoln ("I answer emphatically, as Mr. Lincoln has heard me answer from every stump in Illinois . . .") and supported his doctrine of popular sovereignty. The people of a territory *could*, he said, exclude slavery from their limits—no matter what the Supreme Court said about the "abstract question" whether slavery may or may not go into a territory. This may have been an honest and forthright presentation by Douglas of his political philosophy, and it may well have helped him retain his seat in the Senate, but his "Freeport Doctrine" had disastrous results for his standing as a presidential candidate as far as Southern Democrats were concerned. With his announcement that the Dred Scott decision could be nullified by the will of the people and his statement that "slavery cannot exist a day or an hour anywhere unless it is supported by local police regulations," he was immediately rejected by more radical leaders of the South who expected much more from the prospective leader of their party. The Lincoln-Douglas debates were already having farther reaching effects than those that could have been expected in the state of Illinois.

Following the exchange at Freeport, nearly three weeks went by as the rivals made their way to the southern tip of the state at Jonesboro, just across the line from Kentucky. From Jonesboro they traveled up to Charleston in the east-central region, where they debated before a large and enthusiastic crowd of between 10,000 and 15,000. Another three weeks went by while Lincoln and Douglas, now tiring fast from the grueling pace, made their way northwest to Galesburg for the next debate on October 7. Here the two men lashed out at each other for three hours, with

Lincoln accusing the Democrats of plotting a program of foreign annexation to get more slave territory, while Douglas condemned the Republicans for their sectional views and claimed that Lincoln was not being faithful to either the Constitution or the Union.

After Galesburg, they moved south to Quincy, just across the line from Missouri, where they spoke before some 12,000 people; and following this exchange they traveled southeast to Alton where the last debate took place on October 15. Here Douglas summed up his position by reiterating his Freeport Doctrine and reaffirming his belief in the principle that the people always had the right and the duty to determine their own local institutions. No principle on earth, he stated, was more sacred than that of popular sovereignty. "I will never violate or abandon that doctrine, if I have to stand alone!"

In making his final statement, Lincoln returned to the importance of the fundamental moral issue involved in the decision of whether to retain slavery or to do away with it forever: "It is the eternal struggle between these two principles—right and wrong," he insisted. "The one is the common right of humanity, and the other is the divine right of kings. It is the same principle in whatever shape it develops itself. It is the same spirit that says: 'You toil and work and earn bread, and I'll eat it. . . .'" Only when these principles were faced squarely and the institution of slavery placed on its way to "ultimate extinction" would there be an end to conflict and violence in the nation.

Some idea of the bitterness of the fight and the appeal of the contestants can be seen in the closeness of the final election returns early in November. The Republican ticket in Illinois polled 125,275 votes; the Douglas Democrats received 121,090; and the Buchanan Democrats came in a very poor third with only 5,071 votes. Despite their plurality, however, the Republicans failed to take over control of the state legislature. Because of an outdated system which apportioned seats without taking into account the rapid and recent growth of population in the northern part of the state, the Democrats maintained control of the state legislature and returned Stephen A. Douglas to the United States

Senate for another six years. In marked contrast to the wave of Republicanism that toppled Northern Democrats in Indiana, Pennsylvania, New York, New Jersey, and throughout all of New England, Douglas secured his state for his party despite serious efforts by the leadership of his own party to destroy him.

Douglas's victory was tragic and costly in terms of his long-range hopes and plans for the presidency in 1860. First of all, he became the prime target of the pent-up hatred and frustration of President Buchanan and supporters of the administration. Although the election returns showed that the only hope for Democratic success in the North lay with the principle of popular sovereignty and the leadership of men like Douglas, Buchanan seemed more determined than ever to destroy the political heretic who had openly defied the power of the President. Just how far the administration was prepared to go was demonstrated in December, 1858, when the Democratic caucus voted to strip Douglas of the chairmanship of the Committee on Territories, a post close to his heart and one in which he had made his name and reputation over the years. This was dramatic proof that the Democrats had not only failed to halt the growing split within their own party but were actually widening it.

Second, Douglas emerged from the debates with Lincoln with a serious loss of prestige and support in the South—and for an aspiring presidential candidate this was disastrous. Since the elections below the Mason-Dixon Line did not take place until 1859 (elections were held in the odd years), Southern voters had the opportunity of reviewing the events of 1858 before going to the polls. What they saw gave them cause for alarm.

Although most Southerners had originally supported the principle of popular sovereignty as a means by which slavery could expand freely and without hindrance, the failure of the Lecompton constitution, the victory of the antislavery forces in Kansas, and now Douglas's Freeport Doctrine left them feeling cheated and frustrated. Douglas was not presenting the same kind of popular sovereignty the South believed in. In his debates with Lincoln, Douglas agreed that although the Federal Government had the responsibility of protecting slave property wherever it went, the people of the territories had the final power of deciding whether slavery should remain or not. Southerners—especially the extremists Rhett of South Carolina, Ruffin of Virginia, and Yancey of Alabama—rejected this interpretation as both meaningless and dangerous to the Southern position. They insisted that the Federal Government was obligated to positive and continuing protection to slavery in the territories. Whether the people of a territory *wanted* slavery or not was immaterial, they said. The Federal Government was bound to see that all such property was duly and constitutionally protected.

Disgusted at what they regarded as the timidity of the Freeport Doctrine, and already alarmed by what they considered the veiled threats of Lincoln's house-divided speech, the growing fears of Southern leaders were even further confirmed when they read the reports of a speech given by Seward, the New York Republican leader, on September 25, 1858, in which he spoke about an "irrepressible conflict." Interpreting this to mean that the Republicans were now regarding an intersectional conflict as inevitable many Southerners began to reassess the relationship of their own section to the rest of the country.

With the Republicans growing in strength and in numbers, with the Democrats losing power in the North, with the Buchanan administration tearing apart at the seams, with Douglas preaching popular control, with Lincoln talking house-divided, and with Seward predicting irrepressible conflict, Southerners began to wonder in earnest whether or not their only hope for safety lay in their own hands. Perhaps the time had finally come for the South to break loose from a government that ignored its views and rejected its values, and to strike out on its own. These, certainly, were the ideas and sentiments of men like Rhett, Ruffin, and Yancey, who formed the "League of United Southerners" and called for the South to abandon all compromises and to work for the support of Southern interests—even if that eventually meant secession. This was a climate of opinion that would be far from receptive to the idea of Stephen Douglas as the presidential candidate in 1860.

And finally, in agreeing to the series of joint debates, Douglas had unwittingly provided the mechanism by which his rival could capture the prize he wanted so desperately for himself. Up until 1858, Abraham Lincoln had been fairly prominent in the political affairs of Illinois, but he had none of the political fame or national glamor that characterized the spectacular career of the Little Giant. The novelty of the debates, the publicity they engendered, the significance of the issues, and the dramatic contrast of the speakers brought newspaper reporters from all over the country flocking to Illinois to cover the Senate race. By the time the debates were over, therefore, the name of Abraham Lincoln was almost as well known as Douglas's. For good or for ill, Lincoln had established a political reputation extending from one end of the country to the other; his new prominence brought him to the attention of Republican leaders. Here was a man of unusual personal appeal who supported the basic tenets of the party with greater force and eloquence than any other political candidate in recent memory. Efforts would have to be made to hear more about this rough-hewn Westerner.

In the meantime, the Buchanan administration was closely and anxiously watching the upcoming 1859 elections in the Southern states as a barometer of Democratic strength. The '58 elections had damaged the party badly in the North. If the party could not carry the Southern states in '59, then the Democrats would have little chance in the presidential elections of 1860.

There were many reasons for anxiety in 1859, for various groups were dissatisfied with the Buchanan administration, and they were agitating for a change. Conservative Southern Whigs, for example, thought the Democrats had gone too far in the direction of extremist tactics and were campaigning against them throughout the South. Behind the leadership of John Crittenden of Kentucky and John Bell of Tennessee, they were hoping to revive the old principles of conservatism, organize all those opposed to the Democrats, and build up their forces for the contest in 1860. Others, like those backing the League of United Southerners or promoting the "Gulf Confederacy," felt that the Democratic party had not gone far enough in protecting the rights of the South and were organizing their own forces to take control

away from the Democrats and establish a new and more independent structure. In addition to these major and well-organized
displays of opposition, many Southern states were torn by personal feuds and political factionalism which made it almost
impossible for the administration in Washington to predict the
outcome of the elections below the Mason-Dixon line.

Despite the apprehension that they would fall prey to forces
either of the conservative right or the fire-eating left, the Democrats held on to their control of the South in the fall elections of
1859, and they saw a slate of fairly moderate party regulars
voted into office in most of the states. Still, moderate Democrats
had encountered stiff and often violent opposition from more
militant rivals all through the campaign. It was evident that
ultraists of all types were making plans for the critical Presidential contest of 1860.

While the atmosphere was still tense in 1859, there were some
people who hoped that the worst had passed and that perhaps
things were finally beginning to move in more normal and acceptable channels. There had been a decided lessening of violence during the past year or two, the Lincoln-Douglas debates
were an accepted part of the American political tradition, the
elections of 1858 and 1859 had been conducted according to or-
derly democratic procedures, and conservative parties of considerable substance and support were starting to revive in both
the North and in the South. There were many other signs, for
those who wished to look for them, that people were willing to
work within the political system once again and that relations
between the North and the South might well be readjusting to a
more normal and peaceful pattern. All this was only wishful
thinking, however, a house of cards that was demolished in a
single incident.

On Sunday morning, October 16, 1859, a handful of men set
out from a small farmhouse in Maryland. Moving silently through
the chill morning mists they made their way across a small bridge
spanning the Potomac River and stepped onto the soil of Virginia. At the head of the column, his eyes blazing with a fierce
light, his white beard blowing in the morning air, was John

Brown—fresh from his exploits in Kansas where he had blazed a flaming path of terror and violence.

By the summer of 1859 Brown had completed his mission in Kansas. Moving east, he leased a farm in Maryland, traveled throughout the Northeast collecting several thousand dollars for his cause and then equipped his small band of followers with a supply of guns and pikes. The little band of eighteen men, including three of his own sons and five blacks, struck at a place called Harpers Ferry, seizing the federal arsenal located there, and prepared to distribute weapons from the arsenal to the slaves. Brown believed that a Negro uprising in Virginia—the state where slavery had been introduced in 1619—might be the spark to ignite hundreds of similar uprisings throughout the South and spur the slaves to force their own emancipation.

Brown had not prepared carefully enough, however, and the effort ended in disaster almost before it began. Alarm bells tumbled the local citizens out of their beds, whistles shrieked, and gunfire crashed out as local companies raced to cut off the bridge, which was the only means of retreat for these Abolitionists from the North. Then they closed in. One by one the invaders were shot down, until finally Old Brown and his surviving men were trapped in a nearby engine house. Late that night, federal army officers in the persons of Colonel Robert E. Lee and Lieutenant J. E. B. Stuart arrived with a company of United States Marines. Waiting for daylight, the troops crashed through the doors, cut down the men, and took the old man prisoner after he had been beaten to the floor. Only a week later, Brown went on trial for his life and heard the case against him as he lay on a cot in the Virginia courtroom.

It was not so much that Brown had taken up arms against the Federal Government, or even that he had invaded the soil of Virginia, that created such grave and hysterical demands for his death: it was that he had actually tried to incite a slave revolt. All of their lives, Southerners had lived in mortal fear of slave uprisings; and now a Northern man, a white man, threatened to make that nightmare a reality!

An apprehensive South was put on a war footing. Rigid curfews were established everywhere, and increased appropriations were demanded for tighter local defense measures. Southerners angrily blamed the entire North for encouraging such an attack, and leading Congressmen from the Southland insisted on a full-scale congressional investigation in order to discover exactly how John Brown, a man without any visible source of income, had managed to get the money, the guns, and the support for his out-rageous invasion.

"Mr. Brown," asked the prosecution, "who sent you here?" "How many are engaged with you in this movement?" "Have you had any correspondence with parties at the North on the subject of this movement?" "Who are your advisers in this movement?" Again and again during the course of the trial the prosecution demanded that the prisoner tell them who in the North had con-spired with him. They wanted names, dates, places, sums—but Brown would give them nothing. About himself he admitted everything; but he would not implicate anyone else. Silent, grim, defiant, the wounded prisoner refused to speak. But the South refused to accept his silence. There must have been others in-volved. Any such project involved a great deal of expense, and Old Brown was known to be virtually penniless.

Although there were more than four hundred miles between Harpers Ferry, Virginia, and Boston, Massachusetts, John Brown's raid made that distance seem considerably shorter. Re-ports that soldiers had found four hundred letters in Brown's abandoned farmhouse produced an immediate sense of panic. No one knew to whom the letters were addressed, what they contained, or whom they might implicate. A number of promi-nent New Englanders had been associated with John Brown over the course of the last three or four years, and now it began to look as though they were implicated in a criminal plot of na-tional proportions. Merchants like Amos A. Lawrence and George Stearns of Massachusetts, industrialists like John Carter Brown of Providence, humanitarians like Samuel Gridley Howe, and preachers like Theodore Parker and Thomas Wentworth Higgin-son had not only supported the emigrant aid societies, they had also sent money and guns to Brown during his exploits in Kansas.

When Brown left Kansas and made his tour through the Northeast in 1859, these same men had given him more money and encouragement for his cause. The attack on Harpers Ferry, however, gave many of Brown's former backers cause for alarm.

It was one thing to be snubbed for associating with Abolitionists, for reading the *Liberator,* or even for aiding the free settlers of Kansas Territory. But it was quite another matter to find yourself implicated in a plot involving the invasion of a state, the murder of a number of citizens, the inciting of slaves to rebellion, and an attack upon the property and forces of the United States of America! The Senate had appointed a special investigating committee, headed by Senator James Mason of Virginia and Senator Jefferson Davis of Mississippi, in order to uncover the "higher and wickeder" villains in this nefarious scheme and to make them share in the punishment of John Brown. Many Bostonians, once fearless in their support of Brown, now faced the possible loss of their good names, their businesses, their wealth, their property—and, perhaps, their freedom. While there were some who remained steadfast in their support of Brown and who applauded what he had done (Higginson dared the Southern Senators to call him to the witness stand), there were many more who suddenly decided to pay a visit to Canada "for reasons of health."

John Brown was found guilty of treason against the state of Virginia, and on December 2, 1859, he was led out of his cell and brought to the gallows that awaited him. He was able to take one long, last look out onto the hillsides of Virginia before the sheriff's axe cut the rope that sent his body crashing into eternity. John Brown was dead.

Some rejoiced. Others mourned him. The South was convinced that the Old Man was a symbol of the hatred of the North, and they began making elaborate preparations to see that the Republicans did not win the upcoming elections. If the kind of people who had sent John Brown into the South to spark a slave uprising should succeed in taking over the Government of the United States, then there was no place for the South in such a government. In the North, on the other hand, antislavery spokesmen hailed John Brown as a true Christian martyr—an "angel of light," Henry Thoreau called him—who had become a "new saint" and who would, in the words of Ralph Waldo Emerson, "make the gallows glorious like the cross." Even those who did not approve of his actions agreed that his principles were right and just. Brown's sensational deed stirred the North to its very depths and made the coming elections of 1860 a crucial test, to decide the future of the Union and to determine whether Brown had died in vain.

The Republican National Convention of 1860 met in Chicago, in a huge, wooden, two-story structure known as the Wigwam, especially built for the convention by the Republicans of the city. The building had a seating capacity of 10,000, but still bulged with spectators, delegates, and newspapermen. More people atttended this convention than any previous party gathering. With its pillars festooned with tinder-dry evergreen boughs, as well as with red, white, and blue streamers, the hall was lighted by flaring gas jets. The Civil War historian, Bruce Catton, has suggested that it was perhaps "one of the most dangerous fire traps ever built in America."

➤

CHAPTER 8
TORCHLIGHTS
AND WIGWAMS

ONLY six months after Harpers Ferry, when John Brown's body had been lying in its grave only a little over three months, the Democratic National Convention met in Charleston, South Carolina, on April 23, 1860, to nominate a candidate for President of the United States.

There are times in American political history when a particular city takes on a certain atmosphere peculiar to itself, which can either promote a spirit of unity and harmony or else create a sense of dissension and bitter hatred. This was true of Charleston in the spring of 1860 and it was, too, of Chicago in May of that year. In 1856, when there was general accord within the Democratic party, Charleston might well have been the best city in which to place the name of Stephen A. Douglas in nomination for the Presidency. In 1860 it was probably the worst.

Douglas appeared to be the only strong candidate the Democrats could place in the field. There was little doubt that he would get the party's nomination at Charleston; and most of the Democrats gathered there were sure that he was the only man who could win a national contest. In 1860, a total of 152 electoral votes were needed to win. A Democrat, under ordinary circumstances, could count on picking up all 120 votes from the slave states of the South; and it did not seem unlikely that an experienced politician like Douglas could easily acquire 32 additional votes in the Northeast and the Northwest. The Democrats simply had no other candidate with such wide appeal.

But there were a growing number of delegates from the states of the lower South who threatened that if Douglas did succeed in getting the nomination they would break up the convention and, if need be, break up the Democratic party itself. By 1860 many Southerners had come to view Douglas as a double-dealing cheat, a villainous schemer, and a bare-faced liar who had bargained away the rights of the Southern people for his own mess of pottage. The radicals, Yancey, Ruffin, and Rhett, were tired of

timid compromises and weak-kneed concessions—all for the sake
of party unity. If the Democratic party was not prepared to stand
foursquare for the rights of the South, without apology or equivo-
cation, then they were prepared to reject the party. They would
create a totally independent South and strike out for themselves.

The showdown between the Southern fire-eaters and the Douglas forces came with the writing of the party platform. The main
body of the Democrats, seeking to avoid open conflict over what
they regarded as abstract issues, proposed to adopt basically the
same platform that had been drawn up in Cincinnati in 1856,
which asserted that Congress could not touch slavery in the
states, endorsed the Compromise of 1850, and supported the general principles of popular sovereignty.

But the 1856 platform was not acceptable to the states of the
lower South, and they had already planned the action they would
take. Earlier in 1860, Alabama had passed a resolution emphasizing the "positive protection" idea: the Federal Government had
to *enforce* slavery, and a slave code would have to be established
for the territories. If the Democratic convention would not accept
this resolution, the Alabama delegates were instructed to walk
out. Meeting at night after the opening session of the convention, delegates from Georgia, Florida, Louisiana, Texas, Arkansas,
and Mississippi agreed to follow Alabama's lead. Now, when the
platform was proposed, Southerners insisted that the party go
further than ever before in its support of popular sovereignty.
They demanded that the convention endorse the principles that
neither Congress nor the territorial legislatures had any power
to abolish slavery in the territories, nor could they prohibit the introduction of slavery nor exclude it from territorial soil.

Douglas rejected this platform outright. Not only did it go
against his own concept of popular sovereignty, but from a prag-
matic point of view it would be suicide for the Democratic party.
No Democrat who subscribed to such a platform could carry a
single Northern state, he argued. Contemptuous of the idea of a
Southern political bloc, and not at all fearful of losing one or two
fire-eating states, which might well make him more attractive in
the free states, Douglas agreed to a modified version of the plat-

form accepting the rulings of the Supreme Court on the slavery issue but not incorporating the wording of the Alabama Platform. At this point, most of the delegates from the cotton states walked out of the convention hall in the midst of pandemonium. Since it was impossible to obtain a two-thirds vote of the entire convention for the nomination of Douglas, the party adjourned to meet in Baltimore on June 18, where it was hoped that the atmosphere would be cooler, the exchange of views more reasonable, and the Southern delegates more reconciled to the nomination of Douglas.

While the reconvened convention at Baltimore achieved the two-thirds vote necessary to nominate Douglas, the meeting precipitated another walkout, which left seven Southern states completely unrepresented in the convention and seven others represented by only half their delegations. The breach between the Northern and Southern wing of the party grew even wider when the delegates who had walked out of the convention decided to make their break official. They formed their own political party, held a separate convention of their own at Richmond in June (where they nominated John C. Breckinridge of Kentucky for President and Joseph Lane of Oregon for Vice-President), and adopted a platform calling for the positive protection of slavery in the territories by the Federal Government. Even though no one expected that this Southern Democratic party could win the election, there was a strong possibility that it could produce a deadlock and have the election thrown into the Congress. With two Democratic candidates and at least two other major candidates running for the presidency in 1860, it was quite conceivable that no one man would get the required majority of electoral votes. With no party holding a majority in the House, it was expected that the Democratic-controlled Senate would be able to name a Vice-President who would go into office on March 4.

The Southern Democrats' prospects of creating a deadlock were good, for before the Democratic conventions, Baltimore had been the scene of an earlier political convention when the "Constitutional Union Party" gathered to nominate its candidate for the White House. Composed largely of old-time conservative

Whigs and remnants of the American party anxious to work out a compromise solution to the nation's problems, this was a party that might cut into Northern votes for Douglas as well as for the Republican candidate. Terrified by the rising violence of rhetoric on both sides and appalled at the way in which the party system was becoming polarized according to geography rather than ideology, business and commercial interests in both the North and the South made serious efforts during 1859–60 to revive the old conservative structure. They hoped that if they could pool their political resources and mount an effective response to the national crisis they might be able to offer the American people an alternative to the sectional parties.

With a flurry of correspondence between Northern states like New York and Massachusetts and border states like Kentucky and Tennessee, the conservatives turned to the well-known and highly respected John J. Crittenden of Kentucky as their nominee for President. Running on a platform that emphasized the Constitution, the Union, and the traditional virtues of the American way of life, and deliberately ignoring all the other pressing issues of the moment, the conservatives hoped to appeal to the moderate majority of the nation, the voters who did not want to risk violence and civil war by voting for either the fire-eaters of the South or the militant Abolitionists of the North. Senator Crittenden declined to accept the new party's nomination, however, and his decision came as a terrible blow to conservatives everywhere who had staked their meager hopes on the Kentuckian's vote-getting appeal. Nevertheless, they went ahead and held their national convention settling for the less considerable talents and reputation of Senator John Bell of Tennessee and naming former Senator Edward Everett of Massachusetts as his running mate.

All these developments—the split in the Democratic party, the breakup of the Democratic convention, the walkout of the Southern delegates, the formation of the Constitutional Union party —were grist for the mills of the jubilant and victory-hungry Republicans as they prepared to move into Chicago for their national convention. On May 16, in the huge wooden auditorium known as the Wigwam, the Republican party opened its convention proceedings with delegates who were confident that they were about to nominate the next President of the United States.

There seemed little doubt in anyone's mind but that the front-running candidate was William H. Seward, the popular New York Governor and a well-known antislavery leader. Indeed, after the first day of the convention, there were few spectators who thought that the Seward bandwagon could be stopped. The magic number was 233; and already Seward had received 173½ votes on the very first ballot! The next day would do the trick. That night the New Yorkers paraded noisily through the streets of the Windy City with their big brass bands, celebrating the triumph of William Seward and anticipating that the next day would make it official.

Behind the scenes, however, events were moving swiftly. In the course of his long political career, Seward had made many enemies. His record of radicalism made him unacceptable to many conservative Republicans from the Western states; his opposition to the Know-Nothing movement and his protection of the rights of Roman Catholics made him suspect with Nativists; his association with Thurlow Weed and the New York political machine created a most unsavory image; and the raucous behavior of the hard-drinking New York delegation shocked a good many of the Western Republicans. There were a number of rivals who wanted to block his nomination, but who saw no other candidate at hand to challenge the New Yorker's hold over the convention. Men like Edward Bates of Missouri, Salmon P. Chase of Ohio, and Simon Cameron of Pennsylvania all had solid blocks of votes—not enough to secure their own nominations, to be sure, but enough to stop Seward if they could agree on the right man to oppose him.

At this point the name of Abraham Lincoln was put forward as a possible substitute for Seward. His debates with Douglas had brought him a national reputation, and when he came East to speak in New York City in February, 1860, his carefully prepared Cooper Union speech impressed New York political leaders with its moderation on the slavery issue, its emphasis on constitutional procedure, and its strong appeal for national peace and harmony.

Lincoln's backing in the Western states was already considerable, his growing acceptance by Easterners added immeasurably to his political stature, and his refusal to be drawn into the Know-Nothing party increased his voting power among German and Irish immigrants. Because of his calm, objective, and dispassionate appraisal of the slavery issue, he was regarded by many Republicans as a more reliable and dependable candidate than the more excitable Seward and his militant Abolitionist associates.

Lincoln's managers went to work enthusiastically to complete the work they had already begun on behalf of the lanky rail-splitter from Illinois. An Illinois man, Norman B. Judd (who later placed Lincoln's name in nomination), arranged the seating in the Wigwam to the advantage of the Lincoln people by placing the Seward delegates in the front, surrounded by Lincoln's Illinois and Indiana delegations. This made it almost impossible for the New Yorkers to communicate effectively with the doubtful delegations arranged in the rear of the hall. Other Lincoln managers, directed by Judge David Davis and Leonard Swett, buttonholed delegates for Lincoln, bargained for support on the second ballot, cajoled favorite sons into lining up behind the Illinois candidate, made promises, and offered commitments. And to the candidates Cameron, Bates, and Chase they made binding promises that later affected the makeup of Lincoln's cabinet. While the Seward men were celebrating their triumph, the Lincoln men were hard at work into the wee hours of the convention's second morning organizing a stop-Seward movement to go into effect on the second balloting.

When the convention assembled later in the morning, it was apparent that there had been a major shift in the power structure of the convention and that a serious movement was afoot to defeat the New Yorker. To make matters worse, when the Seward delegates arrived at the Wigwam they found their seats occupied by Lincoln supporters. Although the convention chairman offered a great deal of sympathy, there was nothing that could be done to find seats for all the New Yorkers. When the second ballot was taken, it was evident that Seward had reached the peak of his power and that Lincoln was catching up fast. To the delight of uproarious supporters whose ear-splitting yells made the walls of the Wigwam tremble, Lincoln began to pick up more and more support from delegates who suddenly realized that Seward *could* be stopped and that Lincoln was the man to do it. New Hampshire, then Vermont, then Pennsylvania and Ohio turned over more votes to Lincoln, bringing him within $3\frac{1}{2}$ votes of Seward. On the third ballot, Massachusetts gave Lincoln 4 votes, and Ohio added 15 more to bring the railsplitter within $1\frac{1}{2}$ votes of the required 233 for nomination. Then the chairman of the Ohio delegation leaped to his feet to announce the change of four more votes from Chase to Lincoln! After a moment's silence, the great hall erupted in a tremendous roar. Abe Lincoln had been nominated! Cannon boomed out from the top of the Tremont House, the city of Chicago went wild, and the Republican party had its candidate for the election of 1860.

The election was now a four-cornered race, with each of the candidates—Lincoln, Douglas, Breckinridge, and Bell—claiming to be the man who would preserve the Union and prevent civil war. Although Douglas traveled through New England, the West, and the Southern states in a vigorous one-man crusade, the split within the ranks of the Democratic party proved to be an insurmountable obstacle. With the advantages of a unified organization, a wealthy treasury, and an enthusiastic following, the Republicans took advantage of every opportunity to pile up votes for their candidate.

Like most presidential candidates of the period, Lincoln was content to sit out the campaign in his temporary headquarters in the Illinois statehouse. Beyond discreetly referring visitors and newspaper reporters to his earlier actions and speeches on the issues of the contest, he did little more than grow a set of whiskers—beards had become fashionable by 1860.

While Lincoln waited in Springfield, however, his supporters were active in various parts of the country, and among the Republicans most of the disappointed candidates came to terms with their rivals long enough to work for the party. William Seward took to the stump in New England and in the Northwest; Salmon P. Chase traveled to Michigan to persuade free-soil

Democrats to throw in their lot with Old Abe; and Carl Schurz of Wisconsin did effective work among the numerous German-American communities in the Middle West.

Even though Lincoln had great appeal throughout the New England states because of the slavery issue, there were other factors contributing to strong Republican support. His background as a Whig undoubtedly made him a sympathetic candidate to many of the traditional Whigs in the Northeast. Too, the prospect of having a Republican Congress and the likelihood of higher tariffs undoubtedly appealed to much of the business community. The combination of antislavery sentiment and economics was a significant factor in swinging both New York and New Jersey behind the Republicans; but as the campaign moved westward the slavery issue tended to be pushed more and more into the background. Certainly this was true in the important state of Pennsylvania, the producer of half the nation's iron; and the role of the Republican party as the advocate of protectionism did much to undercut the appeal of the Democrats in that state.

Campaigning in Indiana (a "must" state that Frémont had lost in '56), the Lincoln supporters gave far less emphasis to the slavery issue, insisting that they were fighting for free land for the landless, for the rights of the workingman against the privileges of the aristocrat, and for the end of Democratic rule in Washington. In states like Ohio, Iowa, and Wisconsin, and in Lincoln's own home state of Illinois, Republicans pointed to the plank in their platform which would reduce the residency requirements for immigrants, and they made capital out of their support for free homesteads in the West and extolled the benefits of a transcontinental railroad. By the time they reached California and Oregon, the Republicans were hardly mentioning slavery at all but were stressing such things as the Pacific railroad, the overland mail issue, and the importance of turning the corrupt Democrats out of office.

When all the election returns were finally in in November (Vermont and Maine went Republican in September; Pennsylvania, Ohio and Indiana declared for Lincoln in October) the election of Lincoln was certain. The Republican candidate had carried eighteen states of the North and had rolled up an impressive electoral count of 180 votes. Breckinridge came in second with 72 electoral votes coming from eleven slave states; Bell ran up 39 electoral votes from three of the border states; while Douglas came in a poor fourth with only 12 electoral votes from the states of Missouri and New Jersey. Although it is true that Lincoln polled only 40 percent of the popular vote, and that the combined popular votes of his opponents totalled almost a million more than his, his overpowering electoral vote left no question as to his constitutional victory. At the same time, however, he was clearly a Northern President; only 26,000 out of his 1,800,000 votes coming from the Southern states, and over a million and a quarter Southern votes were registered against him. The political polarization of the 1850's had reached its culmination in the election of 1860.

While his electoral victory was unassailable, Lincoln was not even strongly a Northern President in terms of the support he could expect to receive on a broad popular basis. He had taken the North by the slim margin of 1,800,000 popular votes to the 1,500,000 of his opponents; and the manner in which some Northern newspapers were already assailing the new Republican candidate as "a slang-whanging stump speaker" and a "mole-eyed monster" testified to the problems Lincoln would have in organizing popular support behind his administration during the war years.

But the reactions the new President-elect faced in the North were nothing compared with those that his election produced in the South. There were some Southern leaders who pleaded for time and patience so that they could judge the extent of the damage. After all, said one Kentucky newspaper, "As we have survived the reign of James Buchanan, we can live through the administration of Abraham Lincoln." Noting that the Republicans had actually lost ground in the congressional elections and could not be expected to control either the House or the Senate, they asked their constituents to be "perfectly cool, or as cool as we can be." As one Mississippi newspaper put it: "We do not mean to rebel against the Government because an obnoxious man has been made President."

Others in the South, though, were not so calm about prospects for the future ("We will have trouble"; "The country is in peril"); and there were still others who believed that the "sectional" victory of the Republican party had placed the South in a position where it must definitely break with the Union. "Secession becomes the glory and prosperity of the South," cried a Georgia newspaper, while Mississippi echoed with the battle cry: "Devotion to the Union is treason to the South!" "For ourselves, we are not unprepared for this result," said the *New Orleans Delta* ominously, "nor for the remedy for its consequence."

The "remedy" was, of course, secession. This had always been the ultimate weapon for the advocates of states' rights, and the time had finally come when the South was prepared to use it. The response of the South was not so much a personal reaction against Abraham Lincoln himself as it was an emotional response to the Republicans' having taken over the leadership of the nation. This was the "Black Republican" party, the party of John Brown, the party committed to the eventual destruction of slavery through a containment policy that would place it in the course of ultimate extinction. Regarding the distinction Lincoln and the Republicans made between an attack upon slavery in the states themselves and attack upon the expansion of slavery into the territories as tricky semantics and utter hogwash, Southerners saw the Republican platform as merely the first step toward the destruction of the life, the society, and the culture of the South. "The significant fact which menaces the South is not that Abraham Lincoln is elected President;" said the *Richmond Enquirer* in a lead editorial on November 19, "but that the Northern people, by a sectional vote, have elected a President for the avowed purpose of aggression on Southern rights. The purpose of aggression had been declared. *This is a declaration of war.*"

As soon as the results of Lincoln's election were known, the principal federal officeholders in the state of South Carolina resigned and the two Senators also gave up their posts. In keeping

ELECTION OF 1860

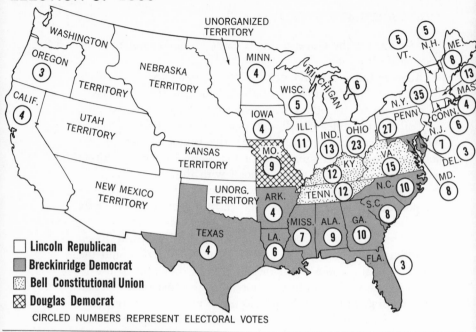

- Lincoln Republican
- Breckinridge Democrat
- Bell Constitutional Union
- Douglas Democrat

CIRCLED NUMBERS REPRESENT ELECTORAL VOTES

SECESSION 1860-1861

- THE CONFEDERACY

with the procedures outlined in Calhoun's theory of nullification, members of the state legislature called upon the voters to authorize a convention to deal with the question of secession. While officials of the state were negotiating with Secretary of War John B. Floyd for the purchase of 10,000 surplus army muskets, the South Carolina convention opened its deliberations at Columbia. The danger of smallpox made them move to Institute Hall in Charleston where the sessions resumed on December 18.

Two days later, "We, the people of the State of South Carolina, in Convention assembled" declared that the ordinance whereby the state had ratified the Constitution back in 1788 was now repealed, and that "the union now subsisting between South Carolina and other States under the name of the United States of America" was dissolved. There was no debate. The motion was put to a vote and was unanimously carried 169 to nothing.

Just as the colonial leaders who revolted against Great Britain in 1776 felt a need to "declare the causes" that impelled them to "separation," so the leaders of South Carolina needed to justify raising their state to its "separate and equal place among nations." A few days later, drawing upon a tradition of states'-rights doctrines that had characterized Southern constitutional opinion from Jefferson to Calhoun, the convention adopted a declaration that accused the Northern states of consistently violating the compact that joined the sovereign states together under the Constitution. The free states, they charged, had not only refused to support national legislation favorable to the South (such as the Fugitive Slave Act) but had kept up a "hostile agitation" against the South for over twenty-five years and had even "assumed the right of deciding upon the propriety of our domestic institutions." Northerners had formed a "sectional combination for subversion of the Constitution," they had drawn a geographical line across the Union, and now, with the election of Lincoln and the Republican party, they were obviously intent upon completing the destruction of the rights of the Southern states.

The question now was: would South Carolina stand alone, as she had when she defied the power of the Federal Government and braved the anger of President Andrew Jackson during the nullification crisis of 1832–33? Or would the other states of the South rally to her side and give her the moral support, the political encouragement, and the military assistance that could transform an idealistic gesture of defiance into a realistic and workable act of rebellion?

Entitled "The Last Moments of John Brown," this painting by Thomas Hovenden shows Brown leaving his cell on his way to the gallows. John Brown is the only American ever executed for the crime of treason in the United States; and, in fact, was executed for treason against a state (Virginia) and not against the Federal government. On the morning of his execution, Brown gave one of his guards a note containing the following words: "I John Brown am now quite certain that the crimes of this guilty land will never be purged away but with blood."

➤

WHETHER the secession of South Carolina would become the signal for a coalition of Southern states depended on the President's exercising the force of his personality and the powerful authority of his office. James Buchanan, however, was neither willing nor able to alter the course of events through his personality or his authority. As a lame-duck President whose party had been defeated in a national election, he questioned his right to establish policies that would bind his successor. An essentially cautious man who was never known for swift thought or decisive action, the seventy-year-old politician was content merely to hold the line and keep the peace until his time in office ran out in March, 1861. Surrounded by a noisy claque of mediocre Cabinet members who pushed him first one way and then the other, the baffled old man did little constructive in the critical weeks that followed Lincoln's election. Ultimately he did send an officer down to report on the situation at Charleston and tell Major Robert Anderson at Fort Moultrie to take whatever steps he thought necessary to protect his isolated garrison. And he drafted his State of the Union message. Some measure of the confusion and uncertainty that gripped the President's mind can be gathered from the annual message, read to the Congress on December 4, 1860, the day after it had convened.

Hoping to appeal to a broad range of opinion as a base for establishing a cooler atmosphere and a more reasonable discussion of the issues, he started out by denouncing the agitation of the Northern Abolitionists and urging them not to interfere any longer with the domestic institutions of the Southern states. Then he went on to denounce those in the South who were calling for secession and warned them that the mere "election of any one of our fellow-citizens to the office of President does not of itself afford just cause for dissolving the Union." Secession, he cautioned in fairly strong language, was nothing less than revolution. But, just at the point where he might have stated in clear and forceful language how he would view such a revolutionary act and what steps he would take to prevent one, Buchanan failed completely. Even though he had denounced secession as revolution and had deprecated any disruption of the Union, he admitted that there was nothing he could do to stop it. As President, he said, he had no powers of coercion that could prevent such a disaster, and he expressed the opinion that Congress itself possessed no powers of coercion. Congress might have a number of means of preserving the Union by "conciliation," he said simply, "but the sword was not placed in their hands to preserve it by force." It was a tragic and forlorn performance. In an effort to please as many different elements as possible, Buchanan ended by alienating everyone and made it abundantly clear that his administration had no intention of using force or coercion to prevent secession. The only hope the President held out was that Congress might submit an "explanatory amendment" to the Constitution on the subject of slavery, or that it might pursue a peaceful resolution of the problem through "conciliation."

It was in the spirit of conciliation that on December 20 the Senate appointed a Committee of Thirteen to investigate the growing crisis—ironically, this was the very day on which South Carolina passed its Ordinance of Secession. It was in the same spirit that Senator Crittenden of Kentucky, one of the members of the committee, proposed a series of six amendments to the Constitution; he hoped these would accomplish in 1860 what Henry Clay had done so successfully in 1850. The first and most critical of the "Crittenden Compromise" proposals was to extend the old 36°30′ line all the way west to the Pacific, prohibiting slavery north of that line while allowing it to the south. Future states would come into the Union under the principles of popular sovereignty, the Fugitive Slave Laws would be strictly enforced, and all personal liberty laws would be repealed. It was Crittenden's intention that his compromise proposals become amendments to the Constitution of the United States; no further amendments allowing Congress to alter slavery in any of the states were ever to be made.

The Southern Democratic members of the Committee of Thirteen preferred to withhold judgment until they were certain that the Republicans, especially those who were taking office in March, would agree to abide by the terms of the compromise proposal. Republican leaders, however, indicated that they would not accept the Crittenden Compromise, and President-elect Lincoln, in particular, made his own refusal crystal clear. Although he indicated that he was willing to make concessions on several points (he would support the Fugitive Slave Laws; he would support an amendment protecting slavery in the states), he would *not* compromise on the question of expansion. The Republican party was committed to prevent the extension of slavery; and for this reason, he told Illinois Congressman William Kellogg, he would "entertain no proposition for a compromise in regard to the extension of slavery." He was absolutely "inflexible" on this point, he informed Thurlow Weed of New York, maintaining that any proposal to have "the Missouri line extended" would lose the Republicans everything they had gained in the election of 1860. This rigid stand killed any chance the Crittenden Compromise might have had of being accepted. The Compromise was defeated in the Committee, it was defeated when it came before the Senate, and when Crittenden recommended that his proposals be submitted to the voters in a national referendum, this too was beaten down. 1860 was not 1850—the day of the compromise had passed.

Convinced that the Federal Government had neither the will nor the courage to act, and assured that the Republicans refused to compromise the issues in favor of a peaceful solution, the South prepared for the worst. On December 28, commissioners from the seceded state of South Carolina called upon President Buchanan, demanded the removal of all United States troops from Fort Sumter in Charleston Harbor, and called upon the government to turn over all federal forts within the state. Even before Buchanan gave his refusal, South Carolina proceeded to take over the United States arsenal at Charleston on December 30. This became the signal for other states throughout the lower South to seize federal military installations and to prepare themselves to follow South Carolina's lead.

On January 9, Mississippi voted in favor of secession by an overwhelming margin, and the next day Florida, after having seized the federal arsenal at Apalachicola four days earlier, also seceded from the Union. On January 4, troops from Alabama took over Fort Morgan and Fort Gaines, and then on January 11, despite the opposition of a substantial minority who wanted to wait for a Southern convention, responded to the appeals of William Lowndes Yancey and voted for secession. Georgia's Governor Joseph E. Brown ordered the seizure of Fort Pulaski on January 3, and on January 19 the secessionists overcame strong opposition and took their state out of the Union. After state forces had taken possession of the federal arsenal and army barracks at Baton Rouge, Louisiana passed an ordinance of secession by an equally strong margin. And on February 1, Texas declared in favor of secession. By the opening of February, 1861, therefore, seven states of the lower South had declared their separation from a compact forming the Union of states, had severed their relations with all the other states, and had announced themselves to be completely free political units.

On February 4, 1861, delegates from all the seceded states except Texas gathered in convention in the state capitol at Montgomery, Alabama, where they formed a new government called "The Confederate States of America" and proceeded to draft a new constitution. Closely following the wording of the Constitution of the United States, the Constitution of the Confederacy contained certain features that were characteristic both of Southern constitutional views and of the current crisis of the Union. The sovereignty of each individual state was emphasized and the right of secession was clearly implied although it was not explicitly guaranteed. No law could ever be passed prohibiting the institution of slavery, and every citizen was guaranteed the right to take his slaves into whatever territory might be acquired by the Confederacy in the future. The President was to be elected to a single term of six years; cabinet members might be granted seats in either house of Congress; the general welfare clause was omitted; Congress could not levy protective tariffs; and internal improvements were restricted to matters involving navigation.

Acting as the provisional legislature of the Confederacy until the regular elections could take place seven months later, the convention chose Jefferson Davis of Mississippi as President of the government, and Alexander H. Stephens of Georgia as Vice-President. A graduate of West Point who had served with distinction in the Mexican War, Davis had combined life as a successful planter with a public career of service to his state and nation. With a background of administrative experience (he was Secretary of War in the Pierce administration), and with extensive legislative service in the United States Senate, he had emerged as one of the most highly respected statesmen in the South. Stephens was a Congressman from Georgia and a relatively mild states'-rights man who originally opposed secession in his own state. He was selected for the second post largely to persuade other Southern moderates to support the confederation movement. A new flag was adopted (the "Stars and Bars") to symbolize that the Confederate States of America was viewed as an entirely new and independent nation—a bona fide nation with its own constitution, its own legislature, its own President, its own flag, and its own authority to do all those things that an independent nation had the right to do.

In the North, the sequence of events—defiance, secession, and then confederation—were met with disbelief. During the three crucial months between the secession of South Carolina and the inauguration of the new President-elect, the fatal weakness of this lame-duck period was nowhere so painfully evident as when the Republican party gained a majority in both Houses of Congress after the representatives from the lower South had withdrawn. At this point, the situation in Washington degenerated into confused activity and inconclusive results.

As President Buchanan's Southern Cabinet members resigned their posts and followed their states into secession, Northern appointees took their place and began to steer the President into the more positive stand reflected in his message to Congress on January 8. Flatly denying that any state had the right, "by its own act," to secede from the Union or to throw off federal obligations "at its pleasure," he warned the Southern states that as President of the United States he would continue to collect public revenues and protect public property. Although he assured the South that he had no authority to "make aggressive war upon any state," he emphasized the fact that he was prepared to use military force "defensively" against any state that resisted federal officers or attacked federal property. He closed with another appeal to Congress to come up with some practical proposition for conciliation as rapidly as possible before events pushed both sides into positions from which they could not retreat.

When Buchanan attempted to convert his policy of defensive protection into forceful action, however, he could not face up to what he feared as the inevitable consequence of conflict. On January 9, 1861, he dispatched a merchant vessel, the *Star of the West*, to reinforce the small federal garrison at Fort Sumter in Charleston Harbor, only to have South Carolina shore batteries on Morris Island and Fort Moultrie open fire on the ship and prevent it from entering the Harbor. The vessel steamed back to New York. The President, strangely silent now, refused to regard the incident as a provocation; and the commander of the fort, Major Robert Anderson, was left to work out whatever arrangements he could with the authorities in South Carolina. It was clear that little further assistance from the White House could be expected to work out a solution of the critical issues facing the nation.

Nor was the Republican-dominated Congress any more ready to offer effective remedies. The new session succeeded in passing the Morrill Tariff which increased duties on iron and wool, and it created the new territories of Colorado, Nevada, and Dakota without even a mention of slavery—apparently assuming that the nature of the terrain automatically excluded it. For the most part, however, Congress was content to await the inauguration of the new Republican President before taking any further action on the question of the seceded states.

Those in the North who feared the approaching cataclysm and who sought ways to avert it had to look beyond the formal agencies of government for aid. Moderates in general, and members of the Northern business community in particular, made extraordinary efforts to dramatize the desire of the vast majority of people for a peaceful solution. The manufacturing, the financing, and the transportation of Southern cotton had become such important parts of the industrial and financial life of the Northeast that secession was regarded as an economic disaster as well as a political crisis. Northern factories depended upon a steady flow of cotton upon which to base their profits. Northern bankers who grew rich by extending liberal credit to Southern planters against the next year's crop insisted upon resolving the issues and maintaining a stable economy. Northern shipowners worried about losing the valuable Southern cotton trade, which accounted for well over sixty percent of the exports of the nation. If the South were permitted to secede from the Union, the textile factories would lose their essential raw material, the ships would lose their largest cargo, and the banks would risk the possibility of a widespread moratorium on Southern debts that would wreak havoc in the financial centers of the Northeast.

Throughout the month of January, delegations of merchants, manufacturers, industrialists, bankers, and railroad men poured into Washington urging Republican leaders to meet the complaints of the South and do everything they could to restore harmony and peace. They displayed gigantic memorials calling for Congress to support one of the compromise proposals under consideration. A New York delegation of prominent businessmen A. A. Low, Peter Cooper, William E. Dodge, and Wilson G. Hunt were entrusted with a memorial signed by forty thousand New York colleagues when they met with Senator William H. Seward on January 30 to plead the cause of compromise. Seward received his constituents cordially, expressed sympathy for their concern, but declined to endorse their proposals. A Boston delegation, headed by Amos A. Lawrence, Edward Everett, and Robert C. Winthrop, and carrying a petition with over twenty-two thousand signatures (described as a hundred yards long and a foot in diameter when rolled up) received even less encouragement when Senator Charles Sumner told the crestfallen group that their efforts were "of no more use than a penny whistle in a tempest." The delegates went everywhere in Washington and spoke with everyone they could find—President Buchanan, Vice-President Breckinridge, General Winfield Scott, ex-President John Tyler, ex-President Millard Fillmore—but to no avail. They found hospitality and sympathy—but not even a promise of any kind of action.

As the businessmen packed their bags and returned North, their mission a failure, the only remaining hope that war might be averted rested with the "Peace Convention" that was assembling at Willard's Hotel at the corner of Fourteenth Street in Washington. First suggested by the state of Virginia as a means of averting the hostilities that now seemed imminent, the Peace Convention received a favorable response from a number of Northern and Border states with the result that twenty-one states were represented at the conference which was scheduled to begin on February 4.

Hopes began to run high. In business circles, stocks started to rise and financial journals reported the disappearance of "panic" and the quieting of "commercial fears." The "political difficulties" would soon be settled, readers were assured, and the crisis would certainly be over "within a short time." This optimism was reflected in an upward swing in New England textile sales during late February and early March, 1861, while the Peace Convention was still holding its meetings.

But it was no use. The conference was presided over by a former President of the United States, John Tyler, and it contained a number of the most prominent political leaders from all over the country; still, little constructive work was accomplished. There was a sense of depression and futility among the members in addition to a lack of encouragement and support from the Republicans who were present. A number of Northern governors, in an effort to demonstrate their willingness to work for peace and avoid the stigma of seeming to be uncooperative, had selected as delegates the kind of antislavery representatives who would refuse to accept any compromise involving the extension of slavery. A meeting with President James Buchanan only deepened the disappointment falling over the entire convention, and it was with only a last faint hope that they prepared to meet the President-elect when he arrived in Washington.

As he packed his trunks, cleaned out his files, ordered some new clothes, and traveled around to say goodbye to his old friends, in Springfield, Illinois, Abraham Lincoln was at work forming his Cabinet. For the top post of Secretary of State he selected his Chicago rival, William H. Seward of New York, hoping thereby to solidify his strength in the Empire State as well as to cultivate the support of the Free-Soil and antislavery forces in the Northeast. To bring radical Western views into his administration he selected Senator-elect Salmon P. Chase of Ohio, a former Whig and Free-soiler, as Secretary of the Treasury. Paying off two political commitments made by his campaign managers at the Chicago convention, Lincoln appointed Simon Cameron of Pennsylvania Secretary of War and Caleb B. Smith of Indiana Secretary of the Interior. The President appointed Gideon Welles of Connecticut Secretary of the Navy, in deference to the wishes of his new Vice-President Hannibal Hamlin of Maine (whom Lincoln had never met in his life until after the convention); Edward Bates of Missouri was named Attorney General; and Montgomery Blair, an old Jacksonian Democrat, became the Postmaster General.

On February 11, 1861, Lincoln made a moving speech of farewell to the citizens of Springfield, where he had lived for a quarter of a century, where his children were born, and where one lay buried. "I now leave" he told his friends as he stood on the platform of the railroad car in a cold drizzle, "not knowing when, or whether ever, I may return, with a task before me greater than that which rested on Washington." A few moments later the train began the long journey that would carry the new President to his rendezvous with history.

Stopping at various state capitals along the route to Washington, he made quiet, prudent speeches, reserving a formal announcement of presidential policy for his official inaugural address. Because of rumors and reports that an attempt would be made on his life, he passed through the city of Baltimore incognito and entered the capital on a secret train after nightfall. Less than twenty-four hours after he arrived in Washington, delegates of the Peace Commission called upon Lincoln hoping to get some positive commitment on his future policies. The reception in

Parlor Number Six of Willard's Hotel was quite informal as the delegates gathered around the strange, tall figure from Illinois, straining to hear any word or phrase that would give hope for a peaceful compromise.

Everything went quietly for a while, as Lincoln chatted affably with the delegates, moving quickly from one to another, shaking hands, renewing old acquaintances, making new ones. To all queries and questions Lincoln held out no other course besides that supplied by the Constitution itself. "My course is as plain as a turnpike road," he told William C. Rives of Virginia. "It is marked out by the Constitution. I am in no doubt which way to go."

The tone of civility was suddenly broken when James A. Seddon of Virginia (later to be Secretary of War in the Confederate government) charged the Republican party with having encouraged John Brown and William Lloyd Garrison to provoke slave insurrections in the South. When Lincoln dryly observed that Brown had been hanged and Garrison had been imprisoned, Seddon blasted the Northerners for not having carried out the statutes calling for the return of fugitive slaves. Again Lincoln quietly parried by pointing out that fugitive slaves *had* been returned—from the very shadow of Boston's Faneuil Hall, in fact. Although people in the North were required to observe the letter of the law, he said, there was nothing in the law that forced them to enjoy their work.

"Your press is incendiary!" cried Seddon, suddenly changing his attack; and he went on to accuse the newspapers of the North of promoting slave uprisings and murder in the South. At this point Lincoln's smile faded and his tone became sharp. "I beg pardon, Mr. Seddon," he replied. "I intend no offense, but I will not suffer such a statement to pass unchallenged, because it is not true. No Northern newspaper, not the most ultra, has advocated a slave insurrection or advised slaves to cut their masters' throats. A gentleman of your intelligence should not make such assertions. We do maintain the freedom of the press—we deem it necessary to a free government. Are we peculiar in that respect? Is not the same doctrine held in the South?"

Passing on to other members of the delegation, Lincoln greeted each one and chatted pleasantly about personal affairs. As he mingled with the New York group, William E. Dodge raised his voice so that he could be heard throughout the room and addressed the President-elect. Obviously hoping to get a preview of what Lincoln intended to say in his Inaugural Address, Dodge asked whether he expected that grass would grow in the streets of the commercial cities of the nation?

Lincoln, however, had maintained his silence all the way from Springfield, and he had no intention of letting down now. As far as he was concerned, he replied with a disarming smile, obviously hoping to brush the question aside, the only place grass would grow was in the fields and meadows where it always grew. But Dodge was on him like a tiger. "Then you will yield to the just demands of the South?" "You will admit slave states into the Union on the same conditions as free states?" "You will not go to war on account of slavery?"

As the room suddenly quieted and the delegates waited in silence for Lincoln's reply, the tall man slowly answered in tones that were stern and measured and thoughtful. "I do not know that I understand your meaning, Mr. Dodge," he said evenly, "nor do I know what acts or opinions may be in the future, beyond this. If I shall ever come to the great office of President of the United States, I shall take an oath. I shall swear that I will faithfully execute the office of President of the United States, of all the United States, and that I will, to the best of my ability, preserve, protect, and defend the Constitution of the United States. . . . It is not the Constitution as I would like to have it, but as it *is*, that is to be defended. The Constitution will not be preserved and defended until it is enforced and obeyed in every part of every one of the United States. It must be respected, obeyed, enforced, and defended—let the grass grow where it may."

No one could answer. No one could think of anything to say. The determined words and the unquestionable tone of authority with which they had been delivered stunned the delegates. The new man was prepared to give one promise, and only one, relating to his future conduct as President. He would obey the Constitution of the United States.

It became evident, day after day, that the members of the Peace Convention could not arrive at any satisfactory grounds for compromise. Every attempt to bring up the Crittenden proposals was fought down by Northerners as outright surrender, while the Southern representatives were determined that they would accept nothing less. "The Peace Congress," observed one New Englander, "was slowly talking against time, and coming to no conclusion." Somewhat less kindly, the *New York Tribune* referred to the gathering as "a convocation of old hens sitting on a nest of eggs, some of which would hatch out vipers, while most were addled."

On February 27, the convention presented to the Congress a plan of conciliation involving seven amendments to the Constitution that incorporated many of the features of the ill-fated Crittenden proposals. These suggestions received little support when they were brought to a vote in a Senate Committee on March 2, and they were not even presented in the House of Representatives. Just before March 4, 1861, the ineffectual Peace Convention concluded its sessions, with most of the departing members convinced that all hopes of reconstructing the Union were gone and that civil war was only a matter of time. With the news that the main purposes of the Peace Convention had failed, the stock market collapsed and business sales plummeted to an appalling low. By Inauguration Day, the entire nation was tense with anxiety, waiting to hear what the new President would say about the historic and unprecedented state of affairs in which the issues of war and peace, life and death, hung in the balance.

CHAPTER 10
THE GUNS
OF SUMTER

THE INAUGURATION of Abraham Lincoln as the sixteenth President of the United States took place amid tense military precautions, with squads of riflemen on the roofs of buildings as President Buchanan and the President-elect rode along Pennsylvania Avenue in an elaborate procession from Willard's Hotel. After first visiting the Senate chamber to see Hannibal Hamlin of Maine sworn in as Vice-President, the presidential party made its way to the Capitol where it was escorted to the east portico and then out onto the platform to face a waiting crowd of over ten thousand people. Sharpshooters peered anxiously from the windows in the wings of the Capitol building looking out for any acts of violence.

Reaching into an inside pocket for his speech, Lincoln smoothed the papers briefly on the rostrum, drew his reading-glasses from another pocket, steadied them briefly upon his nose, and then began his carefully prepared Inaugural Address. Speaking in measured tones, he emphasized the fact that his first duty was to preserve the Union and to uphold the authority of the Government of the United States. To calm the anxieties and apprehensions of the South, he announced that he had no intention of interfering with slavery in the slave states, and insisted that as Chief Executive he would enforce the provisions of the Fugitive

Many Northerners got their information about national events and world affairs from the pages of Harper's Weekly, *a popular illustrated journal which not only contained news and opinions, but pieces of fiction and humorous anecdotes. This contemporary print from the front page of* Harper's Weekly *shows Charlestonians crowded on their rooftops watching the spectacle of Confederate batteries firing on Fort Sumter. The Union fort, with its barracks in flames, is in the center of the harbor. Off to the left are the ships of the Northern relief expedition which made no attempt to enter the harbor, but later carried off Major Anderson and his garrison.*

Slave Law. At the same time, however, he strongly reaffirmed his
belief in the fundamental principle that the Union was "perpet-
ual" and that it could not be dissolved without the consent of all
the states. The Union was unbroken, as far as he was concerned;
and he would continue to act just as any other President would
act in all things affecting the government and the Union. There
would be no conflict, therefore, he concluded, unless the South
itself provoked it. "In your hands, my dissatisfied fellow country-
men, and not in mine, is the momentous issue of civil war. You
can have no conflict without being yourselves the aggressors. You
have no oath registered in heaven to destroy the government,
while I have the most solemn one to 'preserve, protect, and defend it.' "

When he finished speaking, the aged Chief Justice, Roger B.
Taney, slowly moved forward with the open Bible so that Lincoln could take the oath of office. After the solemn words were
read and repeated, the Marine Corps band struck up, the crowd
cheered, and Army artillery over on the nearby slope thundered
out its salute to the new President. The inaugural ceremonies
were over.

Lincoln turned to the task of salvaging some measure of peace,
despite the incessant flood of hungry office-seekers that plagued
him day and night. On March 5, the Senate officially received and
approved the slate of new Cabinet officers that Lincoln had
worked out before he left for Washington. For a brief moment,
just before Inauguration Day, it looked as though Lincoln would
have to find someone else for the post of Secretary of State when
William Seward decided that he could not possibly serve in the
same Cabinet with his political rival, Salmon P. Chase of Ohio,
the new Secretary of the Treasury. A strong personal appeal
from Lincoln, however, soothed the ruffled feathers and led
Seward to accept the top Cabinet post.

Many people appeared to view Seward as the real power in the
new Lincoln administration, as a more experienced and sophisti-
cated leader who would handle the affairs of state for the genial
but limited rail-splitter from Illinois. Indeed, Seward himself

seemed to consider his position as the one to dictate the course of the new President's actions and policies. On April 1, 1861, Seward sent Lincoln a letter entitled "Thoughts for the President's Consideration." He suggested that Lincoln leave all policy decisions to the Secretary of State, that Fort Sumter be evacuated by Federal troops, and that the Government consider going to war with both France and Spain as a means of forcing all sections of the nation to forget their differences and unite against a common enemy. With remarkable self-control, Lincoln set aside these fantastic proposals, and with quiet dignity replied to Seward, leaving no doubt that he, as President of the United States, would be the only one to determine national policy. Thus, Lincoln let it be known that he would be master of his Cabinet.

There were many situations pointing up the conflict of interests between the Federal Government, representing an unbroken Union, and the Confederate States, self-declared independent entities. But few were as critical as Fort Sumter, a federal fort located inside the mouth of Charleston Harbor. The Federal Government regarded this fort as United States Government property which must be maintained and defended. The Confederate States regarded Fort Sumter as the property of a foreign power—a potential threat that had to be removed.

President Buchanan made one attempt to reinforce the federal fort early in January, but when the *Star of the West* was fired upon by shore batteries he quickly backed off, let time run out, and left the problem to the incoming Lincoln administration. On the morning after his inauguration Lincoln studied the dispatches from Major Anderson reporting that the food supplies for his garrison of eighty men would last only about four more weeks and that unless he received reinforcements and provisions he would be forced to turn the fort over to the Confederates. Lincoln faced a deadly dilemma: If he sent a vessel to the relief of Fort Sumter, he would be accused of an act of aggression and he might touch off a bloody conflict. Buchanan's experience in January indicated that the Confederacy would most likely regard reinforcement as an act of war, and recent reports from Confederate territory only confirmed the probability that the South was readying itself to respond to an act of war by the Union government. If, on the other hand, Lincoln did not send relief to the garrison at Sumter, then he was failing in his duty as President and Commander-in-Chief. Not acting would mean he was tacitly agreeing that the Union was, indeed, broken and that he was no longer the President of all of the people of all of the states.

After long and serious thought, Lincoln decided to send aid to Fort Sumter. Notifying Governor Pickens of South Carolina on April 6 that he was going to "supply Fort Sumter with provisions only," he dispatched a small fleet from New York for that purpose.

To the leaders of the South, Lincoln's decision to provision Fort Sumter indeed seemed an overt act of aggression and an invasion of their soil. After an anxious conference at Montgomery, the Confederate Secretary of War directed General P. T. G. Beauregard to demand the evacuation of the Fort. If the demand was refused, he was told to "reduce it." Although Major Anderson offered to surrender after his failing rations had run out, the fact that provisions were on the way caused the Confederates to regard the Major's answer as unsatisfactory. At 4:30 in the morning of April 12, 1861, Confederate shore batteries opened fire on Fort Sumter. After a bombardment of about forty hours which damaged the walls and caused great fires, and with his ammunition nearly gone, Major Anderson surrendered the Fort on April 13. At this point, the relief squadron had little else to do but carry off Anderson and his garrison after the surrender.

The attack on Fort Sumter produced a dramatic change of Northern attitudes, creating a spirit of unity and patriotism at a time when Northern sentiment was marked by weakness and indecision. Democrats rivaled Republicans in public displays of loyalty, and businessmen who had earlier tried to prevent war now supported the Union cause and called for a swift defeat of the secessionists. Abolitionists heartily supported the administration and backed the War, and even pacifists salved their consciences with the explanation that they were not being called upon to fight a war but to suppress a rebellion. Although there were still those who opposed the War and challenged the leadership of Lincoln, their voices were hardly heard amid the clamor and excitement sweeping through the North.

On April 15, three days after the fall of Sumter, the President issued a proclamation calling forth the "militia of the several States of the Union" to suppress "combinations" in seven states that were "too powerful to be suppressed by the ordinary course of judicial proceedings." Lincoln resorted to this particular procedure of calling upon the states to provide the militia, rather than calling out the United States Army, not merely to get the 75,000 men needed to begin military action against the Confederacy but to classify this officially (at least in Lincoln's mind) as a rebellion against a legally constituted government and not, as the Confederacy claimed, a war between two hostile nations.

Lincoln's call for volunteer militiamen to suppress the insurrection of the rebellious states produced a violent reaction throughout the upper South. Until the attack upon Fort Sumter, eight slave states had still refused to leave the Union. Although they generally conceded that slavery was permissible and insisted that the Confederate states had a right to depart from the Union in peace, they themselves had decided to remain with the Union. When the Federal Government announced its intention of bringing the seceded states back into the Union by force of arms, however, four of these states—Arkansas, Tennessee, North Carolina, and Virginia—also seceded from the Union during April and May of 1861. This brought the total number of states in the Confederacy to eleven. When Virginia entered the Confederacy, Richmond was made the capital of the South, and Colonel Robert E. Lee declined a position of high command in the Federal army, resigned his commission in the United States Army, and offered his services for the defense of his native state.

The remaining slave states—the Border States, Missouri, Kentucky, Delaware, and Maryland—although they were divided in sentiment did not secede from the Union. In all these states, however, a bitter contest was waged all through the Civil War; they furnished men for the armies of both sides, and brother was pitted against brother in divided allegiance. About the only bright spot in this otherwise gloomy picture for the North came when a block of forty-six counties in the mountains of northwest Virginia broke away from the rebellious state in June, 1861, and formed the loyal state of West Virginia.

From the outset of the War, the North could count on a numerical advantage in terms of states, population, industrial plants, and railroad lines. Backing the Union cause were a total of 23 states, with an aggregate population of over 20 million. About 110,000 manufacturing plants were to be found in the North, along with 21,973 miles of important railroad lines connecting the Northeast with the Mississippi and Ohio Valleys. The Confederacy, by contrast, could count on only 11 states, with a population of a little over 9 million people—nearly 4 million of whom were Negro slaves. There were fewer than 20,000 factories below the Mason-Dixon line, and the South held less than a third (9,283 miles) of the railroad mileage at that time.

The North also possessed certain obvious military advantages. It had a sizeable regular army, and because of its greater overall population it could be expected to recruit many more men in the years to come. The Union forces had taken over the entire United States Navy, almost intact, and this important factor placed the Confederacy under a considerable handicap from the very start. Since the North was clearly the financial capital of the nation, with strong banks, greater capital reserves, and a more varied economy, in the long run it would be better able to finance the costly operations of a protracted struggle.

But the South, too, possessed certain advantages. First, the Confederacy decided to assume an essentially defensive position, using the mountains, the rivers, and the seacoast to ward off attacks; and this decision automatically forced the North to develop a three-to-one superiority in numbers. Also, some 182 Confederate officers of the rank of brigadier general or higher came from the trained ranks of the United States Army, and these included such brilliant leaders as Robert E. Lee, Thomas "Stonewall" Jackson, and Joseph E. Johnston. The men in the Confederate ranks, too, were more accustomed to outdoor life, were better horsemen, and were more skilled in the use of firearms. Fighting for their homes, their land, and their freedom against hostile aggression and invasion, they comprised a stubborn and formidable foe.

Economically, too, the Confederacy possessed considerable bargaining power. An agrarian section specializing in raw staples —notably cotton—the South wielded enormous influence at home and abroad. Nations like England and France, with large textile industries that employed hundreds of thousands of workers, would find it difficult to ignore the demands of the Confederacy for recognition and support. The South also found considerable sympathy among some Europeans who found much to admire in the chivalry, elegance, and tradition of the antebellum South. This affinity was seen as a possible inducement to bring European aid to the Confederacy.

The regular army of the United States was well trained and efficient, and it had experienced its baptism of fire only a dozen years before in the Mexican War. By March, 1861, though, there were only 13,000 officers and men, and most of these were on garrison duty along the Indian frontier and could not be spared immediately. As a result, the Federal Government found that it had to rely heavily upon the state militias. Since few of these states had enough men to fill their assigned quotas, each governor was forced to issue his own call for troops. Mass meetings were held throughout the states to raise volunteer units, and as soon as companies were filled they were assembled into regiments and promptly sent along to the national government. Company commanders were invariably elected by the men themselves, while regimental officers were usually selected by the governor. Within a surprisingly short time, more than enough men were ready— but the supply of arms was totally inadequate, uniforms were scarce and varied, and the recruits were without the slightest knowledge of military training and discipline.

In the South, recruitment followed much the same pattern. President Davis called for troops to be assembled as fast as possible, and men rushed to volunteer when the drums rolled in the various towns and villages. In order to offset the lack of a navy, the Confederacy issued "letters of marque and reprisal" which authorized her ships to capture merchant vessels flying the Stars and Stripes. Although Southerners were not much better equipped than the Union troops, they were able to start the fighting with a larger supply of small arms, ammunition, and horses. Between December, 1860, and February, 1861, the Confederate States had taken over a score of federal forts and arsenals and had come into possession of some 160,000 rifles, muskets, and cannon. These, added to the millions of small weapons throughout the rural Southland, gave the Confederate troops an initial advantage in firepower over Union troops who, in the early stages of the fighting, were often equipped with foreign weapons that they did not know how to use.

By June of 1861, the lines were clearly drawn, and in the minds of each of the contestants the issues were personal and vital. Northerners were determined to restore the integrity of the Union, needlessly broken into pieces by the South's selfish whim. And many also harbored the conviction that victory over the South would bring in its wake the abolition of Negro slavery. Southerners, on the other hand, were equally determined to defend their homeland against what they regarded as the unwarranted aggression of the "Black Republicans." Convinced of the constitutionality of peaceable secession, the South determined to wage a defensive war of attrition designed to wear down the Union government and force it to recognize the independent status of the South.

Although General Winfield Scott, General-in-Chief of the United States Army, was seventy-five years old, swollen, and infirm, he viewed the essential military strategy with a clear and steady eye. During the secession crisis he had urged Buchanan to reinforce the federal forts to prevent their seizure by the Confederacy, and now that war had come, he advised Lincoln to call for 300,000 men for three-year enlistments—not 75,000 men for three-month terms.

Envisioning a long and costly war at a time when most people were talking about "peace in ninety days," he proposed a coordinated plan to envelop the Confederacy and strangle it. Scott's "Anaconda Plan" (as the press called it, after the huge reptile that crushes its victims in its coils) proposed: (1) to establish an effective blockade around the entire Southern seacoast from Norfolk to Galveston; (2) to seize and control the Mississippi River so that the Union could divide the Confederacy and develop new offensive bases; (3) to use control of the border states to clamp down the lid on the Confederacy below; and (4) to send in well-trained, massive armies to crush the Confederate forces and destroy their resources once they had been effectively boxed in by land and sea. These were the basic ingredients of the Union war plans that were officially adopted by the Lincoln administration just before Congress came into session on July 4, 1861.

Scott's elaborate military plans seemed much too complicated to many Northerners who assumed that a quick march upon the nearby enemy capital at Richmond would bring victory to the Union forces and cause the immediate collapse of the Confederacy. Yielding to public pressure, on July 29 the administration assigned the task to General Irvin McDowell. While General Robert Patterson moved to keep Joseph E. Johnston's Confederate troops in the Shenandoah Valley from moving eastward, McDowell prepared to smash into Beauregard's army with his force of 35,000 men and capture the Confederate capital.

On July 16, 1861, McDowell's army moved out of Washington and headed for the railroad junction at Manassas. His unseasoned recruits were accompanied by Congressmen, newspapermen, sightseers, even women and children, who drove along in gaily bedecked carriages to watch the "Yanks" whip the "Johnny Rebs." Waiting for the Federals was General P. T. G. Beauregard with almost the same number of troops, settled on the southern side of a little stream called Bull Run.

On the morning of July 21, the two armies made contact. McDowell confidently threw his assault against the Confederate left flank in a maneuver that seemed sure to sweep the Southerners from the field by noontime. A "stonewall" defense by General Thomas Jackson, however, followed by a series of unexpected Confederate counterattacks, stalled the Federal assault. At this point, the troops of General Johnston, who had slipped away from Patterson, came pouring into the Confederate lines, at which point McDowell decided to pull his troops back to safer positions. For the inexperienced troops, however, the order to withdraw created panic and the result was a headlong flight. While some regiments held their ranks and kept the pursuers back, the rest of the Union troops rushed pell-mell back to Washington. At one point the capital lay wide open to the enemy, if he had had the means of taking advantage of the opportunity. Stonewall Jackson insisted that he could take Washington with only five thousand men, but President Davis decided not to make the attempt. The Confederates were as badly cut up as the Federals at Bull Run, and almost as confused and disorganized. But the onus of defeat fell on McDowell, who was reported not to have used a reserve division that was available to him.

The defeat at Bull Run rocked the North back upon its heels. But it did serve two important functions: First, it shocked complacent Northerners into realizing that this was not going to be a short war won by untrained recruits. Second, it enabled President Lincoln to get all the three-year enlistments he asked for—and many more. After the initial shock, the North rallied behind the administration, and states competed with one another in furnishing new companies for the defense of the Union.

Bull Run was the end for General McDowell. In order to reorganize the Army of the Potomac, thirty-four-year-old George B. McClellan was ordered to return from West Virginia and was placed in command. Young, dynamic, and brilliant (he was often compared to Napoleon) "Little Mac" restored morale among both the troops and the public at large as he vowed to build one of the greatest fighting machines in history. A skilled organizer and drillmaster, McClellan slowly brought order out of chaos and established a regular routine of discipline and training. When old General Scott retired early in November, 1861, McClellan was placed in command of all Union forces. Through the fall and into the winter of 1861, the city of Washington resounded to the encouraging sounds of marching feet, pounding hooves, and clanging caissons. Into the spring of 1862 the drill and the training continued, the numbers grew larger and larger, the appropriations went higher—but there was no sign that any action was even contemplated. A perfectionist, McClellan pledged not to move until he had a force big enough and strong enough to insure victory.

McClellan's "masterful inactivity" began to annoy the public, the press, and the President when, even after the first of the year, there was no word that the Army of the Potomac was about to move. Also, in the Western theater of operations military developments were taking place at a surprising rate. The Confederate defense line ran west from Virginia to the Mississippi and was anchored securely on the three main rivers that cut into the old Northwest Territory from the South. Fort Henry controlled the Tennessee River, Fort Donelson commanded the Cumberland River, and heavy fortifications on Island Number Ten (one of a chain of islands in the Mississippi River near the Tennessee line) allowed the Confederates to effectively block the Mississippi itself. If Union forces, under the command of General Henry W. Halleck, intended to move successfully against the forces of General Albert Sydney Johnston, Confederate commander in the West, they would have to take these forts first.

Brigadier General Ulysses S. Grant obtained permission from Halleck to launch an assault on Fort Henry just after the first of 1862. Grant, a West Pointer who had won distinction in the Mexican War, had resigned from the peacetime Army when boredom led to too much drinking. Still only thirty-nine years old when the war broke out, Grant offered his services to his state, was commissioned a colonel, and was given command of an ornery district regiment in Illinois. Having whipped his force into shape in a surprisingly short time, Grant suddenly found himself one of three dozen brigadiers created by President Lincoln in August, 1861. With 17,000 men, supported by a squadron of Union gunboats under Flag-Officer Andrew H. Foote, Grant moved up the Tennessee River, and on February 6 his men forced the surrender of Fort Henry. Without waiting for new orders, Grant then marched his men eleven wintry miles overland to Fort Donelson and took the "unconditional surrender" of that strategic fort on February 16, 1862. Grant's bold moves created a sensation in the

victory-hungry North and caused Lincoln to give General Halleck
(who, as theater commander, received much of the credit) command over all the Western armies.

Grant's unexpected victories at Henry and Donelson forced
Confederate General A. S. Johnston to pull his army down toward
Corinth, Mississippi, lest he be outflanked by the Union forces
still moving up the Tennessee River. Halleck ordered General
Don Carlos Buell to proceed south from Nashville and link up
with Grant who had just arrived at Pittsburgh Landing in southern Tennessee, just north of the Mississippi border. Both federal
armies would then move against Johnston. Learning that the
Union troops were massing before him, the Confederate commander came to the conclusion that his only hope lay in smashing Grant before Buell could join him.

On the morning of April 6, a surprise Confederate attack near
Shiloh caught Grant and his men off guard and threatened to
wipe out the whole Union position. Only a hastily organized resistance by Union riflemen and cannoneers managed to stall the
fierce Confederate charge, which slowly became disorganized by
virtue of its own success. When Johnston was mortally wounded,
General Beauregard took over and decided to suspend the attack
for the rest of the day in order to consolidate his gains and reorganize his troops. This brief respite gave Grant an opportunity
to regroup his own shattered forces. Using advance elements of
Buell's troops as reinforcements, Grant did the unexpected and
launched a fierce counterattack the next morning which drove the
Confederate army from the field and forced it to withdraw all the
way south to Corinth to take up new defensive positions.

On the same day as Grant's bloody victory at Shiloh, General
John Pope took the strategic Island Number Ten, thus opening
the upper Mississippi to Union attack. This advantage was followed up by General Halleck himself who moved to Corinth on
May 30 and then turned his attention to the important river city
of Memphis, whose water approaches were guarded by a make-
shift fleet of light, fast vessels, armored with cotton bales, designed to hit hard and run fast. After a series of unsuccessful attempts to take the city, Flag-Officer C. H. Davis led a small force

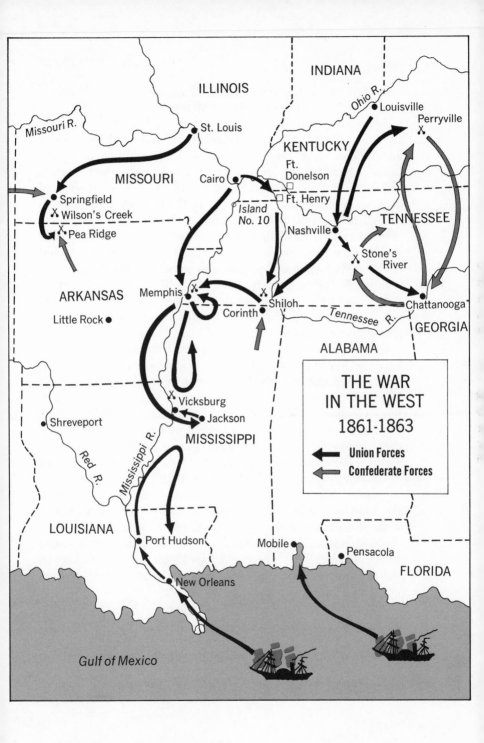

THE WAR
IN THE WEST
1861-1863

➡ Union Forces
➡ Confederate Forces

of Union ironclads against the Confederate ships, blasted them to pieces, and forced the surrender of Memphis on June 6, 1862.

At the same time that Union forces were taking over important positions along the upper Mississippi, elements of the United States Navy were preparing to take decisive action along the lower portions of the great river. Under the able administration of Secretary of the Navy Gideon Welles, a naval blockade had been set up along the 3,000 miles of Confederate coastline. Although it was relatively ineffective at first because there were fewer than a hundred ships in the American Navy, the blockade slowly grew more rigid. Almost every kind of craft that would float and hold a gun was pressed into service to plug the gaps and seal up the Southern ports. The stranglehold continued to press tighter and tighter every month, until in the latter stages of the war it became impossible for the Confederacy to obtain any of the goods it needed to continue the war.

One potential threat to the future of Union naval operations appeared on March 8, 1862, when a Confederate ironclad, the *Virginia* (rebuilt from the Union frigate *Merrimac*), appeared at Hampton Roads, on the Virginia coast. Steaming toward federal blockade ships off Fort Monroe, the ugly vessel with its sides covered by iron plates and its peaked roof slanting up from the deck, proceeded to sink a sloop-of-war and a frigate. When the *Virginia* came back the next day, she found a Union ironclad, the *Monitor,* waiting to give battle. Her flat deck topped by a revolving turret with two cannon, the *Monitor* exchanged shots with the *Virginia* for four hours, after which both vessels withdrew without serious damage. This was the first battle between ironclads; it represented a new type of naval warfare that would change navies all over the world. The *Virginia* was bottled up by the federal fleet and was subsequently destroyed by her commander when Union forces neared Norfolk.

Not content with defensive action alone, the Navy Department made arrangements for an assault on the fortifications along the lower Mississippi. Commanded by Admiral David Farragut, a Southerner who remained loyal to the Union, and ably seconded by Commander David Porter, the fleet began operations against the South. Running his ships past the blazing fire of the shore batteries of Forts Jackson and St. Philip on the night of April 23, 1862, Farragut destroyed the defenses of New Orleans and forced the Confederate troops to withdraw from the city. Leaving behind General Benjamin Butler of Massachusetts as commander of a Union occupation force, where his high-handed excesses made him one of the most hated men in the South, Farragut and the fleet continued to blast their way northward.

In the four months from February to June, 1862, therefore, combined Army and Navy operations in the Western theater had produced impressive results. Mississippi, Kentucky, and western Tennessee were in Union hands, along with important Confederate cities like Memphis and New Orleans. Federal forces controlled most of the Mississippi River, with the exception of Port Hudson and strategically located Vicksburg, Mississippi. Imagination and energy had been displayed by the commanders in the field, the Western armies had displayed courage and determination under fire, and the nation had secured its first major military victories at a time when they were badly needed to sustain Northern morale. As theater commander, General Halleck reaped much of the credit for these successes, and in July of 1862 Lincoln brought "Old Brains" to Washington to take over the post of General in Chief. This, in turn, brought promotion to Ulysses S. Grant who was placed in command of the Union forces in western Tennessee and northern Mississippi. Earlier that same year, Lincoln made another significant administrative change when he removed the ineffectual Simon Cameron as Secretary of War and replaced him with Edwin M. Stanton, a man of violent moods and irascible temper who nevertheless discharged his duties with dedication, honesty, and efficiency.

The unexpected series of successes in the West, however, only served to heighten the public complaints against General McClellan's inactivity in the East. If the armies in the West could win battles, take forts, and capture cities with a bare minimum of support from Washington, people asked, why couldn't McClellan, who received men, money, and material in abundance, begin offensive operations with his Army of the Potomac? Despite his protestations that he was still not ready, that the Confederate forces were too large, and that the logistical problems were too great, McClellan was finally forced to move against the Confederate forces in the spring of 1862.

The Battle of Gettysburg was crucial to Lee's decision as to whether he would break through the Union lines and threaten the cities of the North, or whether he would pull his forces back to Virginia and resume a defensive position. The climax came on the third day of the battle when Pickett's division charged against the Union forces along Cemetery Ridge. This illustration shows Confederate General Lewis A. Armistead, his hat on the tip of his sword, leading his men through the center of the line. A few minutes later Union forces counterattacked, and Armistead was shot down by the side of the cannon he had captured. Today at Gettysburg a monument stands where he fell on July 3, 1863, marking the "high tide of the Confederacy."

➤

CHAPTER 11
HIGH TIDE OF
THE CONFEDERACY

O NLY AFTER the most intensive pressure from the press, from political leaders, and from President Lincoln himself did General George B. McClellan agree to begin offensive operations. On March 28, 1862, Lincoln and McClellan agreed upon plans for a movement against the Confederate capital at Richmond. Although the President personally favored a direct, overland assault that would keep the Union army between Washington and the enemy, he yielded to McClellan's decision to launch a seaborne move to Fort Monroe, Virginia, which would be followed by an overland march of 70 miles to Richmond. Lincoln gave the plan his approval—with the proviso that enough troops be left behind to insure the safety of the capital.

The water movement from Alexandria began on March 17, and by the middle of April McClellan, with an army of some 100,000 men, was ready to move up the peninsula between the York and the James Rivers. Everything depended upon the speed of the Union troops, driving in upon the flank of General Joseph E. Johnston's Confederate forces before they could know whether the action was a feint or the real thing. McClellan lost the main advantage of surprise, however, when he spent four weeks in an elaborate and unnecessary siege at Yorktown against a handful of Confederate defenders. This delay allowed Johnston to move his army down to Richmond to make preparations for an all-out assault, while he sent Stonewall Jackson into the Shenandoah Valley to create such a frightening diversion that Lincoln would not dare to send reinforcements to McClellan—and, indeed, would even divert valuable troops to the Valley in hopes of catching the elusive Confederate leader.

After finally taking Yorktown on May 4, McClellan spent the remainder of the month moving slowly and cautiously closer and closer to Richmond. With his base at White House Landing and his army straddling the Chickahominy, McClellan had penetrated to within five miles of the Confederate capital when, on May 31, the defenders crashed out in a surprise assault that nearly broke through his advance positions. Union artillery fire and a daring cavalry charge by Phil Kearny drove the Confederates back to the city, however, and in the course of the fighting General Johnston was severely wounded. The task of defending Richmond now fell upon General Robert E. Lee, who assumed command when the Army of the Potomac was only about ten miles away.

While McClellan halted his march, reorganized his forces, and waited for the bad weather to clear before resuming his offensive, Lee swung into action. He secretly recalled Jackson to Richmond, sent J. E. B. Stuart on a remarkable cavalry raid making a complete circle around McClellan's army, and then combined with Jackson to smash at the Union force threatening the Confederate capital. For a whole week, from June 25 to July 1, a series of determined Confederate assaults drove McClellan progressively southward, away from Richmond. After furious fighting and enormous losses on both sides, the Confederates succeeded in cutting the Union forces off from their main base of operations at White House Landing, and they forced McClellan to take up defensive positions at Malvern Hill. Coming upon the Union troops in their new entrenchments and assuming that they were about to withdraw, Lee ordered a frontal assault that was poorly delivered and was torn to pieces by massed Union artillery. The following day McClellan withdrew his forces to a new base of operations at Harrison's Landing on the south side of the peninsula and dug in, while Lee pulled his exhausted Army of Northern Virginia back to Richmond for a much-needed rest.

Lincoln clearly was far from satisfied with McClellan's performance on the peninsula and decided that the time had come to try a new commander. To relieve pressure on McClellan and his army of 85,000 men still at Harrison's Landing, Lincoln consolidated the various Union detachments in the Shenandoah Valley (about 45,000 men), called it the Army of Virginia, and placed it under the command of General John Pope. Early in August, McClellan was ordered to withdraw to the Potomac River and join up with Pope at Fredericksburg—a move that would place a Union army of some 130,000 men about 45 miles north of the

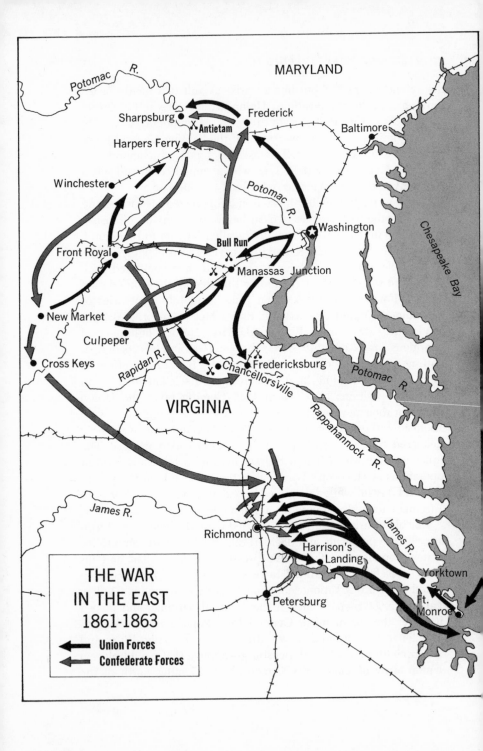

THE WAR IN THE EAST 1861-1863

← Union Forces
← Confederate Forces

Confederate capital, midway between Washington and Richmond. Realizing his danger if these two Union armies were allowed to join forces, Lee decided to throw his army of 55,000 against Pope's 45,000 before McClellan arrived with the Army of the Potomac.

Moving northward toward Pope, on August 25 Lee sent Stonewall Jackson veering around the right flank of the Union army, and a short time later he sent General James Longstreet to follow Jackson's route. Confused at this sudden and unexpected shift of Confederate forces, Pope moved around trying to catch the fast-moving Jackson. He missed him at Manassas, where he destroyed a huge Union supply depot, but he caught up with him near the old battlefield at Bull Run on August 29. While Pope's men were furiously trying to break through Jackson's strongly entrenched force, Longstreet moved up, unseen, and burst in on the flank of the weary Union troops. Pope had to order an immediate retreat back to Washington, and by September 3 the Union troops reached the capital defenses after suffering nearly 15,000 casualties.

Once he had beaten Pope, Lee decided that it was time to carry the war directly into the North. On September 4, 1862, he crossed the Potomac and encamped near Frederick, Maryland, hoping that his daring action would induce the people of Maryland to rise up and put their state in the ranks of the Confederacy. With Maryland behind, he might move on into Pennsylvania, persuade England and France to give official recognition and support to the Confederacy, and perhaps even convince a weary and disheartened Union Government to give up the war as a lost cause. The only immediate threat to Lee's position at Frederick was a strong Union garrison at Harpers Ferry. While he proceeded northwest with his main force toward Hagerstown, he sent Jackson and Longstreet back across the Potomac to guard against any flank attack from Harpers Ferry.

After the disaster at the second battle of Bull Run, Pope was relieved of his command. The various units were placed under McClellan's Army of the Potomac, and "Little Mac" was ordered to intercept Lee on his northern march. With his army of 90,000 men organized into six corps, McClellan marched northwest to pick up the track of the Confederate forces, and on September 12 he arrived at Frederick. The following day he found a copy of Lee's marching orders (wrapped around some cigars) showing how he had dangerously divided his forces. Swift action on the part of the Union commander might have caught a diminished Confederate army strung out on the line of march, but McClellan did not move until the next day—and then at a cautious pace.

Learning that his plans had been captured and realizing his vulnerability to attack, Lee quickly halted his northward march and pulled his army south to Sharpsburg on Antietam Creek on September 15. Although pinned in between the Creek and the Potomac River, hopelessly outnumbered, and with no room to maneuver, Lee decided to make his stand. Stonewall Jackson immediately began a rapid march up from Harpers Ferry to join Lee's forces but reported that his advance columns would not be able to arrive until the 16th. Fortunately for the Confederates, McClellan delayed his attack until the 17th, when he launched a series of uncoordinated assaults at the thin Confederate line. As cautious as ever, McClellan used only five of his six corps (he insisted upon holding Porter's V Corps in reserve), and he refused to let his junior officers lead a final all-out assault against the weakened center of the Confederate line. Jackson's last division arrived in time to head off a final attack, and at the end of twelve hours of bloody fighting, Lee still held his ground. Since he had suffered 12,000 casualties, McClellan decided that he had accomplished his purpose in stopping the invasion of Lee and refused to resume the attack. On the night of September 18, 1862, Robert E. Lee, with 13,700 casualties, was allowed to make his way back across the Potomac to the comparative safety of northern Virginia.

President Lincoln had expected a major victory, which would destroy Lee's army completely and perhaps hasten the end of the fighting. He was disappointed at the final outcome of Antietam and furious with McClellan for having permitted Lee to escape with his army intact. But Antietam was still a Union victory, and it gave Lincoln the opportunity to take an important step he had been contemplating for some time—the emancipation of the slaves.

Throughout his public career and into his presidency, Lincoln had declared that, although he himself was personally opposed to slavery and its expansion into the territories, he could not and would not touch slavery where it existed in the states. When war broke out, Lincoln again stated publicly that the War was being fought to restore the Union—the slavery question was purely incidental. As the War progressed, however, Lincoln came to see a distinct military advantage in an emancipation proclamation. Such a move would create confusion in the Confederate states, it would disrupt their economies and deprive them of a valuable labor supply, and it would certainly appeal to the strong anti-slavery sentiment of many European countries—especially of Great Britain.

As early as July 13, 1862, Lincoln confided to both William Seward and Gideon Welles that he had finally come to see that freedom for the slaves was "absolutely essential" to the preservation of the Union, and on July 22 he informed the members of his Cabinet that he planned to issue an emancipation proclamation. Before making such an announcement, however, he wanted a suitable military victory so that his action would not appear to be a desperate act of reprisal in the face of imminent defeat. The victory at Antietam gave him what he regarded as the most appropriate opportunity; and on September 22, 1862, acting in his capacity as Commander-in-Chief of the armed forces, he adopted what he regarded as "a fit and necessary war measure for suppressing . . . rebellion." Lincoln issued a preliminary announcement declaring that unless the seceded states returned to the Union by January 1, 1863, all slaves in rebellious states would be "then, thenceforward, and forever free." He announced that freed slaves, "of suitable condition," would be used in the armed forces, and he pledged that the government of the United States, both civil and military, would recognize and maintain the freedom of all former slaves.

The Emancipation Proclamation had no immediate or practical effect on the Negroes themselves, since it did not apply to the border states that had not seceded and was not put into effect in the seceded states, still, there can be little doubt of its long-range significance. The document had considerable effect in influencing sentiment, both at home and throughout Europe, that this was no longer merely a political war to defeat a rebellious faction and to restore the power of the official government. The war was now a holy crusade to abolish the scourge of slavery and set all men free. Thus, after January 1, 1863, the nation passed an important milestone in the history of the Black American. Up until this moment, there had always been the possibility that if the Confederate states had given up their rebellion (either by force or persuasion) and the Union had been restored, the institution of slavery would have continued in effect. Certainly Lincoln made it clear in the wording of his Emancipation Proclamation in September that he was willing to allow slavery to continue if the Southern states would give up their rebellion. Even as late as his State of the Union Message in December, 1862, he was still talking about the possibility of a federally compensated program of colonization that assumed the continuity of the institution of slavery. After January 1, 1863, however, there was no longer any question in anyone's mind, North or South, that the defeat of the Confederacy would mean the end of slavery forever.

Just as the Emancipation Proclamation marked a turning point in Lincoln's attitude toward slavery, it also marked a change in his attitude toward the use of Black Americans in the armed forces of the United States. Ever since the beginning of the conflict, Lincoln had taken a dim view of the Negro's capabilities as a fighting man, and he felt that any attempt to incorporate Negroes into the Army (other than as common laborers or service personnel) would produce "more evil than good." Conscious of the hostile reactions of border states like Kentucky and Missouri to the recruitment of black troops, he sharply countermanded moves by Union generals John C. Frémont and David Hunter, who prematurely issued edicts liberating slaves in their military commands.

As the War progressed and with the growing number of Confederate victories in the spring and summer of 1862, however,

Lincoln's ideas about the strategic value of emancipation began to change. When the final Proclamation went into effect on January 1, 1863, former slaves were authorized to be "received into the armed services of the United States, to garrison forts, positions, stations, and other places, and to man vessels of all sorts in said service." Seeing that the blacks could become loyal and brave members of the Union service—as demonstrated by Thomas Wentworth Higginson's First Regiment of South Carolina Volunteers, and Robert Gould Shaw's Fifty-Fourth Regiment from Massachusetts—Lincoln's admiration for black troops reached the point where he declared that they were virtually "indispensable" to the Union war effort and promised that no black man who served the Union would ever be returned to slavery.

While many in the North greeted the Emancipation Proclamation with great rejoicing, there were others who denounced it as only one more blunder of an inept and irresponsible President— for Lincoln was heavily criticized throughout his time in office. Some condemned him for having gone too far and selling out to the Abolitionists. Others accused him of not going far enough, and of hoodwinking the American people with a political trick that had no practical effects at all. The use of black troops in the Union army also proved a source of sharp and constant criticism— from those who felt that Lincoln was too conservative as well as from those who felt he had done too much. Many of the anti-slavery Republican leaders accused the administration of rank discrimination in having delayed so long in allowing black men into the Army in the first place, and then in failing to provide them with the same pay, the same bounties, and the same type of equipment that were provided for white troops. Opponents, on the other hand, condemned the Lincoln administration roundly for daring to use colored troops in any capacity; and the Confederate states, in particular, were outraged at the "barbarous" prospect of the Union Government arming former slaves and sending them back into the South to fight against their former masters. When the Confederate Congress threatened to execute white officers who commanded black regiments, Lincoln promptly retaliated with a proclamation threatening to execute one Confederate soldier for every Union soldier killed "in violation of the laws of war."

The war was obviously not going as quickly or as successfully as the people in the North expected. After more than a year of fighting they were discouraged by repeated Union defeats (at Bull Run, on the peninsula, at Second Bull Run), alarmed at mounting casualty rates, and disappointed at the final outcome of Antietam. It was clear that strong and vocal opposition was increasing against Abraham Lincoln and his Republican administration. The off-year elections of 1862 were coming up, and Northern Democrats were hard at work undermining public confidence in the Republican administration and stumping for a Democratic victory. Loudly they condemned the President's "dictatorial" use of extraordinary wartime powers, they made hay out of disclosures of corruption in the War Department under Simon Cameron, and they called into question Lincoln's ability as Commander-in-Chief in the face of repeated Union failures and Confederate victories over the past year and a half. Coming down hard on the Emancipation Proclamation, the Democrats declared that Lincoln had gone against the express wishes of the people in changing his policy from a war for the Union to a war for the Negro. As a result of their attacks and a strong voter turnout, the Democrats made an excellent showing in the 1862 elections. They took the lead in New York, New Jersey, Pennsylvania, Ohio, Indiana, Illinois, and Wisconsin, and they just missed winning a majority in the House of Representatives. Clearly the political future of Lincoln and the Republicans was in serious doubt unless they could produce some decisive military victories in the field.

Discontent throughout the North grew even more when the Federal Government passed a conscription law in March of 1863. The vagueness of the law and the many abuses that occurred when local authorities tried to administer it resulted in widespread protest, opposition, and outright violence. The provisions of the law were particularly unfair for the poor, because rich young men could either hire substitutes to go in their place or purchase outright exemption for the sum of $300. All through the North—in Ohio, New York, New Jersey, Pennsylvania, Kentucky, Missouri, Indiana, Illinois—there were many instances of disturbances and "insurrections" against the enforcement of the law. But it was in New York City that the most violent reaction occurred. For three days, July 13–15, 1863, a terrible and bloody draft riot took place during which Negroes were murdered, telegraph lines were cut, buildings were destroyed, and property was looted. Order was not restored until Federal troops were brought in to put down the rioting.

Realizing that Northern military successes were necessary in order to restore morale and create some semblance of unity, Lincoln relieved McClellan as commander of the Army of the Potomac early in November, 1862, and replaced him with General Ambrose Burnside, a fine-looking man with resplendent side-whiskers, who took the post with reluctance.

Burnside set out to take Richmond by crossing the Rappahannock River at Fredericksburg and then following the railroad line all the way to the Confederate capital. When he advanced to the Rappahannock, though, Burnside found Robert E. Lee and his Army of Northern Virginia in excellent defensive positions along the heights that overlooked the river. Despite almost insurmountable difficulties of both the tactics and terrain, Burnside proceeded to throw pontoon bridges across the wide river, and on December 13 he sent his infantrymen in a series of suicidal assaults against Marye's Heights. All day long the blue lines struggled across the open waters, crawled up the exposed shores, and crumbled under the withering fire of Confederate cannon and musket, until over 12,000 Union troops lay dead or wounded by four o'clock in the afternoon. The Battle of Fredericksburg was another Union disaster, and when the generals made it clear that they would not order their men into battle again, a furious Burnside had no alternative but to bring his Army of the Potomac back to Washington. Despite his attempts to blame others for his appalling lack of military competence, Burnside was removed from command; and on January 25, 1863, Lincoln replaced him with General Joseph Hooker who had won a good reputation as a division and corps commander. Perhaps this would be a man who knew how to fight.

Hooker did much to restore morale in the badly shattered ranks of the Army of the Potomac through competent training and discipline, and by early spring he was developing plans to envelop Lee and his army in a gigantic pincers movement—his army now numbered more than 150,000 men. On April 27, he sent one force of 40,000 men under General John Sedgwick towards Fredericksburg while he took the rest of the army in a westward arc around Lee's left flank. Thus, General Lee found himself being encircled by two strong Union forces. He had to decide whether to retreat southward, to fight Hooker coming down on his left, or to strike at Sedgwick moving down on his right. Sending about 10,000 men under Jubal Early to hold off Sedgwick near Fredericksburg, Lee turned his own army on "Fighting Joe" Hooker and made contact with the main Union force at Chancellorsville.

On May 1, the two armies met and hammered away at each other throughout the day, with Hooker inflicting heavy losses upon Lee. That night, however, Lee sent Stonewall Jackson racing in a semicircle around Hooker's right flank while the main army poured a diverting fire upon the Union line all through the next day. Jackson and his men worked their way around to the rear of the unsuspecting Northerners, and at 6:00 on the evening of May 2 they came bursting in upon the Union troops while Lee smashed in from the front. Hooker, dazed and confused, pulled his troops back northward even as Lee swung against Sedgwick at Fredericksburg and hammered him back across the Rappahannock. Military historians regard Chancellorsville as Lee's most brilliant battle. Starting with an initial disadvantage, the Confederate commander outwitted, outmaneuvered, outflanked, and outfought a force more than twice his size. The only dark spot in an otherwise brilliant chapter of military history was the fact that Lee lost Jackson. While riding in advance of his lines as he came up in the rear of the Union positions, Jackson and several of his staff officers were accidentally shot and killed by their own men who mistook them for Union officers. This was a loss which the Confederacy could never replace.

With an incredible string of victories to his credit, having more than once beaten forces twice his size, having humiliated every Union general sent to defeat him, General Robert E. Lee once again decided to bring the War into the heart of Union territory. Over the protests of General Longstreet, who wanted to clear Union forces out of Tennessee and to relieve the pressures on Vicksburg, President Davis authorized Lee to strike into Pennsylvania. Early in June he moved his units away from Fredericksburg and funneled them northward through the Shenandoah and Cumberland Valleys. His immediate target was the city of Harrisburg, Pennsylvania. Once there, he was certain that the Union commanders would have to divide their forces into three parts in order to safeguard the cities of Philadelphia, Baltimore, and Washington—any one of which would be a logical target for attack by the Confederate leader.

As had been true the year before, Lee's motives in taking his forces north of the Potomac were as much psychological as they were military. A full-scale Confederate invasion into Pennsylvania might well be the final blow that would force Northerners to accept the idea that the North could never win and the South could never lose. Casualty lists continued to rise, morale continued to fall; and a successful offensive might be all that it would take to tip the scales in favor of a negotiated settlement.

Then too, Lee calculated the effect his daring venture might have upon the nations of Europe, which were still waiting to see, with some degree of uncertainty, whether the Confederacy could sustain itself through its own military efforts before they risked an open break with the Union government. One vital factor throughout the Civil War was the possibility that European nations might give recognition and support to the Confederacy. The Confederate government worked steadily toward this objective for four years, and the Federal Government worked equally hard to prevent it.

Certainly the most influential power, whose weight on the balance scales of the War would go far toward determining its final outcome, was Great Britain. The Confederacy needed British gold, British guns, and especially British ships to offset the great Union advantage in naval power; and from the very outset of hostilities the South threatened to send no cotton to England unless it received gold, guns, and ships. To England, the greatest industrial nation in the world, who received nearly five-sixths of her cotton supply from the South to keep her textile mills rolling, this was a serious threat to the national economy. King Cotton diplomacy presented a powerful and persuasive argument for bringing Great Britain into active support of the Southern Confederacy.

When the Civil War first started, the English press was fairly favorable to the Union cause, assuming the War was intended to free the slaves. But when it became evident that this was a War primarily to preserve the Union, Britain became decidedly more friendly to the South. The landed aristocracy, particularly, sympathized with the plight of the plantation owners and their desire to maintain rigid class and social lines. At the outset, England issued a formal proclamation of neutrality—but she recognized the South as a belligerent power. Secretary of State William Seward reacted violently to this decision, and through the American Minister to England, Charles Francis Adams, he issued an ultimatum that if Britain went a step further and received (even unofficially) any Confederate diplomatic agents, the United States would break off diplomatic relations.

Although the English government withheld formal recognition of the Confederacy for the time being, British maritime interests continued to run the Union blockade, bringing manufactured goods to the Southern states and taking much-needed cotton back to England. This action was upheld by the Secretary of State for Foreign Affairs, Lord John Russell, who maintained that it was permissible for neutral vessels to sell contraband of war to belligerents—and who pointed out that the Americans themselves had made great profits selling to Napoleon when England was at war with France during the early 1800's.

Relations between the United States and Great Britain got a good deal worse in November, 1861. The Confederacy sent two agents, James M. Mason of Virginia and John Slidell of Louisiana, to obtain official recognition from Britain and France. Sailing out of Cuba aboard the British mail steamer, *Trent,* the agents were intercepted by Captain Charles Wilkes of the *U.S.S. San Jacinto,* who stopped the British vessel and took off the two Confederates. Although Wilkes's action was a clear breach of international law, most Americans were not concerned with the niceties of international procedure. Starved for the lack of a military victory (especially after the fiasco of Bull Run), the American public hailed Wilkes as a national hero. Banquets were held throughout the nation, at which prominent dignitaries were present to honor the popular Captain, and the United States Congress passed resolutions in his honor.

On the other side of the Atlantic, the British public was outraged at the flagrant insult to their national honor. War talk filled the air, 10,000 troops were dispatched to Canada, and Lord Russell drew up a strongly worded note demanding the return of the Confederate agents and an apology from the Federal Government. Fortunately, Queen Victoria's consort, Prince Albert, used his personal influence to soften somewhat the wording of the note, and the British Minister at Washington, Lord Lyons, used considerable tact when he presented the note to the American government.

President Lincoln faced a delicate problem: If he did *not* apologize for Wilkes's action, he faced the possibility of war with Great Britain; if he *did* apologize to the British, he risked the anger of the American public to whom Wilkes was a national hero. In a communication skillfully designed to appease both the British government and the American public, Secretary of State Seward apologized to the British for having removed Mason and Slidell from the British vessel. What Wilkes should have done, Seward pointed out, was to bring the ship itself into port for adjudication. Seward closed his note with the additional observation that the United States was pleased to note that Great Britain had at last come around to acknowledge the principle for which the War of 1812 had been fought—freedom of the seas. Although the British government was never quite certain whether it had

received an apology or another insult, it chose to regard the unfortunate incident as closed rather than risk the possibility of an
open conflict with the United States.

While tempers cooled over the *Trent* affair, trouble with Britain
was by no means over, especially since the British continued to
build and outfit vessels for the Confederacy. Over the protests of
Charles Francis Adams, the *Florida* left an English port in 1862,
and the *Alabama,* destined to destroy some $6,500,000 worth of
Northern shipping before the end of the War, sailed out of Liver-
pool the same year. In addition to the ships that were sailing out
of English ports and heading for Confederate waters, Adams was
further alarmed at reports that the shipbuilding firm of William
Laird was constructing some new-style "rams" for the Confederacy. Armored with four and a half inches of heavy iron plate,
and equipped with a seven-foot wrought-iron "piercer" at the
prow, the "Laird Ram" was a potential threat to the Union blockade—especially if Great Britain should decide to recognize the
Confederacy and persuade other European nations to give similar
aid and comfort to the South.

It would not have taken a great deal of persuasion to bring
France into the conflict on the side of the Confederacy. Following
England's example, France too had issued a proclamation of
neutrality at the beginning of the American conflict; but its government recognized the South as a belligerent power and even
allowed French ports to be used as bases for operations against
Northern shipping. With close to 700,000 workers dependent
upon the cotton industry for their livelihood, France was desperate for Southern cotton, and on a number of occasions the
government of Emperor Napoleon III tried to persuade Britain
to join France in shooting their way through the Union blockade.
Although Secretary of State Seward was able to deter Napoleon
III from violence with the threats of a wheat famine (what might
happen if the excitable people of Paris found themselves without
bread as well as without work?), there was a serious question
just how long this kind of threat could work if the Union forces
suffered another military defeat.

In contrast with the strained relations with Great Britain and

France, relations between the United States and Czarist Russia were surprisingly friendly. Fearful of a British or French attack upon her naval bases after the Czar had suppressed a revolution in Poland in October, 1863, Russia sent portions of her fleet into the harbors of New York City and San Francisco hoping to use these ports for naval operations against enemy colonies in the event of war. Despite the fact that the Russians were acting in their own self-interest, most Northerners looked upon the visits of the Russian fleet as a gesture of friendship toward the Union cause. The Russian naval commanders were lavishly entertained during their brief stay, and to accentuate the similarities between the Russian people and the American people it was frequently pointed out that just as Abraham Lincoln freed the American slaves in 1863, Czar Alexander II had freed the Russian serfs in 1861. Although this cordial relationship went far toward establishing the basis for the purchase of Alaska shoftly after the War, for the time being it was only a brief interlude of friendship in the midst of an uncertain international situation.

After the Union disasters at Fredericksburg and Chancellorsville, England and France were dangerously close to throwing caution to the winds and giving the Confederacy the recognition and support it so desperately needed. One last, dramatic display of Confederate military prowess might be enough to convince the European powers that the Confederate States of America could never be defeated and could maintain themselves as a separate nation. It was with this expectation in mind that General Lee and his 80,000 battle-hardened veterans crossed the Potomac in June of 1863, moved through Sharpsburg and Hagerstown, and headed for Chambersburg. Pennsylvania was wild with panic, and official Washington did not know where to turn next. Lee was on the move.

WHILE LEE was moving into the North in June of 1863, the Union troops were still under the command of "Fighting Joe" Hooker, who suggested to President Lincoln that with Lee out of the way he might safely "pitch into his rear" at Fredericksburg and then march directly on and take Richmond. Exasperated that the general should still be thinking of Richmond as his objective rather than the destruction of Lee and his army, Lincoln vetoed Hooker's suggestion. He warned the general to keep his army between the Confederates and Washington, and urged him to try and strike out at the "animal" winding its way northward with its head in Maryland and its tail in Virginia.

The best that Hooker could do, though, was to move his army in a line roughly parallel to that of Lee as he brought his men through Maryland and into Pennsylvania—all the time complaining that he needed more men, more cavalry, more supplies, more reinforcements. On June 26 Hooker crossed the Potomac, established headquarters at Frederick, and then requested that he be given the Union garrison at Harpers Ferry as reinforcements in order to conduct operations against Lee's supply lines. When the War Department refused his request, Hooker angrily submitted his resignation—only to find that Lincoln promptly accepted it. Convinced that Hooker was unable to meet the demands of an

On April 9, 1865, General Robert E. Lee met with General Ulysses S. Grant at a farmhouse belonging to Wilbur McLean at Appomattox Courthouse, to arrange surrender terms for the Army of Northern Virginia. Lee's surrender, however, did not mark the actual end of the fighting. Sporadic resistance continued until the end of May, when General Kirby Smith surrendered his Texas forces to General Edward Canby at New Orleans. The terms of surrender agreed upon by Grant and Lee became the model for most other Confederate capitulations. For their pledge not to take up arms against the Union, Confederate troops were permitted to return to their homes and to keep their horses to aid them in the spring planting.

◄

Army command, Lincoln turned to General George Gordon
Meade, an experienced veteran of Fredericksburg and Chancellorsville, to assume command of the Army of the Potomac—its
fifth commander in little more than ten months.

Moving with speed and determination, the new Union general
marched his force from Frederick northeast toward Harrisburg,
making sure that he covered the Washington-Baltimore area
adequately while he moved to intercept Lee and his Army of
Northern Virginia. On July 1, 1863, advance elements of both
armies made initial contact just outside the little town of Gettysburg, Pennsylvania, where the Confederates were hunting for
badly-needed shoes. While the troopers struck at each other in a
series of sharp engagements all day, they issued calls for help,
and the main forces came up to form the battle lines.

By nightfall on July 1, the Union forces had dug in along a
narrow ridge south of the town called Cemetery Ridge. A fishhook
series of knolls capped the northern end; and two knobby hills,
Big Round Top and Little Round Top, dominated the southern
end of the line. The Confederates, in the meantime, set up their
positions along a second low elevation, Seminary Ridge, which
ran parallel to the Union line three-quarters of a mile away. Although this was not the battleground he would have chosen, Lee
had no alternative but to fight. Either he had to break through the
Union defense lines at Gettysburg and move on his target at
Harrisburg, or else give up his plans to invade the North and
return as quickly as possible to Confederate soil.

On July 2, Lee attempted to drive the Union forces out of their
positions, mounting massive assaults against each end of the
Union line. Longstreet's men just missed taking Little Round Top
when Union troops first scrambled to the top of the strategic hil-
lock; and massed Union artillery drove back a Confederate attempt under General Richard S. Ewell to overrun the northern
end of the line. Although the flank attacks had failed, the Confederates hoped that the effort of beating back the assaults on
both flanks had caused the Union commanders to weaken the
center of their defenses.

Despite heavy losses, Lee reorganized his forces during the

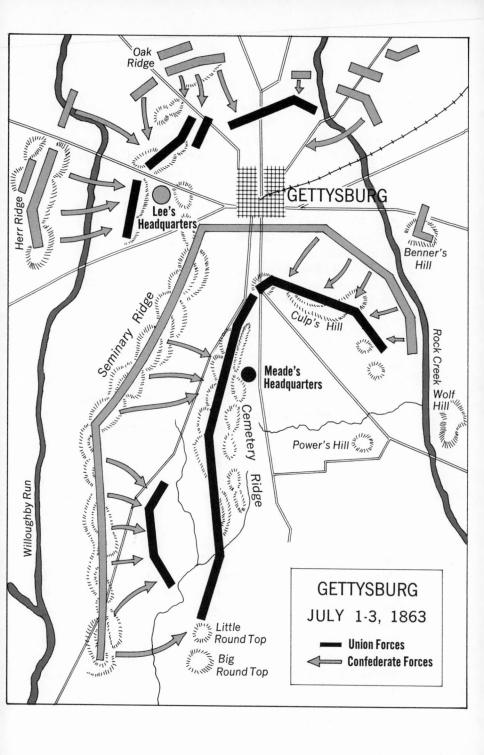

Oak Ridge

GETTYSBURG

Herr Ridge

Lee's Headquarters

Benner's Hill

Seminary Ridge

Culp's Hill

Meade's Headquarters

Rock Creek

Wolf Hill

Cemetery Ridge

Power's Hill

Willoughby Run

Little Round Top

Big Round Top

GETTYSBURG

JULY 1-3, 1863

Union Forces

Confederate Forces

night and prepared to strike directly against the center of the Union line the next day. After a two-hour barrage by Confederate artillery to soften the defenses along Cemetery Ridge, at three o'clock in the afternoon of July 3, some 15,000 veteran infantrymen under the command of General George Pickett began their steady march across the open farmland toward the Northern lines. When they came within range, however, the Union guns opened up on Pickett's advancing columns. Artillery, firing cannister, tore great holes in the Confederate lines, and then a devastating rifle fire sent numbers of Southerners pitching to the ground near the Federal positions.

In spite of heavy losses, the forward point of the Confederate line broke through the blazing center of the Union defense and overran a battery of cannon. But there were not enough of them —the Northern guns had taken too heavy a toll. The ragged gap was quickly plugged with Union reinforcements, and Pickett's men were either killed or put to flight. General Lee himself met the shattered remnants of his Army of Northern Virginia as they staggered back across the bloody fields, and he knew that he had lost decisively. Although forty percent of his men had been either killed or wounded (the Confederates suffered 22,638 casualties in the three-day battle at Gettysburg; the Union lost 17,684), Lee prepared as well as he could to defend himself against the Union counterattack that he knew must come.

But the attack never came. Meade, exhausted by the pressures of the battle, conscious of his heavy losses, and wary of the Confederate guns still in position along Seminary Ridge, decided not to bring his men out of the lines and expose them to possible defeat. Content with having stopped the mighty Lee and having saved the North from invasion, Meade stood his ground and allowed the Confederate general to take his battered army back across the flood-swollen Potomac into Virginia. Although Meade failed to take up the golden opportunity to destroy Lee completely, the Battle of Gettysburg was, nevertheless, an important victory for the North at a most critical moment in the progress of the War. And the rejoicing that greeted Meade's success at Gettysburg on July 3, 1863, was renewed when the news arrived a few days later that General Grant had taken the Confederate stronghold of Vicksburg on July 4.

When General Halleck came east in the spring of 1862 to take over command of the Union armies, and while the Army of the Potomac was still searching for a man to lead it, only the Confederate installations at Port Hudson and Vicksburg prevented Union forces from controlling the entire Mississippi River. In May and again in June, 1862, Admiral Farragut tried unsuccessfully to take Vicksburg; and then in the fall, General Grant decided to try his hand. From October, 1862, and on through the succeeding months, Grant made five futile efforts to capture the heavily fortified city, which sat high on the bluffs overlooking a sharp bend in the Mississippi, its guns commanding all the water approaches. His last attempt came in December when he and General William Tecumseh Sherman planned to advance upon the city in two converging columns. Delayed by political intrigue and administrative confusion in Washington, Grant's winter operation had to be scrapped when Sherman's forces, coming in by water, were beaten back at Chickasaw Bluffs. Grant's own overland assault was so badly cut up by Confederate cavalry attacks that he was forced to pull back.

Early in April, 1863, as soon as the spring thaws were over, Grant launched a new and extremely daring operation. Using a Navy flotilla to run the Confederate batteries and bring his men below Vicksburg, he landed 40,000 men on the east bank of the Mississippi and marched inland. Cutting himself off from his lines of supply and communication, and living off the land, Grant drove midway between two Confederate armies—J. C. Pemberton and his force of 40,000 in the Vicksburg area itself, and Joseph E. Johnston (recovered from his wounds) and his 15,000 men at Jackson, Mississippi. Grant hit Johnston first, drove him out of Jackson, and then left Sherman and a small force to hold him down. Whirling around, Grant then struck at Vicksburg befor the Confederates could organize sufficient reinforcements to come to its defense. On May 16 at Champion's Hill, and on May 17 at Big Black River, Grant beat back the troops of Pemberton and forced them to withdraw into the Vicksburg defenses as he converged upon the target with all his forces. By May 19, Grant had the city completely surrounded, and after a 47-day siege which saw the defenders reduced to absolute starvation, Pemberton surrendered on July 4, 1863, adding another Union success to Meade's victory the day before at Gettysburg. The following day, Washington learned also that General Nathaniel Banks had pushed up the Red River, and after capturing Alexandria, Louisiana, had then turned back to force the surrender of Port Hudson. This meant that the Union now controlled the entire length of the Mississippi River and had effectively sliced the Confederacy in two. It also meant that Union forces possessed a new and much more threatening base for a second front in their battle against the Confederacy.

The Union victories at Gettysburg and Vicksburg not only influenced the course of military operations for the remainder of the War, but they also affected Europe's attitude toward the Civil War. In England, the government announced that no more vessels would be constructed in British ports for sale to the Confederacy, and in September the British authorities confiscated the much talked-about Laird Rams, which had been built for Southern waters. The news of Gettysburg and Vicksburg also seriously undercut the efforts of John Slidell, the Confederate agent to France, who was in Paris trying to arrange a large loan based on cotton futures. The Union victories sent the price of Confederate bonds to a new low, and it was obvious that while many European countries might continue to send their sympathies to the South, their money would not follow.

King Cotton diplomacy had been a powerful and persuasive argument for two years. One more Confederate victory in the summer of 1863 might have convinced England and France that the South could maintain its independence, that the Confederacy was worth the risk of supplying the assistance it had been seeking so desperately. But Lee had gambled and lost—and no one wants to back a loser. From the vantage point of trans-Atlantic perspective it looked as though the high tide of the Confederacy had already started to recede. How long it would take before final defeat came would depend upon how badly the Union government wanted an unconditional victory and what measures it was willing to use to achieve that victory.

The strategic importance of the Mississippi as a base of offensive operations became apparent soon after the fall of Vicksburg when Federal troops moved into East Tennessee and headed toward Chattanooga. The city was a key railroad junction set in a large gap in the Appalachian Mountains, which made it a natural gateway to the East. In Confederate hands, Chattanooga had always provided an effective path into Kentucky and Tennessee enabling Southern forces to strike into the North and to obtain much-needed supplies. In Union hands, Chattanooga could open the way for penetration of the Southeast, an attack upon Atlanta or Savannah, or even a rear assault on the city of Richmond itself.

Late in June of 1863, after months of inactivity, Union General William Rosecrans brought his troops south from Murfreesboro to Chattanooga in hopes of dislodging the Confederate forces of General Braxton Bragg. Learning of the Union plans, Bragg drew up his troops about twenty miles south of the city, and left Chattanooga for Rosecrans. Then, on September 19, Bragg smashed the Union forces when they came after him near Chickamauga Creek. Only the resolute stand of General George H. Thomas, the "Rock of Chickamauga," and his infantrymen saved Rosecrans from complete disaster as the Union forces straggled back to the shelter of Chattanooga. Here they were pinned down by Bragg, who anchored the left flank of his line at Lookout Mountain, southwest of the city. He set up his right flank along Missionary Ridge, which lay to the southeast, and prepared to starve out the Union garrison at his leisure.

Back at headquarters in Washington Lincoln, Halleck, and Stanton concluded that the situation at Chattanooga was critical and drastic steps were necessary. Lincoln named Grant supreme commander of all Union armies in the West, replaced the ineffectual Rosecrans with Thomas, and ordered Hooker to proceed immediately to Tennessee with 20,000 reinforcements. When Grant reached the Chattanooga defenses on October 23, he opened up new supply lines from the north and then organized plans to use Hooker's men and additional divisions being brought in by Sherman to break out of the city in a massive assault against Bragg's mountain positions to the south.

On November 23, Union troops struck at the center of the Confederate line, seizing valuable ground, obtaining a strategic foothold for future engagements, and forcing Bragg to divert men from other parts of his line. The following day, Hooker's men stormed Lookout Mountain on Bragg's left flank and drove the Confederates from the heights. The next day, November 25, Sherman's forces swung in a wide arc against the northern end of Missionary Ridge, but although he had six divisions to the Confederate's one, the ridge was so steep and the Confederates so well entrenched that Sherman could not dislodge them. It was at this critical point that Grant ordered Thomas's men to storm the trenches along the foot of the ridge to the south. A force of 20,000 blue-coated Union troops, aligned in three waves a mile long, charged through the trenches, and then, under heavy fire from the crest of the ridge, they started climbing to the top. In knots, in clusters, in squads, and in companies, they clawed and fought their way to the top of Missionary Ridge and then they swept the Confederates before them as they cheered with newfound confidence.

Confederate forces were now in full retreat, and although Jefferson Davis assigned Joseph E. Johnston to command the Army of the Tennessee in place of Bragg, nothing could stop the Union forces from taking over control of Chattanooga and solidifying their position throughout Tennessee. Grant immediately sent a large force to the northeast to relieve Burnside and his Army of the Ohio at Knoxville. This movement forced Longstreet and his Confederates to move eastward into North Carolina for the remainder of the winter.

So ended operations in 1863. It had been a notable year, starting out on the heels of a devastating Union disaster at Fredericksburg in December, followed by an equally appalling defeat at Chancellorsville in May—only to end up with critical Federal victories at Gettysburg and Vicksburg in July and to climax in successful operations at Chattanooga by the close of the year. With the achievement of this last objective, the road was now open to invade Georgia and the Carolinas and split the Eastern half of the Confederacy in two. But the South fought on; as one military historian has written: "It is clear that the Confederacy had lost the war, but the Confederates were not disposed to admit that fact."

"The Secretary of War directs me to say to you that your commission as lieutenant-general is signed and will be delivered to you on your arrival at the War Department. . . ." So read the telegram Ulysses S. Grant received from General in Chief Halleck early in March, 1864, informing him that Congress had passed a bill creating the office of Lieutenant-General, a rank previously held only by George Washington and Winfield Scott. In appointing Grant to this rank President Lincoln was placing him in command of all Union armies, above all other military officers. For three years Lincoln had been searching for a man who could lead the Federal forces to victory, and in Grant he felt that he had found his general. Only time would tell if his judgment was right; but meanwhile Grant was to be the boss!

Grant saw clearly that a great weakness of the Union war strategy over the past three years was that each theater of opertions was almost completely independent of every other one. As a result there had never been any really concerted effort to co-ordinate Union forces against a single target. In assuming overall command, therefore, Grant worked out plans calling for a series of offensive operations against the Confederacy; these would employ the Union superiority in men and matériel more effectively than ever before. One Union force, under General Franz Sigel, was to raid the Shenandoah Valley, divert the Confederates from Richmond, and perhaps strike Lee from the rear. A second force, under Sherman, would advance southward from Chattanooga, destroy Johnston's Army of the Tennessee, and push into the interior of the Confederacy. A third force, commanded by General Meade but accompanied by Grant himself, would drive southward from Washington and come to grips with Lee and his Army of Northern Virginia.

Union plans to seize the Shenandoah Valley and keep Confederate forces pinned down there while Grant moved on Rich-

mond were painfully slow in developing. After a decisive defeat
at New Market early in May, 1864, Sigel was replaced by General David Hunter, who began working his way up the Valley
toward Lynchburg and a series of railroad lines feeding into
Richmond. Determined to clear the Valley and throw a fright
into Washington that would slow down Grant's offensive in the
East, Lee sent Jubal Early and a brigade of cavalry on a daring
raid northward through the Shenandoah. In mid-June, Early
knocked Hunter back into West Virginia, proceeded to race
through Maryland toward Washington and actually skirmished
in the outskirts of the capital near Fort Stevens on July 11, before
slipping away to safety.

Grant insisted there should be no more of these Confederate
diversions which threatened the capital and stalled his own
operations. He combined all the forces in the Washington-Mary-
land area into a single command, and placed it in the hands of
General Philip H. Sheridan in August with orders to follow Early
to the death. Sheridan doggedly pursued the Confederates, defeated them at Winchester and at Fisher's Hill in September,
and then shattered them completely at Cedar Creek the following month. To prevent the Confederates from using the fertile
countryside as a means of conducting further raids into the
North while living off the land, Sheridan was ordered to destroy
the Valley completely. "If the war is to last another year," Grant
instructed Sheridan, "we want the Shenandoah Valley to remain
a barren waste." Leaving the inhabitants enough provisions to
carry them through the winter, the Union forces put the Valley
to the torch and turned the once beautiful and fertile lands into
a blackened rubble.

While the Shenandoah campaign was getting under way, out
in the West on May 4, 1864, General Sherman moved out of
Chattanooga with a force of 100,000 men, and headed for the
important industrial city of Atlanta, Georgia. Facing him was
the Army of the Tennessee, about 65,000 men under General
Joseph E. Johnston, who employed shrewd and effective delaying
tactics which forced Sherman to halt, deploy, and reconnoiter,
while Johnston fell back and took up new defensive positions.

In this way, the Confederate army slowly backed into positions in front of Atlanta while they were still in good condition and without having suffered major losses. Sherman had been forced to take seventy-four frustrating days to cover little more than one hundred miles.

President Davis, however, had steadily grown more impatient with Johnston's defensive maneuvers and continued withdrawals; and in July, 1864, he replaced him with the more aggressive General John B. Hood. On July 20, Hood drove out of his fortifications and assaulted the Union forces north of the city. Sherman countered quickly by swinging his entire army south of the city, cutting Hood's supply lines and threatening the whole Confederate army with encirclement. Hood had no alternative but to retreat, and so he retired to northwest Alabama as Sherman marched into Atlanta on September 2.

Having come this far, and with no visible opposition before him, Sherman had no intention of remaining at Atlanta. Sending some 30,000 men back to Nashville, Tennessee, under General George Thomas to defend against the possibility of an attack by Hood in his rear, Sherman prepared to cut his lines of supply and communication and march his army of over 60,000 men to the seacoast, through the very heart of the Confederacy. After destroying all military installations in the fire-blackened city of Atlanta, Sherman set out on November 12, 1864, for Savannah, Georgia. Operating on a sixty-mile front and living off the countryside, the Union troops followed a systematic routine of destroying everything that might be considered of use to the Confederate war effort. Crops, machinery, cattle, factories, storage-houses, barns, bridges, railways, were destroyed in the course of the Union march through the Georgia countryside, and only too often personal acts of thievery, plunder, and looting were committed by troops along the lines of march. It was at this time that Sherman's men came across the horrible sight of the Confederate Military Prison near Andersonville, Georgia, where thousands of Union troops, overcome by filth and disease, clothed in rags, and existing on scraps of food, lived like animals and died in droves. After the War the commandant of the prison,

Captain Henry Wirz, was hanged as a war criminal, although historians have continued to debate whether he was a heartless sadist or simply a victim of the desperate circumstances to which the South had been reduced at this stage of the War.

On December 21, 1864, Sherman's armies marched into Savannah. Confederate troops had evacuated the city the night before in an effort to save it, and so the General promptly sent off a dispatch to Washington presenting the President with Savannah as a Christmas gift. Sherman's victory seemed even more complete when news arrived that General Thomas, in a superbly organized assault, had completely shattered the army of General Hood outside Nashville and had driven off the Confederates. From Savannah, Sherman faced his army around, and in January, 1865, he prepared to move northward through the Carolinas to link up with the forces of General Grant.

Sherman's Christmas present to Lincoln was a fitting climax for a year that had started out with a series of political and constitutional problems threatening the personal future of the President and endangering the structure of his party. 1864 was a presidential-election year, and Lincoln had had serious doubts about his ability to get the nomination of his own party, much less to win the national election in November. Despite the Union victories at Gettysburg and Vicksburg the previous summer, opposition leaders within the Republican party had continued to criticize the way Lincoln was directing the war effort; they considered him guilty of failing to bring the Confederacy to its knees. They blamed him for appointing cautious and dilatory Democratic generals like McClellan, who let Lee escape after Antietam, and Meade, who had done the same thing after Gettysburg and who was wasting time sitting in front of Washington when he should have been "on the road" to Richmond.

When Lincoln began to make known the generous and conciliatory terms he had in mind with regard to letting the Southern states back into the Union after the War had been won, these Republican Radicals, as they came to be known, were ready to dump their leader as incompetent and ineffective. Many were prepared to throw their support to Secretary of the Treasury

Salmon P. Chase, who was regarded by Horace Greeley as a much stronger and bolder candidate. There were others who favored John C. Frémont, the disgruntled soldier-adventurer, who attracted considerable support from various antislavery groups in several parts of the North.

For all their backstairs intrigue and elaborate planning, however, the Radicals were frustrated in their attempts to change horses in the middle of the stream. Lincoln was still much too popular with the public to be outvoted, and he was much too astute to be maneuvered out of the picture. By about March of 1864 it was clear that Lincoln could not be sidetracked and that he would probably have to be renominated by the Republican party. Chase quickly read the signs and withdrew his name from candidacy—whereupon the President promptly steered his ambitions in new directions. In June Lincoln accepted Chase's resignation from the Cabinet, but in December he appointed the gentleman from Ohio Chief Justice of the Supreme Court. Although some of the more extreme Radicals still persisted in their search for an alternative, most resigned themselves to the prospect of another Lincoln victory. Much as they would like to have come out in favor of some other candidate, the Radicals were realists who had no intention of ending up on the losing side.

At the regular Republican National Convention at Baltimore early in June, 1864, Lincoln was almost unanimously renominated by his party on a platform calling for the complete eradication of slavery. With defeat of the Confederacy in sight, political leaders worked to reestablish the party on a national basis. To get around the difficulty of the "Republican" label, which by this time was synonymous with "Northern," the name "National Union Party" was adopted. To gain votes from the border states as well as to demonstrate the national character of the party in power, Andrew Johnson, the loyalist Senator from Tennessee, now a "War Democrat," was selected as the vice-presidential candidate.

Some consolation for those Radicals who still had reservations about working for their log-cabin candidate came late in August when, at their Chicago convention, the Democrats nominated General George B. McClellan and then adopted a "peace" platform that had been written by the Copperhead "Peace Democrat") leader, Clement L. Vallandigham. The Radicals may not have been enthusiastic about Lincoln, but this combination of McClellan and Vallandigham was enough to make them abandon their doubts about Lincoln.

By the time the elections were held in November, the victories of Sheridan in the Valley and Sherman's capture of Atlanta had put Lincoln in a much more favorable position. Even more of his erstwhile opponents rallied to his support. Although the popular vote was fairly close, with Lincoln receiving a popular majority of only 400,000 out of 4 million votes, the incumbent President easily carried all the Northern states except New Jersey and took Maryland and Missouri as well—212 electoral votes to McClellan's 21. Lincoln had won an important political victory, and his base of power was secure for another four years. What he wanted now was a military victory that would bring the War to an end and pave the way for the reconstruction of the Union. He was waiting for results from Ulysses S. Grant.

When Sherman's huge Army of the West first began to lumber out of Chattanooga in the spring of 1864, Grant was accompanying the Army of the Potomac on its march toward Richmond. On May 3, the Union forces crossed the Rapidan in a move intended to strike the right flank of Lee's Army of Northern Virginia. Lee did not wait to be attacked; instead he struck out hard at Grant's army as it marched through a dense mass of shrubs and thickets called the Wilderness. Here, on May 5 and 6, both armies fought a furious and bloody battle in the dark gloom of tangled undergrowth, while hundreds of brush-fires flamed about them.

Seeing that he could not break through the wilderness barrier, Grant slid his army farther south against Lee's flank to the vicinity of Spotsylvania Court House. Lee, however, was swift to counter Grant's flanking movement, and he sent his Virginians racing down to take up defensive positions. Starting on May 12, and continuing for five more days, Grant hammered at the

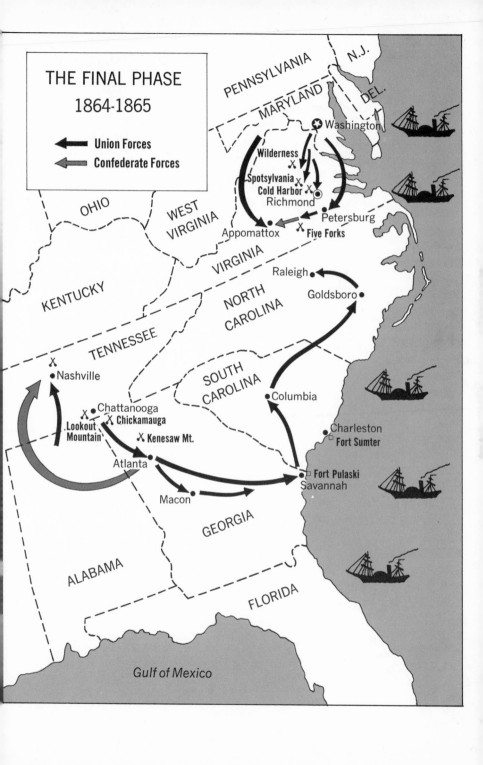

THE FINAL PHASE
1864-1865

← Union Forces
← Confederate Forces

PENNSYLVANIA

N.J.

MARYLAND

DEL.

⊛ Washington

Wilderness X

Spotsylvania X
Cold Harbor X
Richmond ⊚

Petersburg

OHIO

WEST
VIRGINIA

Appomattox

Five Forks X

VIRGINIA

KENTUCKY

NORTH
CAROLINA

Raleigh

Goldsboro

TENNESSEE

X
Nashville

SOUTH
CAROLINA

Chattanooga X
X
Lookout
Mountain
Chickamauga

Columbia

Charleston
Fort Sumter

X Kenesaw Mt.

Atlanta

Macon

Fort Pulaski
Savannah

GEORGIA

ALABAMA

FLORIDA

Gulf of Mexico

stubborn Confederate defense line, only to be thrown back as Lee shifted expertly to meet each attack.

Once again Grant swung his army southward; and once again Lee slipped his defenses down to meet Grant's latest maneuver. Lee's forces were now inside the Richmond defenses, his right flank resting on the Chickahominy while his center was at Cold Harbor. On June 3, Grant sent his forces forward in a massive assault against the Confederate positions at Cold Harbor, only to have Southern cannon drive them back with terrible losses— nearly 7,000 men in a single hour! At this point, Grant's stock was falling steadily in the North. The new General from the West had proved to be no better than all the other Union generals: He had failed to defeat Lee; he had failed to take Richmond. And worst of all, "Butcher" Grant, as some of the newspapers were calling him, had recorded nearly 60,000 Union casualties so far that summer—and it was only June! What the general public did not see was that Grant had also inflicted almost 30,000 casualties upon Lee—nearly 50 percent of his entire army. These were losses the Confederacy could never replace. Lincoln could see what Grant was doing; and for this reason the President refused to yield to those who demanded that he be relieved of his command.

Even while Lee was preparing to meet a new Union attack which he assumed would come directly across the Chickahominy, Grant made a sudden shift of plans. Skillfully screening his movements, he pulled his army away from immediate contact with the Army of Northern Virginia, swung them out past the Confederate flank on a forty-mile march, crossed the James River, and on June 15 struck at Petersburg, about twenty miles due south of Richmond. By seizing this important city and the railroad network that supplied the Confederate capital, Grant hoped either to starve Lee into submission or to force him to come out into the open and fight against superior odds.

Although Grant's maneuver caught Lee by surprise, the Union commanders failed to capitalize on their initial advantage. Bad planning and bungled orders gave Lee enough time to move his forces down to the Petersburg area and set up defense lines.

Both sides dug in, an elaborate series of trenches was developed, and preparations were made for a long siege. Mortars were used extensively and heavy guns were brought up on railway cars as the weary months of trench warfare dragged on through the cold winter months. Lee's lines grew thinner, his ragged veterans hungrier, and his meager store of supplies smaller.

Late in March, 1865, Lee struck out in a desperate effort to break the Union siege. A surprise assault on Fort Stedman staggered the northern end of the Union line, but Grant's men rallied and drove the Confederates back into their defenses with heavy losses. Four days later, Grant himself lashed back with a counterattack which swept far around Lee's southern flank and drove the Confederate defenders back at Five Forks. Fearing complete encirclement, on April 2 Lee rushed a courier to Jefferson Davis with word that he could no longer defend the Confederate capital, pulled his army back from Petersburg, and retreated to the west. Richmond was left practically undefended, and the city fell easy victim to the Union forces. But Grant had no time to waste on empty cities—Lee and the Army of Northern Virginia had always been his principal target, not Richmond. Working in close collaboration with Sheridan and his troops from the Valley, Grant led his army after the retreating Confederates like a hunter on the track of a wounded animal. The Confederate government fled west from Richmond to Danville, Virginia. Before leaving, Davis issued a proclamation to the people of the South asking them not to despair but to meet the foe with "fresh defiance" and fight on with "unconquered and unconquerable hearts."

Lee tried to march, to turn, to feint, to maneuver—but the Union troops were everywhere. He led his exhausted men west toward Appomattox Station where supplies and rations were waiting—only to discover that Sheridan and a strong Union detachment had arrived there first. Lee now saw that further resistance was useless. Grant was in front of him, Sheridan was in back of him, and Sherman was rolling up from the south. Surrender was his only alternative.

On April 7, 1865, Lee requested a meeting with Grant; and on

Palm Sunday, April 9, the two generals met at the McLean House in the village of Appomattox Court House. Having come directly from the battlefield, Grant was dressed in his usual plain uniform, mud-spattered and wrinkled, while Lee was immaculate in his faultless gray uniform and his handsome dress sword. After discussing the general terms of surrender, Grant permitted the Confederate officers to keep their sidearms and the men their horses—in order to "work their little farms." Grant showed no sign of victory or elation—he was simply a professional military man who had completed a difficult assignment. He did not ask for Lee's sword; Lee did not offer it. Expressing his heartfelt appreciation to his men for their "unsurpassed courage and fortitude," Lee bade farewell to the officers and men of the Army of Northern Virginia and rode off toward Richmond.

Although President Jefferson Davis urged his officers to carry on the fighting and, if necessary, to "operate in the interior," General Joseph E. Johnston, who had been trying in vain to stop the Union forces of General Sherman, saw the futility of further resistance now that Lee had surrendered. Two weeks after Appomattox, Johnston met with Sherman at the Bennett House near Durham Station, North Carolina, and agreed to surrender terms similar to those accorded Lee at Appomattox. After the surrender of the Army of Northern Virginia and the Army of the Tennessee, smaller groups of Confederate forces gradually gave up the struggle and the grim years of civil war came to a halt.

No other war in the history of the United States ever had such a direct and personal effect upon so many people. By the time the fighting had stopped, over half a million American men were dead—out of a population of about 31 million people. This conflict between the states killed more Americans than either World War I or World War II, and, because the total population was much smaller, it had a far greater impact upon the nation. This was a war that touched every city, every town, and every family in America.

It was also a conflict that marked the historical transition of warfare from the more romantic and highly personalized epics of the past, with their blaring trumpets, cavalry charges, plumed helmets, and tasseled sabers, into the first of modern war, with such technical innovations as the telegraph, the observation balloon, the Gatling gun, the railroad train, and the ironclad warship. From the point of view of its mechanized operations as well as its military strategy and tactics, the struggle between the Blue and the Gray provides a classic study in modern warfare that has been analyzed by the general staffs of the world for a century.

But in addition to its military implications, the Civil War had a significant impact upon the course of the nation's history. It caused serious dislocations in the national economy and introduced financial modifications that had important consequences for years to come. It established a new constitutional relationship between federal power and state sovereignty, and it provided a base for extraordinary executive authority that has had far-reaching implications. And it revolutionized the established social patterns of nineteenth-century America by giving political freedom to some four million black citizens and calling for the same degree of social equality enjoyed by the white citizens of the nation. The home front, no less than the battle front, was staggered by the shock waves of the Civil War.

CHAPTER 13
"THESE DISTEMPERED DAYS"

$\mathbf{A}$S THE ARMIES of the North and the South struggled along the weary road from Sumter to Appomattox, the mood of the people back home constantly reflected the ebb and the flow of the fortunes of war. The first months of the conflict opened to the noise of blaring trumpets and the cheers of marching throngs. In the cities of the North and the South, men, women, and children were caught up in the excitement of working together as great unified communities for the land they loved. Enlistment tents were pitched in the midst of busy thoroughfares and prayers were offered in every church. Women rolled bandages and sewed quilts, and townspeople took up special collections of clothing, food, and blankets for their boys at the front.

Enthusiasm alone is never enough to sustain a government in a prolonged war for survival, however. Before the smoke of the first engagements had cleared away, both sides realized they would have to consider again how they could maintain economic security and political equilibrium during a conflict that threatened to drain away their every resource. The time had come to face the financial realities of modern warfare!

In 1861 Secretary of the Treasury Chase thought that most of the war expenses could be met through the sale of bonds and

Much of the confusion and mismanagement of the early years of the Civil War could be attributed not only to military inefficiency but also to the greed and corruption of shrewd speculators who overcharged the government outrageously and who delivered spoiled food and shoddy clothing. An awareness of the enormity of this kind of immorality was displayed as early as August 17, 1861, in the columns of Vanity Fair, *a nineteenth-century satirical and political magazine. Here an army contractor who grew rich and fat through public graft is confronted by the ghost of one of his victims. Bitterly, the Union trooper blames him for his death: "I am the bones of a soldi-er, as died in the sickly camp/ Reduced by the pizenous food and the clothes that didn't keep out the damp."*

notes, while the regular expenses involved in governmental operations could be covered by a tax program. It soon became evident, however, that the war would go on much longer than originally anticipated, and that a vast amount of money would have to be raised. The Federal Government began to issue many different kinds of bonds and short-term notes, bearing interest up to 7.3% and payable within a period of five years. Elaborate bond drives were organized throughout the Northern states, and Jay Cooke and Company of Philadelphia undertook to sell bonds for the government on a commission basis. By the end of the War, the United States Government had run up a debt of almost $3 billion, and the debt carried a high annual interest rate.

In order to increase revenue for operational purposes, the Federal Government also established a system of internal revenue taxes. Direct taxes were levied on the various states, and an income tax was exacted from individual citizens in proportion to the amount they earned. Excise taxes were established upon such items as beer, liquors, legal documents, bank checks, and manufactured goods. Beginning with the Morrill Tariff of 1861, the tariff rates were raised several times during the course of the War in order to increase the government's revenue as well as to protect a number of valuable industries that were paying high taxes. By the end of the war, the average rate on dutiable commodities had reached 47 percent—the highest percentage in the history of the nation up to that time.

With expenditures heavy, loans difficult, and taxation inadequate, in February of 1862 Congress passed the Legal Tender Act which authorized the issuance of $150 million in "greenbacks" to meet the wartime needs of the Union government. This was paper currency, backed by neither gold nor silver; each note displayed the promise that the government would redeem it in gold at some future date. Before the War came to a close, the Federal Government had issued a total of $450 million in greenbacks, which drove gold and silver coins out of circulation in the North.

One other emergency measure was the establishment of a more uniform system of banking. Since the days of Andrew Jackson and the struggle over the Second Bank of the United States, the nation's banking system had been controlled by the individual states, which issued thousands of different types of bank notes of varying value. The National Banking Acts of 1863 and 1864 changed this confusing and decentralized structure by setting up a system of national banks; these were required to deposit with the Federal Government bonds worth one-third of their capital. The banks retained their own boards of directors, but they now came under the supervision of the Comptroller of the Currency in Washington. Most state banks were forced into this new arrangement since Congress imposed a 10 percent tax on the circulation of state bank notes. With the two Banking Acts Congress made it possible for the government to dispose of its bonds more effectively, established a national currency on a more stable basis, and organized a more standardized banking system for the country.

If the Northern states, with their broad financial capacity and their increasing industrial productivity, found it difficult to support a prolonged struggle, the South faced financial obstacles that were almost insurmountable. Christopher G. Memminger, the Confederate Secretary of the Treasury, was inexperienced in government fiscal affairs, and he certainly did not anticipate a war that would last four years. He relied heavily upon loans and notes as the basic means of revenue. In February, 1861, the Provisional Congress of the Confederacy authorized a bond issue of $15 million at 8 percent interest, payable in ten years. Although this initial issue was quickly subscribed and provided the Confederacy with the means of purchasing supplies from abroad, it drained the South of so much of its specie that future loans had to be made payable in commodities like cotton, sugar, rice, and tobacco. Early in 1863, a loan was arranged with a French firm for an issue of $15 million worth of bonds which would be redeemed in cotton after the War. But the work of Union agents abroad, coupled with a series of Confederate military defeats, caused less than half the loan to be subscribed.

In an attempt to improve its financial situation, the Confederacy turned to paper money. Although only small amounts were authorized at first, the financial pressures upon the new government were so great that by the end of the War it had issued more than $1.5 billion worth of paper currency. The currency was not based on any kind of specie and it contained no promise of redemption; consequently it quickly fell in value. From time to time during the course of the War, Confederate currency fluctuated in value, rising after a particular military victory and falling after a serious defeat, but by 1864 the Confederate dollar had one-thirtieth the purchasing power of the gold dollar—and then it collapsed completely. By the end of the War, unable to sustain its own paper currency and unable to obtain loans from abroad, the Confederacy was bankrupt, and the entire South was overcome by economic demoralization and financial chaos.

While the Civil War produced financial strain, economic dislocation, and industrial innovation in many parts of the nation, it also resulted in general prosperity throughout the Northern states. The prosperity was destined to continue long after hostilities had ceased. One group, the American farmers, experienced one of the most prosperous periods in their history. The abnormal demands for food required by the huge armies boosted both production and profits. In addition to foodstuffs, farmers provided the woolen goods and the leather products essential for such military material as uniforms, blankets, boots, belts, and saddles. Any initial losses that took place when normal trade with the Southern states was interrupted were more than offset by the sales made, directly or indirectly, to the government. Also, Great Britain, suffering from a series of bad harvests, was forced to import an unusually large amount of wheat from the United States. Unable to procure from Europe, South America, or Egypt a sufficient quantity of wheat to meet domestic needs, Britain depended upon the United States for well over 50 million bushels of wheat per year—three times the normal amount.

As a result of these unusual demands, American agriculture expanded at a remarkable pace. New types of agricultural machinery were employed in the fields, unused lands were cultivated, and old lands were reclaimed. Farmers clamored for even more free land in the West. This pressure, along with the absence of the Southern states from the Federal Government—they could no longer block such legislation—led to the passage in 1862 of a homestead law that set the stage for development of the "middle border" in Iowa, Kansas, Nebraska, and Minnesota directly after the War. According to the new legislation, anyone twenty-one years of age, either a citizen or an alien who had declared his intention of becoming a citizen, might acquire a quarter-section of public land (160 acres). After living on this piece of land for five years and improving it, he would then receive full title to it virtually free of charge.

As farmlands expanded and as use of the soil became a matter of general concern, many people began to advocate a more scientific approach to the problems of agriculture. As early as 1857 Michigan established the first state college of agriculture, followed in quick succession by Iowa in 1858 and Minnesota in 1859. It was also in 1859 that Justin S. Morrill of Vermont, Chairman of the House Committee on Agriculture, pushed through Congress a measure granting public lands to each of the states as an endowment for agricultural education. President Buchanan vetoed the original bill, but in 1862, with Lincoln and the Republicans in power, the Morrill Act became law. Each state was granted as many times 30,000 acres of public land as the number of Senators and Representatives it elected to Congress. Stimulated in this fashion, state after state established agricultural colleges and agricultural departments in state-supported universities.

Farmers were not the only ones who profited from the exigencies of war. Manufacturers, too, experienced unparalleled success in meeting the demands of the armies and navies and in moving the technical operations of plants and factories in new directions. In the course of four brief years, given impetus by this massive modern war, a new industrial age was beginning to take shape. Domestic manufacturing in the United States had begun on a small scale after the American Revolution, and it received both moral and financial support from the national government after the War of 1812. The era of roads, canals, and turnpikes, and then the advent of the railroad, marked the spread of industry to markets far beyond the Atlantic seaboard; and the application of steam power to new mechanical inventions made greater production possible. Individual financiers, businessmen, and railroad entrepreneurs not only amassed great personal fortunes, but they also helped to shape the political destinies of Massachusetts, New York, and Pennsylvania and other states during the 1840's and 1850's. There was a regular and consistent rise in American industrial production in the antebellum decades, and the transformation of America from an agrarian economy and a rural society into an industrial economy and an urban society would surely have come about in a slow and gradual manner.

But the Civil War suddenly produced great changes in industrial patterns. The armies required huge quantities of manufactured goods of every sort—especially clothing, boots, shoes, hats, blankets, tents, wagons, rifles, cannon, ammunition, and means of locomotion by rail and by ship. Never before had manufacturing been called upon to produce such a volume of goods for so many customers in such a concentrated period of time. These demands forced significant changes in production methods and management techniques.

Like the farmers, manufacturers were also greatly assisted by inventions and innovations made during the years preceding the war. The principle of interchangeable parts made the Springfield rifle supreme. The new Sault Sainte Marie Canal now brought more easily to Pittsburgh foundries an unlimited supply of inexpensive iron with which to produce cannon, railroad rails, and iron plating for the new ironclad ships. The sewing machine came into widespread use not only for the manufacture of uniforms and garments, but also to turn out boots, shoes, and other leather products so much in demand. The heavy industries probably made the most rapid advances, as the need for large guns, powerful artillery shells, ironclad vessels, mobile bridges, and railroad locomotives resulted in larger factories, greater investment, mounting capitalization, and increased productivity. In many dramatic ways, the Civil War greatly accelerated the rate of industrial change in the United States and helped to set the stage for the Age of Big Business that followed it.

By 1864 the pattern for the future was clear. The reelection of Abraham Lincoln in November of that year was crucial not only to the conduct of the War but to the economic transformation of the nation as well. If the Democrats had won that election and returned to power at the national level, the transformation would probably have been slowed down, if not actually reversed. The Democrats traditionally blocked such economic measures as protective tariffs, free homesteads, a national banking system, and direct federal aid for internal improvements. But with their return to office in 1864, the Republicans were in a position to continue the programs and policies that were already providing a new stimulus to the changing patterns of American life.

Wartime production meant wartime profits, and extraordinary opportunities for financial investment were the source for individual incomes and fortunes that in turn provided the base for new industrial empires in the postwar years. Government contracts were a major factor in the growth of many war fortunes. Railroads were profitable investments as a result of stepped-up war traffic, and railroad mileage throughout the Northeast and Northwest expanded rapidly. Internal waterways, too—the Great Lakes, the Western rivers, the numerous canals—did an unusually large business throughout the conflict. Financial institutions, which at first suffered heavy losses when their Southern patrons seceded from the Union, found more than adequate compensation in the growing commercial activity of the Northern states.

All too often, however, the very scale of financial dealings and the heavy investment created opportunities for fraudulent contracts and corrupt manipulations. Millions of dollars, for example, were derived from selling uniforms made from "shoddy," a textile processed from refuse and sweepings, which commonly disintegrated on the backs of the soldiers as they marched through rains and mud. Individuals regularly made profits from the sale of war bonds. Freight rates were hiked to incredible levels, broken-down horses were sold to the Army, and many of the natural resources of the nation were generally regarded as the exclusive property of the shrewd, the clever, and the quick.

Wartime profiteering often bred a spirit of extravagance and frivolity in the North, in contrast to the growing casualty lists in daily newspapers. Social life reached a dizzy whirl, with more fancy-dress balls, parties, and musical extravaganzas than ever before. Public interest in sports as a diversion in wartime grew noticeably. Besides regular sporting attractions like horse-racing and prizefighting, baseball had its crude beginnings. The newly rich spent lavishly, flaunting gaudy jewels, flashy carriages, and elaborate gowns. Their purchase of foreign luxury items, rather than the government's buying war matériel, resulted in an unfavorable balance of trade with Europe. Fifty-four million dollars worth of American gold was sent abroad in 1863, and the figure went as high as $91 million in 1864.

Wartime prosperity, however, was not evenly distributed, and the working classes in particular failed to obtain their share of the new wealth. Increased profits, higher wages, and lavish spending pushed up consumer prices. As a result, most working people, as well as the families of Union soldiers whose base pay was only $13 a month, suffered hardships and privations on the home front. Their incomes failed to keep pace with the climbing costs of commodities, and they often could not afford even the basic necessities of life, as the price of foodstuffs, dairy products, coal, and gas soared higher and higher. Tangible evidence of growing dissatisfaction with the wartime economic picture is seen in the labor disorders which grew more frequent as the War progressed. Coal miners in Pittsburgh, dry-goods clerks in New York City, shop girls in Boston, and newspaper workers in Chicago engaged in strikes against management policies. These disputes set the stage for the confrontation of labor and management that came about after the War had ended.

If the War brought extraordinary prosperity to the North, it brought unparalleled depression to the South. Because the welfare of the section was so intimately bound up with cotton culture, the failure of Southern cotton to find a normal market was nothing short of disastrous, and the fall of cotton sales provided a tragic barometer by which to gauge the economic decline of the Confederate States.

Confident that the European nations would come to their aid as soon as their textile mills were short of cotton, the Confederate government tried in the early months of the War to prevent all shipments of cotton abroad. To impress upon Europeans the South's determination to stand by its King Cotton diplomacy, as well as to reduce temptation for those who might try to make private deals, cotton planters were urged to burn their cotton supplies; it is estimated that this policy cost the South about a million bales of cotton. Had exportation been stimulated rather than discouraged, the South might well have been able to build up credit abroad for use in later stages of the War. By 1863, the Confederate government realized the failure of its cotton policy and was prepared to reverse it, but by that time the Union naval blockade had made shipments from the South almost impossible.

With the outbreak of war and the threat of a Union blockade, the Southern states realized that they might not be able to import manufactured goods and foodstuffs either from Europe or from the Northern states. They tried to make their economic life more diverse than ever before. Corn and sweet potatoes were grown in place of cotton in many areas, sugar and rice were brought under cultivation in new regions, and even small kitchen gardens were encouraged as a means of supplementing the dwindling food supply. "Confederate coffee" was manufactured from things like parched peas and corn ground together, a form of tea was concocted from blackberries and huckleberries, rope was made from Spanish moss, and leather was pieced together from cotton cloth and shoetops. Saltworks were established wherever possible, ironworks were geared to wartime needs, and cotton mills, boot and shoe factories, munitions plants, and the like were started in spite of inadequate capital, defective machinery, and poorly trained workers. But it was too little and too late, and the South was unable to make up the deficiencies that were moving its government toward bankruptcy and ruin.

At first the War did not produce too many changes in the

everyday life of the people at home, and even when shortages began the civilians responded with ingenuity and determination. The women of the South, especially, displayed a courage and gallantry that did much to keep up spirits on the home front while they supported their men on the battlefield. They formed sewing circles, knitted socks, worked long hours in the hospitals, and raised money for war relief by organizing musicales, auctions, and minstrel shows. To keep up a semblance of the gay social life they loved so well, they arranged fancy-dress balls, formal teas, and picnics—even though in the later stages of the War these were called "starvation parties." Women took over the complicated tasks of operating large plantations; and on small farms women did the plowing, planting, and harvesting, while their husbands were at war. Some, like Belle Boyd and Rose O'Neal Greenhow, risked their lives as Confederate spies; and others smuggled medicines and other scarce goods through the Union lines.

In the early stages of the fighting, the theaters were active and crowded, gentlemen were able to enjoy an occasional hunt or a horserace, and a prize fight always drew an enthusiastic audience. But as the War drew off more and more men, and as the horses were requisitioned for the cavalry, it became more difficult to find escape from the pressures of suffering and privation. The people stoically tightened their belts and adjusted to the wartime scarcities, but the deteriorating Confederate economy was fast chipping away at their morale. Even when scarce products became available, a soaring inflation drove prices to fantastic heights. Butter sold at $15 a pound, bacon was $9 a pound, potatoes went as high as $25 a bushel, the price of a pair of boots was $200, a pair of pants cost $100, and at the end of the War a barrel of flour was sold in Richmond for $1000. The inflationary spiral demoralized men on fixed salaries, planters whose incomes had fallen when they could no longer export their produce, and ordinary workingmen who protested that they could no longer purchase even the necessities of life. Especially hard hit were the families of private soldiers whose base pay was only $11 a month, and those widows and dependent parents whose pension of $10 a month could not provide for their basic needs.

A sense of panic and desperation gradually began to settle in among the civilian population, and it became so widespread that during 1863 a series of food riots were reported from such cities as Richmond, Atlanta, Macon, and Mobile, when large companies of women and children broke into shops in search of bread, flour, and clothing. There was also the growing spectre of illness and disease which could not be controlled. As a result of the Union blockade, drugs, medicines, bandages, and medical instruments were in desperately short supply even for the Confederate army, and on the home front they were scarcely available at all. As a result, the civilian population was nearly helpless to cope with the periodic epidemics of diphtheria, typhoid, dysentery, small-pox, and yellow fever. Although the spirit of the Confederacy was still willing, its flesh had been seriously weakened by hunger and disease, and its morale was crippled by an economy rapidly falling to pieces.

The economic and financial problems were only symptoms of the lack of political leadership which made it impossible for the Southern states to work together to achieve their independence from the North. The political problems stemmed from the diffi-culties faced by a head of government attempting to organize unity, solidarity, and disciplined obedience in order to win a war that supported the principles of revolution, secession, and state sovereignty. This would have been a demanding task for any chief executive, and Jefferson Davis lacked both the finesse in politics and the breadth of view to make it work at all.

Overly concerned as he was with legalisms, propriety, and his own sense of his prerogatives as Commander in Chief, Davis greatly diminished his effectiveness as a political leader. He sat at his desk too much trying to take care of inconsequential ad-ministrative details himself; but he did not provide the type of direct, personal leadership the Confederate revolution required. Then too, although Davis was highly respected because of his tenacity, his bravery, his intelligence, and his determination, he was never loved and was never really popular among his people —especially with state leaders who defended their own prerogatives jealously and guarded against any encroachments upon the cherished principles of state sovereignty.

Without a warm personality or instinctive tact, always sensitive to criticism and too rigid for change, Davis made enemies of those who could have done much to aid the Confederate cause. Some critics accused him of favoring West Pointers and their formalized style of fighting and of ignoring those Southerners who emphasized the superior fighting qualities and enthusiastic élan of the Confederate soldier. Others claimed that he had appointed too many "Yankees, foreigners, and Jews" to high positions in his administration, and pointed to his Jewish Secretary of State Judah P. Benjamin, his German-born Secretary of the Treasury C. G. Memminger, and his Quartermaster-General Abraham Myers, a Pennsylvania Jew, as "outsiders" who were directing the affairs of the South. State governors quarrelled incessantly about political appointments, allocation of troops, the commissioning of officers, the suspension of habeas corpus, and the policy of conscription; and Davis never developed a satisfactory mechanism for dealing effectively with his war governors, who remained a source of irritation and frustration down to the end of the War.

But, always, the great dividing force in the structure of the Confederacy was the principle of states' rights. Southern leaders emphasized that this was a constitutional war and demanded that their constitutional rights be preserved at all costs if the goals of the War were to be achieved. They fought off every attempt by Davis and his Confederate government to impose centralized controls, suspend habeas corpus, and establish conscription as violations of their constitutional prerogatives. They wanted the Confederacy to win its independence, of course, but they refused to sacrifice the principle of states' rights to help Davis achieve that goal. If victory had to be achieved at the expense of states' rights—then they would rather accept defeat.

Abraham Lincoln, too, was confronted with the inevitable constitutional problems of a President in wartime, and his views on the extent and limitations of presidential authority created as much discussion and dissension a century ago as these issues still do today. Throughout the North there was considerable opposition to Lincoln, to the Republican party, and to the War itself. Much of this opposition was forceful and vocal, and some of it was highly organized. One of the largest and most active of the opposition groups were the "Peace Democrats"—the Copperheads, whose platform the Democrats adopted for the election of 1864. Among their leaders were Clement L. Vallandigham and Alexander Long of Ohio, Fernando Wood of New York, and B. G. Harris of Maryland. In 1864 the Copperheads formed a secret society called The Sons of Liberty, reputed to have some 3,000 members who supported states' rights and who were sworn to oppose any "unconstitutional" measures of the Federal administration. They charged Lincoln with violating fundamental provisions of the Constitution and infringing on the basic rights of American citizens in his conduct of the War.

At the very outset of the fighting, when Maryland secessionists tried to prevent Union forces from reaching Washington, Lincoln had ordered a number of the rebel leaders seized and imprisoned without benefit of trial. One of these citizens, John Merryman, petitioned Chief Justice Taney for a writ of habeas corpus so that he could be brought to trial immediately. Taney issued such a writ—*Ex parte Merryman*—and demanded the release of the prisoner. The commander of the military prison at Fort McHenry, however, informed the Chief Justice that the President had ordered the suspension of habeas corpus in cases such as Merryman's, and returned the writ. Although Taney wrote an opinion denouncing Lincoln's action as unconstitutional, pointing out that habeas corpus could only be suspended by act of Congress, the legal technicalities were ignored and Merryman remained in custody. Two years later, in 1863, Congress passed the Habeas Corpus Act which officially authorized the President to suspend habeas corpus in cases arising out of the War. But even as early as the Merryman case Lincoln assumed he already had the power to take whatever measures were necessary to suppress the rebellion and prevent the disruption of the Union.

Closely related to the problem of irregular imprisonment was the issue of irregular trials. In May, 1863, Clement Vallandigham was arrested for speaking out in violation of orders given by General Burnside. He was tried in a military court, found guilty, and ordered imprisoned for the duration of the War. Although Lincoln eventually commuted Vallandigham's sentence and ordered him banished beyond the Union lines to avoid making him a martyr to his cause, the action provoked a serious debate over freedom of speech and the trial of civilians by military courts. The Vallandigham case further inflamed those who felt Lincoln had assumed the powers of a dictator. For his own part, Lincoln insisted that he was simply carrying out his duties as Commander in Chief in suspending statutory laws in order to protect the public safety and in upholding his official oath of office to support the Constitution and defend the Union. Since both houses of Congress were still fully operative and the civil processes of political elections were still functioning, he was willing to leave it up to his "rightful masters," the American people, to decide whether he had acted wisely and well.

In addition to political assaults from those Democrats who felt that he had gone too far in exercising his presidential powers, Lincoln also faced substantial opposition from those elements within his own party who felt that he had not gone far enough —with regard to the War, to slavery, and to the treatment to be accorded the South once the War had ended.

From the very beginning of the fighting, long before their opposition in the 1864 election campaign, there were a number of militant antislavery leaders, the Radicals, who opposed Lincoln's refusal to declare the War a crusade to free all the slaves immediately. Further, they felt that the President was not pressing the War against the seceded states with sufficient vigor and vehemence. Early in the War, the Radicals took a leading role in the Joint Committee on the Conduct of the War, which Congress created in December, 1861, to investigate the prosecution of the War and to control the actions of the President. Always in the background, however, was their conviction that Lincoln was not sincerely interested in working for the civil and political rights of the Negro. When it became evident that his Emancipation Proclamation did not apply to all slaves everywhere in the nation, Senator Charles Sumner of Massachusetts and such prominent Congressmen as Benjamin Wade of Ohio, Henry Winter Davis of Maryland, and Thaddeus Stevens of Pennsylvania concluded that their deep-seated fears of the President's weakness on this issue were more than justified.

The division between Lincoln and the Radicals became even more dramatic after the Union victories at Gettysburg and Vicksburg in the summer of 1863 showed that the Confederacy could not hold out much longer and that the Federal Government should be preparing policies for the postwar South and the reconstruction of the Union. In December of 1863, Lincoln issued a Proclamation of Amnesty and Reconstruction in anticipation of the end of the conflict; he offered to take the Southern states back into the Union when ten percent of the population of each state had taken the oath of allegiance.

This presidential approach smacked too much of "conciliation" and "easy" reconstruction, so far as the Radicals were concerned, and they saw that they had one more basic conflict with presidential policy. The South, the Radicals felt, had committed high treason and ought not to be readmitted to the Union until proper sanctions had been applied and until the South had demonstrated repentance. The Radicals' answer to Lincoln's Amnesty Proclamation came on July 2, 1864, in the Wade-Davis bill, which would reestablish civil government in the South only when 50 percent of the citizens (not 10 percent) had taken the oath of allegiance, and which denied the right to vote and hold office to all those who had fought for the Confederacy. When Lincoln pocket-vetoed the Wade-Davis bill, a break occurred between the President and the Radicals the results of which would influence events during the next four years. The President tried to minimize the effects of the controversy by giving at least partial recognition to the Wade-Davis plan in his Proclamation Concerning Reconstruction on July 8. He assured the nation that he was not yet "inflexibly committed to any single plan of reconstruction" and presented the Radical plan as one possible approach to the problem. In a further attempt at concession, he reluctantly agreed to sign a joint congressional resolution excluding all eleven Confederate states from the electoral count of 1865, even though the exclusion applied to states that had already consented to follow his own program of reconstruction. Although Lincoln could see serious troubles ahead over the manner in which the Union would be reorganized, he was already taking steps to keep the channels of communication open between the executive and the legislative branches of the government.

But in November, 1864, Lincoln was more concerned with winning reelection than speculating about future conflicts with members of his own party. Once he had been safely returned to office, he focused his attention upon Grant, Sherman, and the Union armies in the field as they fought through the weary winter of 1864–65, drawing the ring tighter around the Confederate armies and bringing the awful conflict closer to an end.

On April 9, 1865, Lincoln received official notification of Lee's surrender at Appomattox, and with the end of the terrible bloodshed, he was able to turn his thoughts again to the question of how the Union could be brought back together. To a crowd of jubilant people celebrating the end of the War on Tuesday night, April 11, he spoke in thoughtful, sober terms, not revelling in the military victory but dwelling upon the serious and complex problems to be solved in the months ahead. Urgently he pleaded that the nation restore the Union as quickly, as peacefully, and as painlessly as possible. He asked that legislators not become embroiled in arguments over the legal technicalities of whether the Confederate states had actually been "in" or "out" of the Union. The important thing, he emphasized, was that the Southern states were *back*—and the nation should return to the normal processes of government as soon as possible.

With the horrors of civil war now behind him, and with the controversial problems of reconstruction lying before him, a fatigued Lincoln agreed to a respite from the cares of office and accompanied his wife to Ford's Theater on Friday night, April 14, to take in the relaxing witticisms of *Our American Cousin*.

As the President leaned back in the comfortable rocking chair to enjoy the comedy, the silent figure of John Wilkes Booth stepped into the box, raised an arm, and sent a single bullet crashing into the unprotected head of Abraham Lincoln. The President was carried across the street from the theater to a private house where he lived through the night and passed away the next morning without ever regaining consciousness. Draped in black, a funeral train carried the body of the rail-splitter back to his home in Springfield, Illinois, while weeping crowds of people watched silently until the mournful caravan had puffed slowly into the West.

The Civil War had ended. Abraham Lincoln was dead.

CHAPTER 14
THE ORDEAL OF
RECONSTRUCTION

THE ASSASSINATION of Abraham Lincoln brought to the White House Andrew Johnson, a War Democrat who had worked his way up from poverty to become a leader in Tennessee politics. A confirmed Jacksonian, Johnson regularly took up the cause of the poor farmer against the rich planter, and when he went to Congress he pressed for homestead acts to provide more land for small farmers. The only Senator from a Confederate state to remain loyal to the Union, he was appointed military governor of Tennessee in 1862; and in 1864 Lincoln agreed to his nomination as the Republican vice-presidential candidate. A man of courage, tenacity, and determination, Johnson was nonetheless insecure and impulsive. His belligerency made him disregard the opinions of others and his stubbornness prevented him from engaging in effective political accommodation.

Despite his Southern background, his Democratic affiliations, and his reputation as a hot-tempered demagogue, Johnson assumed the Presidency on good terms with congressional leaders. Determined to punish those Confederate aristocrats who he believed had led the unsuspecting people of the South into a war they never wanted, Johnson took office denouncing secession as a "crime before which all other crimes sink into insignificance,"

A sketch from another popular weekly of the period, Frank Leslie's Illustrated Newspaper, *shows a scene of South Carolina's House of Representatives in session during the Reconstruction period. It obviously features the unusual number of black members who were elected to the state legislature. In the South Carolina constitutional convention blacks outnumbered the whites 76 to 48, and seven blacks were elected to the federal Congress from that state. But South Carolina was clearly the exception to the rule. In no other Southern state were the blacks in the legislative majority. No black was ever elected governor, only fifteen were elected to the House of Representatives, and only two blacks won seats in the United States Senate during Reconstruction.*

and threatening to reconstruct the South "with fire and hemp."
The Radicals, especially, were delighted that they had a President who would not adopt a "soft" program of reconstruction;
and their encouragement gave Johnson a golden opportunity to
build up an effective base of confidence and support among the
more moderate Republicans. Senators like William Fessenden of
Maine, Lyman Trumbull of Illinois, and John Sherman of Ohio,
as well as Representatives like James G. Blaine of Maine, Elihu
Washburne of Illinois, and Rutherford B. Hayes of Ohio, were
known to favor relatively painless readmission of the Southern
states after sufficient guarantees that Confederate leaders would
not resume political control. With the backing of those Democrats and Republicans who already favored strong executive
leadership in restoring the Union, Johnson might well have
cultivated the support of the moderates in curbing the power of
the Radical minority and moving ahead toward a reasonable and
cooperative program of reconstruction. Instead, he set out alone,
on his own initiative, and gave the Radicals their first opportunity
to gather support from more conservative elements within the
party.

After the initial shock of his first weeks in office, Johnson had
settled down to his responsibilities in a sober mood. Although he
still retained his hatred of the planter-aristocrats, he became convinced that justice for the plain people of the South, as well as
the future welfare of the Union, could best be achieved through
the principles outlined by Lincoln. Without calling a special session of Congress, and without even consulting congressional leaders, he offered his own terms for the return of the seceded states,
disenfranchising only those Confederates who had taxable property worth at least $20,000. He ordered states to reorganize their
governments, repeal their ordinances of secession, and repudiate
all Confederate debts. He also required them to ratify the Thirteenth Amendment abolishing slavery, passed by Congress in
January, 1865. Following Johnson's directives, the Southern states
conducted elections and assembled constitutional conventions
before November, 1865. Before the close of the year Johnson had
formally recognized the newly organized governments in all

eleven Rebel states and prepared to watch their new Senators and Representatives join the incoming Congress of the United States.

When Congress convened in December, 1865, the Radical leaders were in a furious mood, and even the moderates were displeased with the consequences of Johnson's actions. The spokesmen and leaders of the Radical faction were Senator Charles Sumner of Massachusetts, the powerful antislavery orator who had gone down under Brooks's club in 1856, and 73-year-old Representative Thaddeus Stevens of Pennsylvania, who was dedicated to the cause of black equality and fearsome in his determination to remake the South. First, they denied that the President had any authority to deal with matters they considered the exclusive right of Congress. According to Stevens, the Confederate states were merely "dead carcasses" at this point in their history. "Dead men cannot raise themselves. Dead States cannot restore their existence. . . ." "Congress," he insisted, "is the only power that can act in the matter."

Second, they maintained that Johnson's program, like Lincoln's, was much too conciliatory and did not provide adequate punishment for an unrepentant South. Not only had Southern states elected prominent Confederates to state and local offices, but they had also sent them to Washington to sit in the national Congress! Several Southern conventions still refused to admit that secession had been illegal, and although they repealed their ordinances of secession, they refused to repudiate them. The Johnson legislature in Arkansas voted pensions for Confederate veterans, South Carolina would not repudiate the Confederate debt, and Mississippi still refused to ratify the Thirteenth Amendment.

Perhaps more than any other single factor, Radical leaders were outraged by reports that Southern states had passed laws, known as the Black Codes, which set up stiff fines and penalties for unemployment, vagrancy, unlicensed preaching, and carrying of arms. If an accused Negro could not pay his fine, his services were sold to any white who contracted to pay it for him. Thus the codes had the effect of binding an accused black man to the

land. Southerners insisted that these laws were essential to the
preservation of law and order in the turbulent postwar South;
but the Radicals saw the measures as thinly veiled attempts to
evade the letter of the Thirteenth Amendment and to refasten
slavery on the South in a slightly different form. Several Radicals
demanded a program of land confiscation that would punish the
Rebel leaders and at the same time compensate the black man
for his centuries of bondage. Sumner wanted the plantations,
which he called "nurseries of the Rebellion," broken up and
parcelled out to freedmen; and Stevens called for former slaves
to receive sufficient economic support to make their freedom
meaningful. "Forty acres and a hut," he announced realistically,
would be more beneficial to the black man than "the right to
vote."

Determined that the Confederate states should not be readmitted until their rebellious leaders had been weeded out and the
principle of secession repudiated, the House voted to establish a
Joint Committee on Reconstruction to investigate conditions in
the Southern states and determine whether their elected officials
were entitled to be represented. When the Senate approved this
resolution, the newly-elected Senators and Representatives from
the South were ordered to stand aside while their "proper status"
was determined.

The growing impasse between Johnson and the Radicals came
to a climax in February, 1866, when Congress, by a substantial
vote, passed a measure extending the life and enlarging the powers of the Freedmen's Bureau. This was a federal agency established by Congress in 1865 as a part of the War Department to
protect the interests of former slaves "newly placed in society
without background, skill, or friendly hand." Authorized for a
period of one year under the direction of General Oliver O.
Howard, the Freedmen's Bureau helped emancipated slaves
find homes, obtain employment, settle labor disputes, and resolve
family difficulties. It sent hundreds of agents into all parts of the
South to carry out the functions of the Bureau, and to do additional work setting up special educational facilities, distributing

rations, providing medical care, and furnishing legal assistance for the freedman.

Johnson promptly vetoed the Freedmen's Bureau bill on the grounds that it had been passed by a Congress in which eleven states were not represented. Although the Radicals could not yet muster a two-thirds vote of the Senate to override the President's veto, moderates were so surprised by the uncompromising nature of the veto message that many of them began to lose all confidence in Johnson's ability to work with the legislative branch. The Radicals, led by Sumner and Stevens, struck back with a concurrent resolution asserting that no Congressman from a seceded state should be seated until Congress formally declared his state entitled to representation.

A short time later, in order to nullify the effects of the Black Codes, Congress passed the Civil Rights Act, which stated that all persons born in the United States were citizens of the United States and therefore had equal rights in the security of person and property in every state and territory. Although Johnson vetoed the bill on the grounds that it was an unwarranted invasion of states' rights, this time enough moderate Republicans joined with the Radicals to override his veto and pass the bill into law. Only a few weeks later, Congress easily passed a second version of the Freedmen's Bureau Act over the President's veto. It was evident that Johnson's inflexible stubbornness had alienated congressional leaders and had driven most of the moderates into the ranks of the Radicals.

Despite their recent successes, however, there were several legislators who were doubtful of the constitutionality of the new Civil Rights Act, and suggested a constitutional amendment as a means of establishing their policies on a more secure and permanent basis. On June 13, 1866, Congress approved what was to become the Fourteenth Amendment, and submitted it to the states for ratification.

Fundamentally, the Fourteenth Amendment consisted of four parts establishing the rights of the Negro and setting down the standards by which Congress would readmit the Confederate states. The first section incorporated the "dual citizenship" provisions of the Civil Rights Act, stating that all citizens of the United States are also citizens of the state in which they reside. This made the Negroes citizens and prohibited states from interfering with their rights and privileges. The second section provided that representation in the House of Representatives was to be based upon the *total* population of each state, and that if a state denied any adult male the right to vote, its representation would be reduced proportionately. The third section disqualified from state and federal office any person who had once taken an oath to uphold the Constitution and had then participated in the rebellion; and the fourth section outlawed the Confederate debt and denied all claims arising out of the Emancipation Proclamation or the Thirteenth Amendment.

Given encouragement by President Johnson as well as by many Northern Democrats, the Southern states defied the Radicals and, except for Tennessee, refused to ratify the Fourteenth Amendment—even though the Radicals made it clear that acceptance of the Fourteenth Amendment was the fundamental condition for readmittance. This was the way matters stood as the congressional elections of 1866 approached. Johnson was convinced that the American public would approve his "soft" plan of reconstruction and would vote the Radicals out of office if they knew all the facts. The Radicals, on the other hand, were equally convinced that the public wanted "hard" reconstruction, since the South had shown itself to be unconvinced and unrepentant.

The campaign of 1866 was vicious and bitter, with troubles at the polls and riots in many Southern cities. Appealing directly to the people, Johnson took to the stump in person and gave a series of impassioned speeches in a "swing around the circle" from Washington to Chicago. Knowing the explosive nature of Johnson's temper, the Radicals placed hecklers in the audiences; Johnson rose to the bait and on a number of occasions made intemperate remarks which were widely publicized and reflected on the dignity of his office. It was a disastrous defeat for the President, who had badly misjudged Northern public opinion. The Radicals captured more than a two-thirds majority in both houses of Congress in an election that settled the question of reconstruction. Henceforth the Radicals would set the standards and establish the rules. Jubilant in victory, the Republican leaders now formulated plans to punish those who had defied their policies and ignored their directives—Johnson and the South.

The Radicals had no doubt but that the people had given them a mandate to punish the South and promote the interests of the black man. In March, 1867, therefore, they passed the Reconstruction Act—over Johnson's veto—and established military rule in the South. The former Confederate states, regarded as a "conquered province," were divided into five military districts, each under the control of a major general who was directly responsible to the General of the Army, Ulysses S. Grant, and not to President Johnson. Under the authority of these military governors, conventions were to be called in the Southern states. Male Negroes over twenty-one were to be registered as voters, and delegates to the conventions were to be chosen by all citizens who had not lost their franchise by having participated in the rebellion. After each state legislature ratified the Fourteenth Amendment and sent a delegation to Congress whose members had not participated in the rebellion, its Senators and Representatives would be allowed to take their seats and military rule in that particular state would come to an end.

In spite of all the arguments, however, the program of confiscation and land reform to benefit the freedman was voted down. Most Republican Congressmen simply could not see the necessity of going that far. They assumed that political emancipation itself was sufficient to permit the black man to succeed on his own. Many also saw the very idea of confiscation, no matter what good purposes it might serve, as a dangerous violation of the sanctity of property and an interference with individual initiative. They felt quite confident that with the rigid military controls and elaborate political supervision outlined in the Reconstruction Act, the Negro, through hard work and perseverance, would be able to achieve full equality in the American democratic system.

Once they had passed the Reconstruction Act as a means of bringing the South into line, the Radicals turned their attention to President Johnson. More than once he had defied the authority of Congress. He had challenged its role in determining reconstruction policy, and he had persisted in using his veto to block its legislation. The time had come for the legislative branch to strike back. The same day that Congress passed the Reconstruction Act, it also adopted (again over Johnson's veto) the Tenure of Office Act, which stated that the President could not remove a federal officeholder without Senate approval if such an appointment had originally required Senate approval.

Although he consented to execute the provisions of the Reconstruction Act, Johnson refused to adhere to the Tenure of Office Act. He judged this to be an unconstitutional and unwarranted interference with his prerogatives as President, and in August of 1867 he defied the Radicals by demanding the resignation of Secretary of War Edwin M. Stanton. When Congress came together in December, the Senate refused to consent to the removal of Stanton and accused Johnson of having violated the Tenure of Office Act. On February 24, 1868, the House voted to impeach Johnson for "high crimes and misdemeanors in office," and a week later they presented eleven articles of impeachment to the Senate. The majority of the articles dealt with Johnson's violation of the Tenure of Office Act. The tenth article charged that Johnson had used disgraceful language in the campaign of 1866 and had attempted to bring "ridicule and contempt" upon the Congress. The eleventh article, drawn up by Thaddeus Stevens, was a blanket indictment which charged that the President had tried to prevent the execution of the acts of Congress and thereby was failing in his constitutional responsibilities as Chief Executive.

In a holiday atmosphere, the trial of President Johnson began in March, 1868, with Chief Justice Salmon P. Chase presiding and the Senate sitting as a "court of impeachment." Johnson's defense attorneys had little difficulty proving that the major charge —violating the Tenure of Office Act—was ridiculous simply on procedural grounds. Since Johnson had never requested the Senate's approval for Stanton's appointment (Stanton had been appointed by Lincoln), he had not violated the technical provisions of the act at all. But the Radicals, with Stevens serving as chief prosecutor, pressed for a vote on the eleventh article—the blanket indictment—hoping that the Republican-dominated Senate would vote "guilty" on the basis of personal conviction if not of legal fact. When the vote was taken, however, seven Republicans, despite pressure put on them, joined with twelve Democrats and voted against conviction.

By the margin of a single vote (35 to 19), the Senate failed to obtain the two-thirds vote necessary for conviction. Johnson was acquitted, and the United States was saved from what might have been a serious and even dangerous development. The conviction of Johnson could have established the precedent that Congress, at its pleasure, could remove a President with whom it disagreed politically, and the delicate system of checks and balances would have been destroyed. The Tenure of Office Act was later modified by Congress during the Grant administration and repealed altogether during the Cleveland administration. For the time being, however, although Johnson had been formally acquitted, his political power was badly crippled. The Radicals had their revenge: Johnson was in disgrace, and the South was prostrate under the terms of military rule.

The military defeat of the Confederacy had been complete. Its proud armies had suffered a humiliating ordeal, and the South itself was a scene of devastation. Cities lay in ruins; financial institutions were bankrupt; railways had been torn up; crops had been destroyed; farms were depleted; and the entire labor force was disrupted. The women of the South mourned the loss of their fathers, their husbands, and their sons; and the men who had not died in battle roamed the streets in idle desperation. Hundreds of thousands of black men, most of them without land, without food, without money, and without skills and trades of any kind, were at a loss to know where to go or what to do. Some loafed about their cabins in idleness; others gathered about army posts, living on scraps and rations; still others roamed the countryside, scavenging for food and enjoying their first experience of freedom.

The leaders of the South had no alternative but to acknowledge their defeat and submit to the will of the national government. For the most part they accepted the terms laid down by Lincoln and Johnson, since these seemed to offer the most reasonable opportunities for the future. Although they would be required to admit defeat, repudiate secession, and accept emancipation as a fact of life, they assumed that they would be left relatively free to determine their own domestic policies. Except for emancipation, most Southerners looked forward to a revival of the lifestyle that had prevailed in the Southern states before the war. They would reelect their former political leaders, they would keep the black man as a propertyless rural laborer under strict controls, and they would see the economic life of the South continue to revolve about the plantation system and farming.

The Radical program of reconstruction struck at the very heart of what the postwar South expected. No longer would the region be represented by its traditional leaders—plantation aristocrats and well-to-do Whigs—but by men of far lower station. With the threat of land confiscation, the breakup of plantations, and the allocation of land to the black man, the South faced the possibility of a basic change in its way of life. Further, it was likely that effective Republican control would mean high tariffs, centralized banking, and increased industrialization below the Mason-Dixon Line. But the vast social changes that might come in the wake of the Radicals' civil rights legislation frightened the average Southerner most. Emancipation was regrettable—but acceptable as the inevitable spoils of war. Equality, however, was unthinkable; and the idea that the Radical program would grant the emancipated black man not only political rights but also social equality was terrifying in its implications. Dreading any change in the basic traditions of their society, Southerners viewed the program of Radical construction, together with all those who supported it, with fear and contempt.

The political situation in the South, too, was a source of frustration. Since they were prevented from electing former Confederate leaders to office and could not bring themselves to vote for any black candidate, Southerners saw their political offices

fall into the hands of hated "carpetbaggers" and "scalawags."
Carpetbaggers were a part of the large number of Northerners
who had come south in the wake of the Union armies with little
else than their personal belongings stuffed into a carpetbag. Although some proved to be opportunists and adventurers, many
of these Northerners were sincerely interested in helping the
South regain its political and economic balance; many of them
were federal agents, missionaries, social workers, teachers, and
civil service workers. Scalawags, on the other hand, were native-
born Southerners who helped to establish Republican governments in the former Confederate states, who were allied with the
Radicals in Congress, and who cooperated with the Union military authorities in the South. While a number of these scalawags
were poor whites who used the opportunity to gain political
power and economic advancement, more of them came from the
planter, mercantile, and industrial classes of the South. Many
were former Whigs, relatively affluent and socially secure, who
had opposed secession during the 1850's, supported John Bell
and the Constitutional-Union ticket in 1860, and assisted their
states reluctantly through the war years. Now they began to re-
assert themselves as the natural, moderate leaders of their section, and saw the Republican-sponsored reconstruction governments as a means of rebuilding the South on a broader base than
the plantation aristocracy of the antebellum period. Southern
Democrats, too, from regions with industrial potential like western Virginia and northern Alabama, were persuaded to support
Republican governments in the South because they favored
higher tariffs, expanded railroad facilities, internal improvement
programs, and sound money. Although few showed any interest in expanding civil and political rights for the black man, they
were willing to work with the Radical governments as a means of
eventually returning the South to its rightful place in the Union.
    Southerners felt that their fear for the future of traditional
Southern life was best demonstrated in the new state governments, established under the control of these carpetbaggers, a
number of scalawags, and some blacks. State budgets rose to unprecedented heights and state debts soared to incredible sums as

appropriations and expenditures expanded alarmingly. In South Carolina the public debt went from $7 million to $29 million in only eight years. Taxation increased about 800 percent in Louisiana, and almost 1400 percent in Mississippi; while the bonded debt of the eleven Confederate states grew by well over $100 million during the postwar years. Unparalleled taxation and expenditure were frequently accompanied by widespread fraud, embezzlement, and corruption. In part, this situation was caused by the administrative incompetence of men who had no training and little experience in legislative work; in part, it was due to the presence of unprecedented sums of money, passing from hand to hand during a period of high turbulence and wholesale confusion. Southerners were convinced that the results were the natural outcome of Republican politics, Negro suffrage, and carpetbag rule. Only when these factors were removed, they insisted, could honesty and efficiency be returned to the South. This is a theme that was well established in American historical literature for well over a century.

In more recent years, historians have taken issue with the traditional view of reconstruction governments as being little more than a "carnival of corruption." They point out that the abnormal expenditures of this period were necessary in light of the social, economic, and educational problems facing the postwar South. Roads, dikes, levees, bridges, factories, and buildings had to be repaired and replaced after the destruction of war. Hospitals, orphanages, and asylums had to be constructed to meet the needs of the moment; and all kinds of social services had to be created to confront long-range problems. Above all, a whole new system of public education had to be established not only for the white children of the South but for thousands of black children as well. In South Carolina, to take but one example, there had only been 20,000 children enrolled in public schools in 1860. By 1873, there was a total of 120,000 (50,000 white and 70,000 black) who were being educated at state expense. Granting that expenditures during the reconstruction era were abnormally high, there were peculiar and pressing needs that made high spending necessary.

Furthermore, since there were few private sources of credit, most of the Southern states used state credit to finance the rebuilding and expansion of their railroad systems. Most of the large debt increases can be traced to financial grants, charters, and subsidies to railroad promoters; and these issues were regularly supported by influential Democratic members of Republican legislatures. In Florida, for example, more than 60 percent of the state debt went for railroad bonds; North Carolina issued millions of dollars for the same purpose; and $18 million of Alabama's $20.5 million Reconstruction debt went to subsidize railroad construction.

Legislation, in turn, was affected by business groups, contractors, land speculators, and railroad promoters who used their influence to obtain contracts, franchises, or subsidies from state legislatures. In Virginia, the Baltimore and Ohio Railroad tried to control elections and manipulate legislators to prevent the Southside Line from gaining control of the Virginia and Tennessee Railroad. A New York railroad and steamship company exerted tremendous pressure upon the Louisiana legislature to prevent the state from subsidizing a competing line between New Orleans and Houston; and in Alabama rival railroad companies fought for years to control the state legislature and gain access to valuable ore deposits around Birmingham. In addition to the direct and official costs of promoting industrial expansion in the reconstruction era, therefore, the indirect costs of fraud and bribery helped to increase expenditures even further.

Admitting that the postwar years witnessed an unprecedented amount of bribery, incompetence, and corruption in government, nevertheless, historians question whether malfeasance in the Reconstruction governments was any worse than the corruption in many Northern states during the same period. On the contrary, they suggest that the Radical governments can cite many pieces of progressive legislation to their own credit. They provided Southern states with new and liberal constitutions, they abolished imprisonment for debt, they eliminated property qualifications for voting and officeholding, and they readjusted the voting districts in many areas of the South. They rebuilt many of the public facilities, they provided for public education for blacks and

whites, and they allowed the black man to participate in government for the first time in history. "Granting all their mistakes,"
writes Kenneth Stampp, "the Radical governments were by far
the most democratic the South had ever known."

Historians have also modified the popular misconception of
Reconstruction as a time when large numbers of uneducated, inexperienced, and irresponsible freedmen established Negro rule
throughout the South and took the lead in political mismanagement and financial corruption. While it is certainly true that slavery had not prepared the black man adequately for life in a
democratic society, many intelligent and educated Negroes served
in public office during the reconstruction period. Blanche K.
Bruce of Mississippi, for example, the only Negro to serve a full
term in the United States Senate, was an escaped slave who was
educated at Oberlin College in Ohio. Hiram R. Revels, Mississippi's other Senator, who served a one-year unexpired term, was
an ordained minister and former school teacher who had attended
Knox College in Illinois. James D. Lynch, secretary of state in
Mississippi, had been educated in Pennsylvania; and Jonathan C.
Gibbs, secretary of state in Florida, was a Dartmouth College
graduate who was largely responsible for establishing Florida's
public school system. Francis L. Cardozo, secretary of state and
later treasurer in South Carolina, had attended the University
of Glasgow; and Robert Brown Elliott, a member of the South
Carolina legislature, had studied at Eton. Granting that these
men were prominent exceptions to the rule, and that most blacks
who held state and local office during Reconstruction lacked education and political experience, their accomplishments were impressive.

There is even less evidence to support the old myth of a white
South lying prostrate under Negro rule while vindictive blacks
manipulated the political machinery in an effort to "Africanize"
the entire region. Actually, at no time did Negroes come close to
controlling reconstruction policies in the South. Except for the
South Carolina constitutional convention where the blacks outnumbered the whites 76 to 48, in all other Southern states the
blacks were in the minority. In Mississippi, for example, there

were only 17 blacks out of 100 representatives at the constitutional convention. In Alabama there were 8 out of 108; in Georgia
there were 33 out of 170; and in Virginia there were 25 out of
104. The percentage of blacks in the various state legislatures was
about the same, with a tendency to decrease with each session.
On the basis of these one-sided ratios, it is difficult to sustain
the traditions of "Black Reconstruction." Although, to be sure,
there were dishonest blacks who cooperated with equally unscrupulous whites to pilfer funds and accept bribes during their
brief stay in office, there was no way that blacks could control
the policies of state legislatures or determine the overall management of municipal budgets. With few notable exceptions, Negroes
were relegated to minor state and local offices, and in none of
the Southern states was there any serious attempt to reform the
economy or change the society to benefit the black man.

In view of the emotional impact of the War and the bitterly
contested issues that followed it, however, there were few Southerners at the time who could take an objective view of a system
of government they were afraid would Africanize the region and
destroy the Southern way of life. Deprived of military power,
shorn of political representation, and discouraged about prospects for the future of White America, many Southerners came to
feel that their only hope for survival lay in a struggle against
carpetbag rule. Although there was nothing they could do to prevent the passage of reconstruction legislation, Southerners felt
that they might halt the execution of such legislation through
extralegal activities.

With secret societies Southern whites sought to prevent the
execution of Radical laws, to stop the black man from exercising
his franchise, and to maintain white supremacy. The most important of these societies was the Ku Klux Klan, organized in
1866 at Pulaski, Tennessee, as a social club for Confederate veterans. The Klan expanded quickly throughout the South as an
effective organization to prevent crime and maintain law and
order in vigilante fashion. Gradually, however, it became an in-
strument of repression used by Southern whites to terrify the Negro and intimidate those carpetbaggers and scalawags who oper-

ated the state governments. Dressed in white robes, masks, and cone-shaped hats, the men of the Klan rode the night. They warned blacks against voting or running for office, and they were ready to resort to beatings, whippings, and lynchings if their warnings were not heeded. With blackmail and brutality, some persistent Southerners hoped to make Northern reconstruction plans so ineffective that the national government would give their affairs back to the South to manage.

With leaders of the national government demanding recognition of war guilt and black equality as the price of readmission, and with the leaders of the White South steadfastly refusing to yield on either of these two points, the prospects for reunification on a peaceful basis seemed extremely dim. Under the 1867 legislation the Southern states came back into the Union, and soon the white population of the South began to regain control of the various state governments. It was certain that before long the South would once again emerge as a practical political reality and demand full participation in national affairs on its own terms. Upon what basis of accommodation—if any—the reconstruction-minded leaders of the North would be prepared to deal with the emerging new South was by no means clear. In 1867, some form of reunification was foreseeable and even acceptable. But unless some major adjustments were made in the attitudes of both sides, the resulting relationship was bound to be unsatisfactory from all points of view.

"Can you hold your state?" asked the Republican campaign chairman, Zachariah Chandler of Michigan, in his telegram to Republicans in Louisiana, Florida, and South Carolina. What looked like an easy victory for Democrat Samuel J. Tilden in 1876 turned into an explosive political controversy when it was discovered that there were nineteen electoral votes in dispute from these three Southern states. When a special congressional commission finally gave all twenty votes to the Republican candidate, Rutherford B. Hayes, Democrats threatened open rebellion until a final compromise was arranged just before Inauguration Day. This sketch from Frank Leslie's Illustrated Newspaper *shows Democratic members of Congress signing the protest to the counting of the Louisiana electoral votes on February 19, 1877.*

➤

CHAPTER 15
THE PRICE OF REUNION

WHILE THE Radicals were pressing their program of military reconstruction in the South, and at almost the same time that the impeachment trial of President Johnson was taking place in Washington, the Republican party held its national convention in Chicago in May, 1868, to select a candidate for the Presidency. Bypassing several obvious candidates, like Chief Justice Chase, the party leaders made the popular war hero Ulysses S. Grant their nominee.

The Democrats realized they faced an uphill struggle as they gathered for their convention in New York in July. One of their greatest problems was selecting a candidate acceptable to the numerous factions within their ranks. A few members wanted to nominate Johnson, some favored Senator Thomas Hendricks of Indiana, others preferred Senator George Pendleton of Ohio, and still others moved toward Chase, who indicated that he would accept a nomination by the opposition party. After many ballots, the Democrats settled on a compromise candidate, Horatio Seymour, the wartime governor of New York. In their platform they declared the issues of slavery and secession to be "settled for all time," demanded restoration of all rights to the states, called for amnesty for former Confederates, denounced the protective tariff, and called for the end of military rule in the South.

During the campaign of 1868, issues and platforms were pushed into the background in favor of smear tactics and exaggerated displays of patriotism. Reminding voters that Seymour had been governor at the time of the New York draft riots, the Republicans emphasized their role as the saviors of the Union, waved the "Bloody Shirt" aloft, and pictured Grant as the man of action and decision. Although Grant won a one-sided victory by capturing 214 electoral votes to Seymour's meager 80, he received only 53 percent of the popular vote, with a majority of a mere 300,000 votes. Considering that he received nearly 700,000 votes from newly enfranchised Negroes, and that six of the eight reconstructed Southern states voted Republican that year, it was obvious that the Radicals had put through their reconstruction policies none too soon. The question was how long they could sustain their reconstruction program in the face of growing opposition in the South. After considerable debate, in February, 1869, Congress passed and sent to the states for ratification the Fifteenth Amendment, which forbade any state to deny the vote to anyone "on account of race, color, or previous condition of servitude." The Amendment was calculated to assure the Negro's political rights in the South as well as to solidify the basis of Republican voting strength in the Southern states.

Despite his campaign slogan, "Let us have peace," Grant supported the reconstruction policies of the Radicals during his first administration and made little attempt to modify military rule in the South. He gave his approval and support to the Force Act which Congress passed in May, 1870, to help protect Negro voting rights in the South. The following year, when Congress passed the Ku Klux Klan Act, he used the extraordinary powers of the Act to place nine counties in South Carolina under martial law for engaging in terrorist tactics against freedmen.

Fundamentally, however, Grant was not concerned about the intricacies of legislative politics, nor was he particularly committed to the cause of the black man. He was much more interested in reducing national tensions and bringing the North and the South together in a more normal relationship. By the end of his first four years in office, he was weary of responding to the frequent appeals for more federal troops to patrol the South; and he became discouraged about the ability of the Federal Government to shore up carpetbag governments which could not support themselves. In the congressional elections of 1870, the Democrats made substantial gains; and the following year, despite Radical controls and military occupation, Southern whites recaptured control of the state governments in Tennessee, Virginia, North Carolina, and Georgia.

Even Congress was beginning to show signs of losing interest in the plight of the black man as the difficulties of maintaining Republican control in the South became more evident every day.

The old Radical leadership was fast disappearing—Henry Winter Davis and Thaddeus Stevens were dead, Benjamin Wade had gone back to Ohio, Charles Sumner was in terrible health—and with the elections of 1872 coming up, party leaders were less concerned with humanitarian principles than with the hard facts of survival. In May, 1872, Congress passed a liberal amnesty act which restored voting and officeholding privileges to most former Confederates, and they permitted the important Freedmen's Bureau to pass out of existence without any kind of substitute. Although most of its work ended on December 31, 1868, after the Southern states had come under the congressional plan of reconstruction, the Bureau continued to function until June 30, 1872, when it finally closed its books.

The American public, too, was losing interest in the welfare of the black man. Old-time Abolitionists like William Lloyd Garrison, Wendell Phillips, and Henry Wilson tried earnestly to "call the battle roll anew," revive concern for the plight of the freedman in the South, and promote support for reconstruction governments; but they encountered only apathy and indifference. Former antislavery workers agitated for enforcement of the Fourteenth and Fifteenth Amendments and pressed for new forms of educational and economic assistance for the Negro; but they got nowhere. Northerners were tired of hearing about the old slavery issue all over again. Many were disgusted at the widespread stories about graft and corruption in the carpetbag governments in the South, and they washed their hands of the whole affair. Others were convinced that their fundamentally racist convictions about the inferiority of the black race were demonstrated by the way the Negro's brief involvement in the democratic process apparently produced only ignorance, incompetence, and malfeasance. Even committed Abolitionists and well-meaning Northern liberals had become so disillusioned with the failure of Republican attempts at reconstruction in the South that they were ready to write it off as one of history's lost causes.

Fascinating new developments in the United States and throughout the world were also beginning to absorb much of the Northerner's attention. As the Civil War receded into memory, he had less time to concern himself about the problems of a black minority. Daily newspapers carried stories of the Indian wars in the Frontier West, discussed Grant's plans for the annexation of Santo Domingo, and weighed the prospects of a Cuban rebellion against Spain. Diplomatic observers debated the success of American negotiations with Great Britain over the *Alabama* claims as Grant's capable secretary of state, Hamilton Fish, carried on conversations with Sir Edward Thornton and Sir John Rose during the summer of 1871.

Closer to home, large-scale industrialization was sweeping over the nation, as the United States moved from fourth place in industrial production in 1860 to first place in 1894, when its factory production exceeded that of Great Britain and Germany combined. With more capital to be invested and greater profits to be realized than ever before, the money question became all-consuming. The Democrats, supported by a large farm bloc from the West, insisted that war bonds be redeemed in paper greenbacks in order to bolster farm prices. The Republicans, on the other hand, had run on a platform promising that war bonds would be repaid in "hard" coin. Two weeks after Grant's inauguration, therefore, Congress passed a law stating that the government would redeem all obligations in coin or its equivalent— meaning gold. This measure meant that people who had purchased bonds with depreciated greenbacks during the War would now be able to reap a substantial profit on their original investment. Under the Grant administration, the tariff question, too, was settled to the general satisfaction of the business interests of the country. The Morrill Act of 1861 had increased tariff rates, and during the course of the Civil War the rates continued to rise, to a high of 47 percent, to protect those industries—notably iron and wool—which paid high excise taxes to the national government. After the War, excise taxes were reduced; but lobbyists representing leading manufacturing interests put heavy pressure on the Grant administration to maintain tariff rates at their wartime levels.

The currency question and the tariff issues were only a small part of the vast economic revolution already transforming the nation. The Civil War had produced large accumulations of capital that could be used to exploit the valuable resources of the nation; and the growing population furnished an ample labor supply to work the machinery created by American inventiveness. The resulting products were carried through the nation by an elaborate system of water transportation and a growing network of railroad lines. During the late 1860's and the early '70's, construction was in full swing of a series of transcontinental railroads, with financial aid and generous land subsidies from the Federal Government paving the way. The Union Pacific was inching its way through Nebraska to Utah, while Leland Stanford and Collis Huntington were sending their Central Pacific eastward from the Pacific Coast. The Atchison, Topeka, and Santa Fe was pushing along the old Santa Fe Trail from Kansas into New Mexico, and the Northern Pacific was making its unsteady way westward to Portland and Seattle. John D. Rockefeller was beginning to establish his industrial empire based on oil. Andrew Carnegie was organizing the steel industry as a multimillion-dollar enterprise, and the managerial skills of C. C. Washburn, Charles Pillsbury, Gustavus Swift, and Philip Armour were transforming the processing of food and the packing of meat into new and flourishing businesses.

But it was soon evident that the national administration was too weak, too inept, and often too corrupt to understand or appreciate the industrial revolution that was taking place—or even to influence its impact very much. President Grant was particularly ineffective because of his inexperience and his lack of training in economic matters. Personally honest, he placed his faith in friends and associates who were not honest, and he apparently never realized that he was the innocent dupe of scoundrels who used his naïveté as an opportunity to make a dishonest dollar. Cronies, party stalwarts, and confidence men paraded through the White House, professing their loyalty to the General and disastrously influencing his judgments and decisions. With an uninformed President, a Cabinet filled with mediocrities, and a self-seeking Congress, there was political chaos. And unfortunately it was the kind of chaos that permitted politicians to make crooked deals and encouraged businessmen to manipulate the nation's economic resources with little restraint or regard for the social and political consequences of their actions.

One serious episode of political tampering occurred shortly after Grant took office, when James Fisk and Jay Gould turned from milking the Erie Railroad to devote their considerable talents to cornering the nation's gold supply. They planned to buy up all the gold on the New York Stock Market, but their plan could succeed only if they prevented the Treasury from releasing its periodic supply of federal gold. Operating through Grant's brother-in-law (who pocketed $25,000 on the deal), Fisk and Gould persuaded the gullible President that if he withheld federal gold he would keep farm prices up and help the poor farmer. Grant was effectively bamboozled, and he ordered the Treasury Department to hold the government gold. Without a new supply of the metal the price of gold shot up, and speculators found that they could buy gold only from Fisk and Gould, at exorbitant prices. Wall Street went into a state of panic that climaxed on September 24, 1869—known as Black Friday. Although the government became suspicious and released enough federal gold to burst the bubble, scores of men were ruined before the disastrous affair finally ran its course.

A second scandal involved the construction of the Union Pacific Railroad, which was receiving liberal grants of public lands and loan money from the Federal Government. A group of Union Pacific leaders formed a subsidiary company called the "Crédit Mobilier," through which they made contracts with themselves and paid themselves enormous dividends. When Congress became suspicious of the operations of this organization and proposed an investigation in the fall of 1867, Congressman Oakes Ames of Massachusetts, one of the directors of the Crédit Mobilier, distributed shares of valuable stock to a number of influential members of Congress. The Congressional investigation failed to materialize, but enough disturbing information had leaked out to implicate numbers of highly placed officials in the Republican hierarchy.

While Democrats were delighted by the disclosure of corruption within the Grant administration, many Republicans were alarmed about conditions within their party. What had started out as a group of idealists dedicated to the eradication of slavery and the restoration of the Union was fast degenerating into a collection of selfish politicians dedicated only to maintaining themselves in power. Senator James W. Grimes of Iowa labeled the Republicans "the most corrupt and debauched political party that ever existed"; and a Congressman from Ohio compared the House of Representatives to "an auction room where more valuable considerations are disposed of under the speaker's hammer." In 1868, the *Nation* complained that there was hardly a legislature in the entire country that was "not suspected of corruption; there is hardly a court over which the same suspicion does not hang."

An active group of "Liberal" Republicans, first coming to prominence in Missouri, began to agitate for reform within their party. They felt that the first and most critical step in their crusade was the removal of President Grant himself. In the early stages of this protest movement, the best known Liberal leader was Carl Schurz, a German political refugee of 1848, a journalist, and a Civil War veteran who became United States Senator from Missouri and stood in opposition to the continued policy of coercion in the South. Decent citizens and reform-minded political leaders from many parts of the country gathered behind the new Liberal party and prepared to "Turn the Rascals Out." The Liberals met at a separate convention at Cincinnati in the spring of 1872 to select a candidate who could beat Grant and start the nation on a new course. They called for an end to disabilities against Confederates and a return to self-government in the South. With a slate of well-known candidates including Schurz, Charles Francis Adams of Massachusetts, former wartime minister to Great Britain, Lyman Trumbull of Illinois, a leading Republican moderate, and Judge David Davis, a party stalwart from Lincoln's time, the Liberals presented a serious challenge to the Grant administration.

Unfortunately, however, control of the turbulent Liberal convention slipped into the hands of well-intentioned but ineffectual reformers, amateur politicians, and newspaper people who by-passed the professional politicians and chose the prominent editor of the *New York Tribune*, Horace Greeley, as their presidential candidate. B. Gratz Brown, governor of Missouri and a strong supporter of Greeley, was nominated for the vice-presidency. The Democrats, hungry for victory and willing to use any means to defeat Grant and the Radical wing, threw in their lot with Greeley and his call for an end to the "bloody chasm" between the separated North and South. Although he was a fearless moral crusader and a skillful journalist, Greeley was a disastrous choice as a presidential candidate. Emotional, erratic, and controversial, his odd and somewhat Pickwickian appearance made him a favorite target for cartoonists, and the variety of causes he had championed in his newspapers over the years were lampooned severely by the opposition press.

The regular Republican party, as expected, renominated Ulysses S. Grant, and the election of 1872 turned into a bitter campaign that saw both sides engage in mudslinging. Greeley was called an atheist, a communist, a vegetarian, and a congenital idiot (with eleborate phrenological charts to "prove" the charge), while Grant was labeled a drunkard, a butcher, a dictator, and a "depraved horse jockey." In addition to his personal liabilities, however, Greeley also lost ground for political reasons. Because of his history as an extreme protectionist and advocate of high tariffs he was unacceptable to many leading Democrats, while even Liberal Republicans had serious doubts about his devotion to the cause of civil service reform. When the votes were counted, Grant emerged as the winner, with an electoral count of 286 to 66, and a popular margin of over 750,000 votes.

Although the Republican leaders had succeeded in getting Grant reelected, they worried about the future. The policies of reconstruction in the South and the protection of Negro rights already seemed far less important than the necessity of keeping the party in power, and recent reports of disturbing economic fluctuations offered little basis for confidence. The eight years following the Civil War had been years of prosperity in the North and economic recovery in the South. In the burst of business activity that came with peace, speculation was reckless, expansion was unlimited, and credit was extended with abandon. When European investors withdrew their money from the American market in the late 1860's and early '70's, the system's supports were pulled away and the whole financial structure came crashing down.

In September, 1873, only six months after Grant began his second term, several important Eastern firms went into bankruptcy. This set off a panic on Wall Street so severe that the New York Stock Exchange was forced to close down for the first time in its history. The Panic of 1873 spread rapidly throughout the nation. Prices fell, factories shut down, businesses went bankrupt, and banks failed. Business failures were followed by widespread unemployment, and there were only a few private charitable organizations to meet the needs of the hungry and destitute with soup kitchens and bread lines. Occupations such as mining and textiles were among the hardest hit by the panic; and when employers tried to alleviate the situation by cutting wages, they were answered with widespread labor violence. A series of strikes flashed through the mill towns of New England, and the great railroad strike of 1877, which spread from the Atlantic coast all the way to Chicago, is still considered one of the most destructive in American history.

The Panic of 1873 contributed to the Democrats' decisive victory in the congressional elections of 1874. With control of more than two-thirds of the House of Representatives, the Democrats set in motion a series of investigations calculated to reform the operations of the national government and provide ammunition for the presidential election of 1876. The scheme of Fisk and Gould to corner the nation's gold had already created a national scandal during Grant's first administration; and his second term was hardly under way when the *New York Sun* exposed the sordid details of the Crédit Mobilier affair. In the investigations which followed, such prominent Congressmen as Oakes Ames, James Brooks, and James A. Garfield were implicated and former Vice-President Schuyler Colfax himself was shown to have accepted stocks and dividends in the enterprise.

Exposure followed exposure, with each incident demonstrating the dangerous alliance between business and government that had developed under the Grant regime. The Internal Revenue Service was found to be honeycombed with corruption, as taxes on such items as tobacco, cigars, and distilled liquors went uncollected. One investigation uncovered a "Whiskey Ring" composed of high government officials, including Grant's private secretary, Orville E. Babcock, which defrauded the Treasury of enormous sums. Secretary of the Treasury William A. Richardson was forced to resign when it was disclosed that he let a federal tax agent keep half of the $427,000 he had collected in back taxes. Secretary of War William W. Belknap resigned in order to avoid prosecution for dishonest management of army posts in the West. Corrupt officials in the Post Office were shown to have been working with Western stagecoach lines, making fraudulent reports of their operations in order to get appropriations from Congress for firms that did not exist. Robert Schenck was found to have used his post as Minister to the Court of St. James as a means of foisting bogus mining stock on unwary British investors; and James G. Blaine was accused of having compromised his position as Speaker of the House by accepting favors for aiding a Southern railroad to secure a land grant from the national government.

Shortly before the elections of 1876, it was considered a foregone conclusion that the Republican party could not win another presidential contest. The financial depression and the scandals had badly damaged the party in the North, and its control over the electoral machinery in the South was rapidly weakening. Only three states—Louisiana, Florida, and South Carolina—remained under Republican rule; surely it was only a matter of time before the entire South would be back in the old Democratic fold once again. Although there was some talk of running Grant for a third term, such ideas were squelched as Republican leaders came to realize that Grant had become a liability. At the same time, the House of Representatives by vote of 233 to 18 passed a resolution stating that a third term for the President of the United States would be "unwise, unpatriotic, and fraught with peril to our free institutions."

The demand for reform and clean government could no longer

be ignored, and the Republican leaders realized they had to nominate a prominent figure who was not tainted with suspicion. Their first choice was the personable James G. Blaine of Maine, who had just completed seven years as Speaker of the House. But the "Plumed Knight," as he was called in the nominating speech, was painfully unhorsed in the spring of 1876. When the news broke that Blaine had been involved in a railroad scandal, the Republicans had to come up with a candidate with cleaner hands. At the national convention at Cincinnati, they chose Rutherford B. Hayes of Ohio. A relatively obscure candidate, dubbed by the press "the Great Unknown," Hayes nevertheless was a man of considerable ability. He had risen to the rank of major general in the Civil War, had been elected governor of Ohio three times, and had earned a reputation as an able, honest administrator interested in political reform.

In late June, 1876, the Democratic party gathered in St. Louis and selected Samuel J. Tilden of New York as the man to oppose Hayes and help the Democrats return to an office they had not held since the days of James Buchanan. Tilden was a slight, quiet man, a successful corporation lawyer, who had earned a national reputation by helping to break the notorious Tweed Ring and who had been elected governor of New York in 1874. Running on a platform denouncing the past eight years of Republican misrule and corruption, Tilden promised a program of civil service reform and clean government.

The campaign of 1876 was a vigorous one, with the Republicans questioning Tilden's patriotism and the Democrats questioning Hayes's honesty. Early returns seemed to indicate that Tilden had won the Presidency by a comfortable margin. A total of 185 electoral votes was necessary for election in 1876. Tilden had already polled 184 votes to Hayes's 165. Only 19 votes from the states of Louisiana, Florida, and South Carolina were left to be recorded. Hayes would have to get all 19 to win, and considering that Tilden had polled 264,292 more popular votes than Hayes, most observers felt he was certain to get at least one of the necessary votes from these Southern states.

The Republican leaders had not given up the fight, though,

and they set to work to prevent Tilden from getting any of the 19 votes. Claiming fraud, trickery, and intimidation in the three Southern states, they demanded all 19 votes for Hayes and insisted that he was the rightful President-elect. The nation was in an uproar. Republicans refused to yield their claim, and Democrats vowed that Hayes would not live long enough to be inaugurated. Talk of violence and civil war reverberated throughout the nation, and President Grant strengthened the military garrisons in Washington.

After a few weeks elapsed, while Republicans and Democrats in each of the disputed states filed opposing returns and claimed victory for their side, it looked impossible to untangle the political knot that had developed. Even Congress could not offer much help in this disputed election. The Constitution states only that the electoral votes "shall be counted" in Congress; it does not say *who* is to do the counting. If the president of the Republican-controlled Senate were to count the votes, he would obviously discard the Democratic returns. If the Speaker of the Democratic-controlled House of Representatives were to count the votes, he would just as obviously discard the Republican returns. Thus, congressional leaders were as confused as the people.

The deadlock showed no signs of solution. No one was certain who would be inaugurated on March 4, 1877—if, indeed, anyone would be allowed to get that far. Alarmed at the prospect of being without a President, congressional leaders finally proposed the establishment of an Electoral Commission which was approved by Congress early in 1877. This body consisted of fifteen men— five from the Senate, five from the House of Representatives, and five from the Supreme Court. The Commission was equally divided between Democrats and Republicans, seven to seven, with the fifteenth man, Justice David Davis of Illinois, reported to have Democratic leanings. At the last minute, however, Davis resigned his seat on the Supreme Court to accept a post in the Senate, and his place on the Electoral Commission was taken by Justice Joseph P. Bradley, a New Jersey Republican. By a partisan vote of eight to seven, the Commission gave every one of the disputed votes to Hayes. Congress accepted the final verdict of the

Commission on March 2, 1877, only two days before Inauguration Day. Since March 4 fell on a Sunday, Hayes was privately
sworn into office on Saturday; and the public ceremonies on
Monday, March 5, went off without violence or incident.

Congressional approval of the Electoral Commission's report
had not come easily. Behind the scenes, negotiations were in
progress between Southern Democrats, former Whigs, and leading Republicans—negotiations that had a significant effect on the
outcome of the crisis. The situation was this: the South needed
federal funds to control floods along the Mississippi, to clear
harbors and river channels, to repair bridges and levees, and to
reconstruct public buildings. Then, too, during the wartime years
the South had not received the kind of federal subsidies that had
been handed out to such Northern Railroads as the Union Pacific
and the Central Pacific. Hopeful now for a Texas and Pacific
Railroad that would contribute greatly to the revival of their
region, they were informed by railroad entrepreneurs Thomas A.
Scott of the Pennsylvania Railroad and Grenville Dodge of the
Union Pacific that Hayes would support this and other internal
improvement programs in the South if he were elected President.
Interested Southerners also received assurances that Hayes would
withdraw the last remaining federal troops from the former Confederate states if he were President—with the obvious implication
that the Federal Government would be willing to stand by and
see the carpetbag governments go out of existence.

Both economic and political considerations, however, were
based upon a more subtle but crucial consideration—that the
Federal Government would no longer act as the guardian of
Negro rights, that it would allow the South once again to handle
the problem in its own way. Once it was understood that the
South would accept emancipation but that the North would no
longer press for equality, the stage was set for all the other points
of agreement to fall into line. Summing up the situation, Southern
Senators and Representatives concluded that Hayes and the Republicans could do more for their section than Tilden and his
reform-minded associates from the Northeast. In a Tilden admin-

istration, Southern Democrats would be a minority group entitled
to no particular consideration and no unusual concessions. In a
Hayes administration, however, they would hold the whip hand
because they had made it possible for the Republicans to stay in
office four more years.

And so it was arranged. Hayes was no sooner safely installed
in office than the distinctive features of the compromise became
apparent. The Grant wing of the Republican party was no longer
represented in the new administration, and the last vestiges of
old-time Radicalism had also disappeared from view. Hayes kept
his pledge, ordered federal troops out of the South, and watched
the Republican-controlled governments collapse of their own
weight.

With the Compromise of 1877, the Northern Republicans had
welded the final link in a successful and highly significant political
alliance with former Whigs and Democrats of the South who
were now often referred to as Conservatives—although they preferred to refer to themselves as the "Redeemers" who had finally
liberated the South from carpetbag rule. Composed largely of
industrialists, railroad men, textile owners, coal and iron mag-
nates, bankers, bondholders, and corporation lawyers, the Southern Conservative party represented a new type of social leadership that differed sharply from the old planter aristocracy. It also
marked a decisive change in Southern political strategy and economic ideology. Quietly but effectively the Redeemers made
common cause with the Northern Republicans on such questions
as finance, currency, banking, and internal improvements. Thus
they could convert temporary expediency into long-range policy.
At home, they established new state constitutions providing liberal subsidies and grants for railroads, industries, and utilities,
but cutting back on such tax-supported public services as schools
and prisons. Powerful, uncontested, and secure, the Redeemers
fell into complacency and produced political graft and corruption equal to the scandalous practices of Republican governments
in the North.

The basis for reconciliation had been established, the Union

was restored once again, and the nation was in a position to em-
bark upon a period of growth that carried well into the twentieth
century. The ironic and tragic feature is that in 1877 national
unity, which had split wide open in 1860 over the Negro question,
was achieved at the expense of the Negro. In the South, the
blacks were taken under the paternalistic wing of the Southern
Conservatives who relegated them to an inferior and segregated
position, but who represented their only source of protection now
that they had been abandoned by the Federal Government. For
the time being blacks were permitted to vote in fairly large numbers, and they were even allowed to hold minor political offices.
But the stage was being set for a program of disenfranchisement
and social segregation that left the Southern Negro without status
and without hope by the time the nineteenth century came to a
close.

In the North, the future of the black man was hardly brighter.
No one any longer spoke about Negro suffrage; no one any longer
espoused the cause of black equality. No agency of the Federal
Government took on the responsibility of safeguarding the civil
rights of the freedman; no tribunal set itself the task of defining
and defending human liberty. The most disheartening indication
of how far the North had changed showed in the Supreme Court's
support for white supremacy and states' rights in a long series of
decisions that virtually nullified the Fourteenth and Fifteenth
Amendments. In 1876, Chief Justice Morrison R. Waite, in *United
States* v. *Cruikshank*, declared that the Fourteenth Amendment
"adds nothing to the rights of one citizen against another," and in
the same year, in *United States* v. *Reese*, he declared that although the Fifteenth Amendment prevented discrimination on
the basis of race or color, it did not actually confer suffrage on
anyone. The course of black disillusionment reached a low point
in 1883 when the Court denied that the Federal Government
could protect the Negro by bringing charges against private individuals who operated railroads, theaters, or restaurants; and on
this basis it struck down the Civil Rights Act of 1875 as unconstitutional. The price of political compromise had been paid in full.

The wounds of the Civil War had already begun to close, and in time even the scars of reconstruction would slowly heal. But the diseased tissue of racism festered secretly and silently under the surface of the American body politic, like a deadly cancerous growth; and it erupted a century later in all its terrifying symptoms. In the 1870's, though, the operation was regarded as a success, and the patient seemed to be on the road to recovery.

CHAPTER 16
"WE CANNOT
ESCAPE HISTORY"

Fellow CITIZENS, we cannot escape history," wrote Abraham Lincoln in his Annual Message to Congress in December, 1862. "The fiery trials through which we pass will light us down in honor or dishonor to the latest generation. . . . We shall nobly save or meanly lose the last best hope of earth."

Our own generation is passing through its own fiery trials; it has witnessed the alienation of its youth, the assassination of its leaders, race riots in its cities, and violence in its streets on so great a scale that the National Advisory Commission on Civil Disorder has warned that "the future of every American" is threatened and "the destruction of basic democratic values" is possible. To our world Lincoln's sober words are particularly appropriate. At a time when the life of the United States is marked by all kinds of discord, when many observers are predicting a new Civil War, a study of the events of America's earlier catastrophe can hardly be thought futile. Even a casual review of the events of a hundred years ago, in the light of today's events, cannot help but produce a chilling sense of *déjà vu*—the terrible feeling that we have passed through this nightmare once before.

History, of course, never really repeats itself; and it is presumptuous and often dangerous to use the past too literally as a means of understanding the present or to superimpose the norms of the present upon the events of the past. Each time-period possesses political, social, intellectual, and economic characteristics so distinctive that they can never be duplicated exactly. Nevertheless, it is possible for history to provide the citizen with a dimension of time. Historical understanding can enable him to view present-day problems in a broader perspective and help him to cope with complicated issues with a greater measure of wisdom and tolerance. During the 1840's and 1850's, the national government allowed many fundamental social, political, and economic problems—slavery, states' rights, the tariff issue—to go unattended and unresolved. Without adequate care or suitable remedies, these problems festered and grew into ugly sores that impeded the functions of government at every level. Certainly this example of failure in government must attract the attention of people today who see the need to take decisive action in dealing with modern problems that are equally serious in their size and equally terrifying in their implications.

Recent scholarship has done a remarkable job not only in providing more factual information and documentary evidence, but also in suggesting new ways of looking at old facts. Young historians, for instance, have taken a completely new look at early American radical movements, and they have shown a special interest in the ideas and techniques of the Abolitionists. They have found new meaning in the individualist philosophy of Henry David Thoreau; they have reclaimed William Lloyd Garrison as an intrepid forerunner of the civil-rights movement; they have turned John Brown into a latter-day folk hero; and they have rescued the "savage and vindictive" Radical Republicans from their roles as villains in the melodrama of Reconstruction and recast them as the "vanguard" of social justice and civil rights.

At a point in our history when we have seen extremism on a larger and more frightening scale than ever before, there is no more pressing responsibility than to gain an understanding of human behavior under abnormal stress. Through the study of past behavior we can perhaps better understand why men lose control of their emotions, why certain issues can be compromised at one point in history and not in another, why the political processes can work at one period and fail at another, why passionate appeals can produce mass response at one moment and lethargic indifference only a short time later—these are all questions as directly related to the problems of the twentieth century as they were to the difficulties of the 1860's.

"If we could first know where we are, and whither we are tend-
ing, we could better judge what to do, and how to do it," said
Lincoln in his famous house-divided speech in 1858. Something
of this spirit of thoughtful reflection, viewing present circumstances in terms of future goals and past traditions, can do much
to help our own society develop a sense of history that is positive
and constructive. With roots that stretch more solidly and com-
fortably back into the past, the nation should be better able to
resist strain, accommodate itself to change, accept new ideas, and
withstand the pressures of irrational demands and intemperate
assaults. History will not make our decisions for us. It cannot tell
us what to do, or where we should go. But history can at least
show us that a period of extreme crisis and high emotion demands
the best efforts of all its citizens working together.

BIBLIOGRAPHY

GENERAL WORKS

James G. Randall and David Donald, *The Civil War and Reconstruction* (Boston: D.C. Heath, 1961; 1969) is the most detailed and informative one-volume treatment of the entire period; while Roy Nichols, *The Stakes of Power, 1845–1877* * (New York: Hill & Wang, 1961) offers a brief but highly interpretive treatment of the same era. Allan Nevins's eight-volume series, *The Ordeal of the Union* (New York: Charles Scribner's Sons, 1947–71) is the most thorough treatment of American history from the close of the Mexican War to the end of the Civil War. Charles Crowe, ed., *The Age of the Civil War and Reconstruction, 1830–1900* * (Homewood, Ill.: The Dorsey Press, 1966), Robert W. Johannsen, ed., *Democracy on Trial, 1845–1877* * (New York: McGraw-Hill, 1966), and Irwin Unger, ed., *Essays on the Civil War and Reconstruction* * (New York: Holt, Rinehart & Winston, 1970) offer collections of documents and interpretive readings which cover the period of the Civil War and Reconstruction. Joel Silbey, ed., *National Development and Sectional Crisis, 1815–1860* * (New York: Random House, 1970) concentrates his readings on the antebellum period; and William B. Hesseltine, ed., *The Tragic Conflict* * (New York: George Braziller, 1962) contains documentary material dealing with the war years.

THE ROAD TO DISUNION

THE OLD SOUTH

On the subject of the Old South, Monroe L. Billington, ed., *The South: A Central Theme?* * (New York: Holt, Rinehart & Winston, 1969)

---

* Books available in paperback editions are designated by an asterisk.

offers interpretations by leading historians. Clement Eaton, *The Growth of Southern Civilization, 1790–1860* ° (New York: Harper & Brothers, 1961) is an excellent survey of the antebellum South. Avery Craven, *The Growth of Southern Nationalism* ° (Baton Rouge: Louisiana State University Press, 1953) is especially good on the politics of the '50's; while Charles Sydnor, *The Development of Southern Sectionalism* ° (Baton Rouge: Louisiana State University Press, 1948), and John Hope Franklin, *The Militant South* ° (Cambridge, Mass.: Harvard University Press, 1956) concentrate on other aspects of Southern life before the War. C. Vann Woodward, *The Burden of Southern History* ° (Baton Rouge: Louisiana State University Press, 1960) presents a series of essays on central themes in Southern history; William R. Taylor's *Cavalier and Yankee* ° (New York: George Braziller, 1961) is an important analysis of Southern society; and Howard Floan, *The South in Northern Eyes, 1831–1861* ° (Austin: University of Texas Press, 1953) shows the way in which leading Northerners viewed conditions in the South.

THE PLANTATION SYSTEM

Slavery was an indispensable element of the antebellum South, and Eric L. McKitrick, ed., *Slavery Defended* ° (Englewood, N. J.: Prentice-Hall, 1963) provides a convenient summary of the views of leading white Southerners defending that institution, while Harold Woodman, ed., *Slavery and the Southern Economy* ° (New York: Harcourt Brace & World, 1966) contains valuable sources and readings dealing with the slave economy. Frederick Law Olmstead, *The Cotton Kingdom* ° (New York: Alfred A. Knopf, 1861; 1953) is a firsthand account of life and society in the slave states; and both William E. Dodd, *The Cotton Kingdom* (New Haven: Yale University Press, 1921) and Ulrich Phillips, *Life and Labor in the Old South* ° (Boston: Little, Brown, 1929) are standard works on slavery and the plantation system. David Cohn, *The Life and Times of King Cotton* ° (New York: Oxford University Press, 1956) is a highly readable account of the importance of cotton to the Southern way of life; and Eugene Genovese's two works, *The Political Economy of Slavery* ° (New York: Random House, 1965) and *The World the Slaveholders Made* (New York: Pantheon Books, 1969) provide significant insights into the nature of Southern life and society from a Marxian point of view. Frank Owsley, *Plain Folks of the Old South* ° (Baton Rouge: Louisiana State University Press, 1949) is extremely valuable for its treatment of those who did not belong to the ranks of the great slaveholders.

SLAVERY IN AMERICA

Allen Weinstein and Frank Otto Gattell, eds., *American Negro Slavery* * (New York: Oxford University Press, 1968) have published a very useful collection of interpretive essays on the subject of slavery; and Harvey Wish, ed., *Slavery in the South* * (New York: Farrar, Straus & Giroux, 1964) contains contemporary documents dealing with the nature of the "peculiar institution." David B. Davis, *The Problem of Slavery in Western Culture* * (Ithaca, N. Y.: Cornell University Press, 1966) provides a broad perspective on slavery as a world phenomenon: Kenneth Stampp's *The Peculiar Institution* * (New York: Alfred A. Knopf, 1956) is an outstanding analysis of the effects of slavery upon both the master and the slave; and Stanley Elkins, *Slavery: A Problem in American Institutional and Intellectual History* * (Chicago: University of Chicago Press, 1959) is a fascinating and provocative study of human bondage. Richard C. Wade, *Slavery in the Cities: The South, 1820–1860* * (New York: Oxford University Press, 1964) and Robert S. Starobin, *Industrial Slavery in the Old South* * (New York: Oxford University Press, 1970) show the influence of new trends in urban history; and Leon Litwack's *North of Slavery* * (Chicago: University of Chicago Press, 1961) provides a much-needed study of the life of the free Negro in the Northern states before the Civil War.

THE ABOLITIONIST BRIGADE

Recent developments in the civil rights movement and in the techniques of civil disobedience have brought about a renewed interest in the Abolition movement and have stimulated several editions of documents with appropriate subtitles. Richard O. Curry, ed., *The Abolitionists: Reformers or Fanatics?* * (New York: Holt, Rinehart & Winston, 1965), Hugh Hawkins, ed., *The Abolitionists: Immediateness and the Question of Means* * (Boston: D. C. Heath, 1964), and Bernard A. Weisberger, ed., *Abolitionism: Disrupter of the Democratic System or Agent of Progress?* * (Chicago: Rand McNally, 1963) concentrate on the motives and tactics of the early antislavery leaders. William and Janet Pease, eds., *The Antislavery Argument* * (Indianapolis: Bobbs-Merrill, 1965) offers a broad range of documentary source materials; and Truman Nelson, ed., *Documents of Upheaval* * (New York: Hill & Wang, 1966) contains selections from Garrison's newspaper, the *Liberator*. Alice Felt Tyler's *Freedom's Ferment* * (Minneapolis: University of Minnesota Press, 1944) provides an excellent summary of the numerous reform movements which occurred during the 1830's and '40's; and Russel B. Nye, *William Garrison and the Humanitarian Reformers* ° (Boston: Little, Brown, 1955) places the Abolitionist movement against the background of this period of reform. Gilbert Barnes, *The Anti-Slavery Impulse* ° (New York: Appleton-Century, 1933), Louis Filler, *The Crusade Against Slavery, 1830–1860* ° (New York: Harper & Brothers, 1960), and Dwight Dumond, *Antislavery* ° (Ann Arbor: University of Michigan Press, 1961) provide accounts of the background and history of the Abolitionist movement. Russel B. Nye, *Fettered Freedom: Civil Liberties and the Slavery Controversy* (East Lansing: Michigan State College Press, 1949) and Elbert B. Smith, *The Death of Slavery* ° (Chicago: University of Chicago Press, 1967) offer more interpretive insights. Walter M. Merrill, *Against Wind and Tide* (Cambridge, Mass.: Harvard University Press, 1963), and John L. Thomas, *The Liberator: William Lloyd Garrison* (Boston: Little, Brown, 1963) are excellent biographies of the antislavery leader; and Ralph Korngold, *Two Friends of Man* (Boston: Little, Brown, 1950) describes the relationship of Garrison and Wendell Phillips with Abraham Lincoln. Irving Bartlett, *Wendell Phillips: Brahmin Radical* (Boston: Beacon Press, 1961) and Oscar Sherwin, *Prophet of Liberty* (New York: Bookman Associates, 1958) are significant studies of Garrison's close associate, Wendell Phillips; and Tilden G. Edelstein's *Strange Enthusiasm: A Life of Thomas Wentworth Higginson* ° (New York: Atheneum Publishers, 1970) is an excellent portrait of a dedicated Abolitionist.

Martin Duberman, ed., *The Antislavery Vanguard* ° (Princeton, N. J.: Princeton University Press, 1965) is an exciting series of essays on the impact of the antislavery movement; and Aileen A. Kraditor, *Means and Ends in American Abolitionism* ° (New York: Pantheon Books, 1969) focuses upon the tactics and strategy of Garrison. The story of Northern opposition to the Abolition movement may be found in Laurence Lader, *The Bold Brahmins* (New York: E. P. Dutton, 1961), Lorman Ratner, *Powder Keg* (New York: Basic Books, 1968), and Leonard L. Richards, *"Gentlemen of Property and Standing": Anti-Abolition Mobs in Jacksonian America* ° (New York: Oxford University Press, 1970). John Hope Franklin, *From Slavery to Freedom* ° (New York: Alfred A. Knopf, 1947), Benjamin Quarles, *Black Abolitionists* ° (New York: Oxford University Press, 1969) and *Frederick Douglass* (Englewood Cliffs, N. J.: Prentice-Hall, 1968) provide valuable information on the role of the black man in the

Abolition movement; and Henrietta Buckmaster, *Let My People Go* °
(New York: Harper & Brothers, 1941) is especially good on the operations of the Underground Railroad.

POLITICS OF THE FIFTIES

Two two-volume works by Allan Nevins, *The Ordeal of the Union* °
and *The Emergence of Lincoln* ° (New York: Charles Scribner's Sons,
1947 and 1950—both sets are part of Nevins's eight-volume magnum
opus, also called *The Ordeal of the Union*), provide a comprehensive
account of the events of the 1850's. H. H. Simms offers a briefer
summary of the turbulent decade in *A Decade of Sectional Controversy*
(Chapel Hill: University of North Carolina Press, 1942); and Holman
Hamilton, *Prologue to Conflict* ° (Lexington: University of Kentucky
Press, 1964) is a well-written and definitive account of the Compromise of 1850. Chaplain Morrison, *Democratic Politics and Sectionalism* (Chapel Hill: University of North Carolina Press, 1967)
analyzes the party structure of the period, while Herbert Donovan,
The Barnburners (New York: New York University Press, 1925),
focuses on events in New York state. Philip Foner, in his *Business and
Slavery* (Chapel Hill: University of North Carolina Press, 1941)
concentrates on the New York merchants and bankers and the coming
of the War; and Thomas H. O'Connor, in *Lords of the Loom* (New
York: Charles Scribner's Sons, 1968) traces the history of the Cotton
Whigs of Massachusetts. George Mayer, *The Republican Party, 1854–
1964* ° (New York: Oxford University Press, 1964) is a good general
history of the modern Republican party; and Eric Foner, *Free Soil,
Free Labor, Free Men* ° (New York: Oxford University Press, 1970)
concentrates on the history and ideology of the Republican party
before 1860. Stanley Campbell, *The Slavecatchers* (Chapel Hill:
University of North Carolina Press, 1970) describes the efforts to
enforce the Fugitive Slave Law and the response of American public
opinion. Alice Nichols, *Bleeding Kansas* (New York; Oxford University
Press, 1954) is a readable account of the violence in Kansas Territory;
and James A. Rawley, *Race and Politics* ° (Philadelphia: J. B. Lippincott, 1969) has given new and greater attention to the issue of race
in the westward movement. Gerald M. Capers, *Stephen A. Douglas* °
(Boston: Little, Brown, 1959) and George Fort Milton, *Eve of Conflict: Stephen A. Douglas and the Needless War* (Boston: Houghton
Mifflin, 1934) are both sympathetic to the controversial Illinois statesman. Vincent C. Hopkins, *Dred Scott's Case* ° (New York: Fordham

University Press, 1951) gives a basic account of the famous court case; and Stanley Kutler, ed., *The Dred Scott Decision: Law or Politics?* ° (Boston: Houghton Mifflin, 1967) supplies appropriate documents and readings. Carl B. Swisher, *Roger B. Taney* (New York: Macmillan, 1935) is the most expert treatment of the Chief Justice and the constitutional issues of the trial; while Walker Lewis, *Without Fear or Favor* (Boston: Houghton Mifflin, 1965) is a more readable and general biography of the Chief Justice. George W. Van Vleck, *The Panic of 1857* (New York: Columbia University Press, 1943) is a skillful analysis of the economic crisis of 1857.

PERSONALITIES OF CONFLICT

David Donald, *Charles Sumner and the Coming of the Civil War* (New York: Alfred A. Knopf, 1960) is a superb biography of a complex Northern statesman; and Glyndon Van Deusen's studies of *Horace Greeley* ° (New York: Hill & Wang, 1953) and *William Henry Seward* (New York: Oxford University Press, 1967) are indispensable to an understanding of the politics of the 1850's. Roy Nichols, *Franklin Pierce* (Philadelphia: University of Pennsylvania Press, 1958) and Philip Klein, *President James Buchanan* (University Park: Pennsylvania State University Press, 1962) provide studies of two Democratic presidents; Hudson Strode, *Jefferson Davis, American Patriot, 1808–1861* (New York: Harcourt, Brace, 1955) recounts the early life and career of the future Confederate President; and Joseph Parks, *John Bell of Tennessee* (Baton Rouge: Louisiana State University Press, 1950) is an interesting study of a Southern moderate. Older studies of the controversial John Brown, such as Oswald Garrison Villard's sympathetic portrayal, *John Brown* (Boston: Houghton Mifflin, 1911), or James C. Malin's hostile account, *John Brown and the Legend of Fifty-Six* (Philadelphia: American Philosophical Society, 1942), have been brought up to date by such recent studies as Stephen Oates, *To Purge This Land with Blood* (New York: Harper & Row, 1970) and Jules Abels, *Man on Fire* (New York: Macmillan, 1971). Louis Ruchames, ed., *John Brown: The Making of a Revolutionary* (New York: Universal Library, 1969) is a valuable source of contemporary accounts dealing with this complex personality.

Allan Nevins, *The Emergence of Lincoln* ° (2 vols., New York: Charles Scribner's Sons, 1950) supplies an excellent background for the period leading up to the Civil War; Carl Sandburg, *Abraham Lincoln: The Prairie Years* ° (2 vols., New York: Harcourt, Brace,

1926) is a warm and moving literary biography; and Don Fehren-bacher's *Prelude to Greatness* * (Stanford, Calif.: Stanford University Press, 1962) provides a detailed study of Lincoln's career during the 1850's. Jay Monaghan, *The Man who Elected Lincoln* (Indianapolis: Bobbs-Merrill, 1956) and Willard L. King, *Lincoln's Manager, David Davis* (Cambridge, Mass.: Harvard University Press, 1960) trace Lincoln's rise to political prominence; and Robert W. Johannsen, ed., *The Lincoln-Douglas Debates of 1858* * (New York: Oxford University Press, 1965) provides a convenient collection of documents on the great debates. Richard N. Current, *The Lincoln Nobody Knows* * (New York: McGraw-Hill, 1958), David Donald, *Lincoln Recon-sidered* * (New York: Alfred A. Knopf, 1947), and J. G. Randall, *Lincoln: The Liberal Statesman* * (New York: Dodd, Mead, 1947) are collections of interpretive essays that deal with various aspects of Lincoln's life and career.

THE SECESSION CRISIS

Roy Nichols, *The Disruption of American Democracy* * (New York: Macmillan, 1948) is a brilliant analysis of the Buchanan administra-tion; and Kenneth Stampp, *And the War Came* * (Baton Rouge: Louisiana State University Press, 1950) is a fascinating interpretive study of the confrontation that led to violence. Emerson D. Fite, *The Presidential Campaign of 1860* (New York: Macmillan, 1911) is still the most detailed account of the crucial election. David Potter, *Lincoln and his Party in the Secession Crisis* * (New Haven: Yale University Press, 1942) deals with the crisis from the Northern point of view, while Dwight Dumond, *The Secession Movement, 1860–61* (New York: Macmillan, 1931) and Ollinger Crenshaw, *The Slave States in the Presidential Election of 1860* (Baltimore: John Hopkins Press, 1945) tell the story from the Southern point of view. H. C. Perkins, ed., *Northern Editorials on Secession* (2 vols., Gloucester, Mass.: Peter Smith, 1964), and Dwight Dumond, ed., *Southern Editorials on Secession* (New York: Century, 1931) are indispensable for their coverage of public opinion on both sides; and P. J. Stauden-raus, ed., *The Secession Crisis, 1860–61* * (Chicago: Rand McNally, 1963) contains valuable primary source materials on the breakup of the Union. Mary Scrugham, *The Peaceable Americans of 1860–61* (New York: Columbia University Press, 1921) describes the futile efforts at peace negotiations. Richard N. Current, *Lincoln and the First Shot* * (Philadelphia: J. B. Lippincott, 1963) is a detailed and balanced study of the outbreak of the War; and Bruce Catton, *The Coming Fury* ° (Garden City, N. Y.: Doubleday, 1961) is a dramatic account of the critical months from the political conventions of 1860 to the first battle of Bull Run.

THE CIVIL WAR

THE QUESTION OF CAUSATION

The causes of the Civil War are a never-ending source of discussion and dispute among historians, and Thomas Pressly, in his *Americans Interpret Their Civil War* ° (Princeton, N. J.: Princeton University Press, 1954) describes the various interpretations suggested by American scholars over the course of a century. George H. Knoles, ed., *The Crisis of the Union, 1860–61* ° (Baton Rouge: Louisiana State University Press, 1965), Edwin Rozwenc, ed., *The Causes of the American Civil War* ° and *Slavery as a Cause of the Civil War* ° (Boston: D. C. Heath, 1961 and 1963), Kenneth Stampp, ed., *The Causes of the Civil War* ° (Englewood Cliffs, N. J.: Prentice-Hall, 1959), and Hans L. Trefousse, ed., *The Causes of the Civil War: Institutional Failure or Human Blunder?* ° (New York: Holt, Rinehart & Winston, 1971) are source-collections and readings that focus on this question. Arthur C. Cole, *The Irrepressible Conflict* (New York: Macmillan, 1938), and Avery Craven, *The Coming of the Civil War* (New York: Charles Scribner's Sons, 1942) and *The Repressible Conflict, 1830–1861* (Baton Rouge: Louisiana State University Press, 1939) are among the most prominent works to deal with the subject of causation.

GENERAL WORKS

Fletcher Pratt, *A Short History of the Civil War* ° (New York: Pocket Books, 1951) is a popular and readable introduction to the military aspects of the War, although R. E. and T. N. Dupuy, *Compact History of the Civil War* ° (New York: Hawthorn Books, 1960) and W. B. Wood and J. S. Edmonds, *Military History of the Civil War* ° (New York: G. P. Putnam's Sons, 1960) are much more detailed in their material and more expert in their approach. Joseph B. Mitchell, *Decisive Battles of the Civil War* ° (New York: G. P. Putnam's Sons, 1955) and James Rawley, *Turning Points of the Civil War* ° (Lincoln: University of Nebraska Press, 1966) present selected battles and campaigns. Bruce Catton's series of military histories, *Glory Road,*° *Mr. Lincoln's Army* ° and *Stillness at Appomattox* ° (Garden City, N. Y.:

Doubleday, 1951, 1952, and 1953) provide a colorful account of Union military operations throughout the War.

CAMPAIGNS AND BATTLES

Robert Johnson, *Bull Run* (Boston: Houghton Mifflin, 1913) analyzes the first major battle of the War; and Clifford Dowdey, *The Seven Days* (Boston: Little, Brown, 1964) is a fine account of the emergence of Lee during the peninsula campaign. Bruce Catton, *Grant Moves South* (Boston: Little, Brown, 1960) describes Union operations in the West from Forts Henry and Donelson to Vicksburg; and his *Terrible Swift Sword* * (Garden City, N. Y.: Doubleday, 1963) gives a view of the broader aspects of the War from Bull Run to Fredericksburg. Edwin B. Coddington, *The Gettysburg Campaign* (New York: Charles Scribner's Sons, 1968), James Montgomery, *The Shaping of a Battle: Gettysburg* (Philadelphia: Clinton Co., 1959), Edward Stackpole, *They Met at Gettysburg* (Harrisburg, Pa.: Eagle Books, 1956), and Glenn Tucker, *High Tide at Gettysburg* (Indianapolis: Bobbs-Merrill, 1958) are a few of the works that tell of Lee's critical defeat in the summer of 1863. Fairfax Downey, *Clash of Cavalry* (New York: David McKay, 1959) is a study of the battle of Brandy Station during the Gettysburg campaign; and Frank Vandiver, *Jubal's Raid* (New York: McGraw-Hill, 1960) is an exciting account of Early's attack on Washington in 1864. Fairfax Downey, *Storming the Gateway: Chattanooga, 1863* * (New York: David McKay, 1960) describes the action in Tennessee; and Ludwell Johnson, *The Red River Campaign* (Baltimore: Johns Hopkins Press, 1958) analyzes the effects of Union operations in the Gulf region. Bruce Catton, *Grant Takes Command* (Boston: Little, Brown, 1969) traces the history of the fighting from Vicksburg to Appomattox.

Margaret Leech, *Reveille in Washington* * (New York: Harper & Brothers, 1941) is a fascinating study of the Union capital throughout four years of the war. Gerald Capers, *Occupied City: New Orleans* (Lexington: University of Kentucky Press, 1965) and Burton Milby, *The Siege of Charleston, 1861–65* (Columbia: University of South Carolina Press, 1970) describe Union operations against two Southern cities; and A. H. Bill, *The Beleagured City: Richmond, 1861–65* (New York: Alfred A. Knopf, 1946) and Rembert Patrick, *The Fall of Richmond* (Baton Rouge: Louisiana State University Press, 1960) tell of the eventual collapse of the Confederate capital. John Barrett, *Sherman's March Through the Carolinas* (Chapel Hill: University of

North Carolina Press, 1956), Clifford Dowdey, *Lee's Last Campaign* (Boston: Little, Brown, 1960), and Burke Davis, *To Appomattox* (New York: Holt, Rinehart & Winston, 1959) trace the last days of the Confederate armies in the field.

THE WAR AT SEA

Virgil C. Jones, *The Civil War at Sea* (3 vols., New York: Holt, Rinehart, & Winston, 1961) and Bern Anderson, *By Sea and River* (New York: Alfred A. Knopf, 1962) provide valuable accounts of naval operations during the Civil War. Clarence Maccartney, *Mr. Lincoln's Admirals* (New York: Funk & Wagnalls, 1956), James Merrill, *The Rebel Shore* (Boston: Little, Brown, 1957), and Richard S. West, Jr., *Mr. Lincoln's Navy* (New York: Longmans, Green, 1957) concentrate upon Union naval power; while Philip Van Doren Stern, *The Confederate Navy* (Garden City, N. Y.: Doubleday, 1962) Murray Morgan, *Dixie Raider: The Saga of the CSS Shenandoah* (New York: E. P. Dutton, 1948), and Edna and Frank Bradlow, *Here Comes the Alabama* (Cape Town, South Africa: A. A. Balkema, 1958) are works that deal with Confederate efforts on the high seas. H. Allen Gosnell, *Guns on the Western Waters* (Baton Rouge: Louisiana State University Press, 1949) and Fletcher Pratt, *The Civil War on Western Waters* (New York: Holt, Rinehart & Winston, 1956) are useful for their descriptions of naval operations in the interior. Jay Monaghan, *The Civil War on the Western Border* (Boston: Little, Brown, 1955) and Aurora Hunt, *The Army of the Pacific* (Glendale, Calif.: A. H. Clark Co., 1951) describe military activities west of the Mississippi.

THE UNION GOVERNMENT AT WAR

Volumes 5 through 8 of Allan Nevins's *Ordeal of the Union* series, entitled *The War for the Union* (New York: Charles Scribner's Sons, 1959–1971), are well-written and highly informative on the Union government at war. Carl Sandburg, *Abraham Lincoln: The War Years* ° (4 vols. New York: Harcourt, Brace, 1939) is an eloquent tribute to the wartime President; J. G. Randall, *Lincoln the President* ° (4 vols., New York: Dodd, Mead, 1945) is a more balanced and thorough study of the presidential years; and Benjamin Thomas, *Abraham Lincoln: A Biography* (New York: Alfred A. Knopf, 1952) is the best one-volume treatment. David Donald, ed., *Inside Lincoln's Cabinet: The Civil War Diaries of Salmon P. Chase* (New York:

Longmans, Green, 1954) and Burton Hendrick, *Lincoln's War Cabinet* (Boston: Little, Brown, 1946) provide insights into Lincoln's relations with his Cabinet; and Benjamin Thomas and Harold Hyman's *Stanton* (New York: Alfred A. Knopf, 1954) and Richard S. West, Jr.'s *Gideon Welles* (Indianapolis: Bobbs-Merrill, 1943) supply additional information on Lincoln's administrative associates. H. Carman and R. Luthin, *Lincoln and the Patronage* (New York: Columbia University Press, 1943) demonstrate the pressures on a wartime President; and William B. Hesseltine, *Lincoln and the War Governors* (New York: Alfred A. Knopf, 1948) is an excellent study of Lincoln's astuteness in time of crisis. George Fort Milton, *Abraham Lincoln and the Fifth Column* (New York: Vanguard Press, 1942), Wood Gray, *The Hidden Civil War* ° (New York: Viking Press, 1942), and Frank L. Klement, *Copperheads in the Middle West* ° (Chicago: University of Chicago Press, 1960) analyze the influence and extent of subversive activities. James G. Randall, *Constitutional Problems under Lincoln* (Rev. ed., Urbana: University of Illinois Press, 1951) is still the definitive study of Lincoln's handling of civil liberties in wartime; and Harold M. Hyman, *Era of the Oath* (Philadelphia: University of Pennsylvania Press, 1954) traces the progress of Northern loyalty tests during the Civil War and Reconstruction.

Edward C. Kirkland, *The Peacemakers of 1864* (New York: Macmillan, 1927) and W. F. Zornow, *Lincoln and the Party Divided* (Norman: University of Oklahoma Press, 1954) are helpful in dealing with the events of the presidential election year. T. Harry Williams, *Lincoln and the Radicals* ° (Madison: University of Wisconsin Press, 1941) skillfully traces the origins of party controversy during the war years, while Charles H. McCarthy, *Lincoln's Plan of Reconstruction* (New York: McClure Philips, 1901) and William B. Hesseltine, *Lincoln's Plan of Reconstruction* ° (Gloucester, Mass.: Peter Smith, 1963) offer differing views on Lincoln's ideas concerning the restoration of the Union. Jonathan Dorris, *Pardon and Amnesty under Lincoln and Johnson* (Chapel Hill: University of North Carolina Press, 1953) is a valuable study of the subject.

MILITARY LEADERS OF THE NORTH

Kenneth P. Williams, *Lincoln Finds a General* (4 vols., New York: Macmillan, 1956) is a comprehensive account of Lincoln's involvement in the military operations of the Union war effort. T. Harry Williams, *Lincoln and His Generals* ° (New York: Alfred A. Knopf, 1952) is an extremely useful summary of the Northern military effort set against the background of political history; and his *McClellan, Sherman, and Grant* (New Brunswick, N. J.: Rutgers University Press, 1962) is a provocative comparative study of three Union generals. Warren W. Hassler, Jr., *General George B. McClellan* (Baton Rouge: Louisiana State University Press, 1957), Lloyd Lewis, *Sherman: Fighting Prophet* (New York: Harcourt, Brace, 1932), James M. Merrill, *William Tecumseh Sherman* (Chicago: Rand McNally, 1971), Stephen E. Ambrose, *Halleck: Lincoln's Chief of Staff* (Baton Rouge: Louisiana State University Press, 1962), Richard O'Connor, *Sheridan the Inevitable* (Indianapolis: Bobbs-Merrill, 1953) and Freeman Cleves's life of George H. Thomas, *The Rock of Chickamauga* (Norman: University of Oklahoma Press, 1948) are some of the best studies of Northern military leaders. Robert Holzman, *Stormy Ben Butler* (New York: Macmillan, 1954) and Fred H. Harrington, *Fighting Politician: General Nathaniel N. P. Banks* (Philadelphia: University of Pennsylvania Press, 1948) are studies of two of Lincoln's best known political generals. For glimpses into the everyday life and duties of the enlisted man in the Union army, Bell I. Wiley's *The Life of Billy Yank* (Indianapolis: Bobbs-Merrill, 1952) is extremely valuable.

THE WAR ON THE HOME FRONT

Allan Nevins's *The Organized War* (New York: Charles Scribner's Sons, 1971) is the third volume of *The War for the Union,* Volume 7 in the entire *Ordeal of the Union* series; it is especially good on the organizational progress of the Union government in the later stages of the War. Fred A. Shannon, *The Organization and Administration of the Union Army, 1861–65* (2 vols., Cleveland: Arthur H. Clark, 1928) and W. Q. Maxwell, *Lincoln's Fifth Wheel: The Political History of the United States Sanitation Commission* (New York: Longmans, Green, 1956) are detailed accounts of lesser known aspects of the Union war effort; and Robert V. Bruce, *Lincoln and the Tools of War* (Indianapolis: Bobbs-Merrill, 1956) has produced an outstanding study of the technological aspects of the War. George Turner, *Victory Rode the Rails* (Indianapolis: Bobbs-Merrill, 1953) and T. Weber, *Northern Railroads in the Civil War* (New York: King's Crown Press, 1952) describe the role of railroads in the Union war strategy; Emerson D. Fite's classic *Social and Industrial Conditions in the North During the Civil War* (New York: Macmillan, 1910; 1963) is still the best treatment of the subject; and Bray Hammond, *Sovereignty and an Empty Purse* (Princeton, N. J.: Princeton University Press, 1970) has provided a much-needed study of banks and politics during the Civil War. George W. Adams, *Doctors in Blue* ° (New York: H. Shuman, 1952) is a good account of the medical history of the Union forces; and William B. Hesseltine, *Civil War Prisons* (Columbus: Ohio State University Press, 1930) explores a complex and tragic aspect of wartime suffering. Jack Leach, *Conscription in the United States* (Rutland, Vt.: C. E. Tuttle, 1952) places the Civil War experience in historical perspective; George M. Fredrickson, *The Inner Civil War* ° (New York: Harper & Row, 1965) analyzes the reactions of Northern intellectuals to the coming of the War; Louis M. Starr, *The Bohemian Brigade* ° (New York: Alfred A. Knopf, 1954) gives an account of Northern journalists during the conflict; and Robert S. Harper, *Lincoln and the Press* (New York: McGraw-Hill, 1951) shows how Lincoln was treated by the press during his public career.

THE BLACK MAN AND THE CIVIL WAR

Herbert Aptheker, *The Negro in the Civil War* (New York: International Publishers, 1938), Benjamin Quarles, *The Negro in the Civil War* ° (Boston: Little, Brown, 1953), and Dudley Cornish, *The Sable Arm* ° (New York: Longmans, Green, 1956) provide histories of the black man's contribution to the Northern war effort. Thomas Wentworth Higginson, *Life in a Black Regiment* ° (Boston: Lee & Shepard, 1869; New York: Houghton Mifflin, 1900; New York: Collier Books, 1961) is an invaluable primary source for the subject; and James M. McPherson, *The Negro's Civil War* ° (New York: Pantheon Books, 1965) draws upon a wide variety of contemporary sources to recreate the black experience. John Hope Franklin, *The Emancipation Proclamation* ° (Garden City, N. Y.: Doubleday, 1963) analyzes the background and consequences of the famous document. Benjamin Quarles, *Lincoln and the Negro* (New York: Oxford University Press, 1962) and John S. Wright, *Lincoln and the Politics of Slavery* (Reno: University of Nevada Press, 1970) explore the broader aspects of Lincoln's relationships with the black man; while James McPherson, *The Struggle for Equality* ° (Princeton, N. J.: Princeton University Press, 1964) describes the work of Abolitionists and Negroes to obtain equal rights during the period of war and reconstruction. Bertram Korn, *American Jewry and the Civil War* ° (Philadelphia: Jewish Publication Society of America, 1951) and Ella Lonn, *Foreigners in the Union Army and Navy* (Baton Rouge: Louisiana State University Press, 1951) provide additional information on other national and ethnic groups who fought on the Union side.

THE CONFEDERACY AT WAR

On the Confederate side, E. Merton Coulter, *The Confederate States of America* ° (Baton Rouge: Louisiana State University Press, 1950) and Clement Eaton, *A History of the Southern Confederacy* ° (New York: Macmillan, 1954) are solid and readable studies. Clifford Dowdey, *The Land They Fought For* (Garden City, N. Y.: Doubleday, 1955), Frank Vandiver, *Their Tattered Flags* (New York: Harper & Row, 1970), Charles Roland, *The Confederacy* ° (Chicago: University of Chicago Press, 1960), and Emory Thomas, *The Confederacy as a Revolutionary Experience* ° (Englewood Cliffs, N. J.: Prentice-Hall, 1971) contribute additional insights into the history of the Confederacy. Albert D. Kirwan, ed., *The Confederacy* ° (Cleveland: World, 1959) offers a useful collection of documents; and William J. Kimball, ed., *Richmond in Time of War* ° (Boston: Houghton Mifflin, 1960) contains sources and readings on the Confederate capital in wartime.

Elizabeth Cutting, *Jefferson Davis: Political Soldier* (New York: Dodd, Mead, 1930) and Hudson Strode, *Jefferson Davis, Confederate President* (New York: Harcourt, Brace & World, 1959) are sympathetic biographies of the Confederate President. Burton Hendrick, *Statesmen of the Lost Cause* (Boston: Little, Brown, 1939) and Rembert Patrick, *Jefferson Davis and his Cabinet* (Baton Rouge: Louisiana State University Press, 1944) are valuable for their political background, while Robert Meade, *Judah Benjamin: Confederate Statesman* (New York: Oxford University Press, 1943) and Joseph Durkin, *Stephen Mallory: Confederate Navy Chief* (Chapel Hill: University of North Carolina Press, 1954) are sound biographies of two of Davis's leading Cabinet members. Wilfred Years, *The Confederate Congress* (Athens: University of Georgia Press, 1960) is a much-needed study of Confederate legislative activities.

MILITARY LEADERS OF THE SOUTH

Douglas Southall Freeman, *R. E. Lee* (4 vols, New York: Charles Scribner's Sons, 1935) is the definitive study of the great Confederate general; and his *Lee's Lieutenants* (3 vols., New York: Charles Scribner's Sons, 1942) is an excellent account of the Confederate high command. Frank Vandiver, *Rebel Brass* (Westport, Conn.: Greenwood Press, 1956) is a useful analysis of the Confederate command structure; and Jennings Wise, *The Long Arm of Lee* (New York: Oxford University Press, 1959) is a good study of Lee's artillery. Gilbert Govan and James Livingood, *A Different Valor: The Story of General Joseph E. Johnston, C.S.A.* (Indianapolis: Bobbs-Merrill, 1956), Frank Vandiver, *Mighty Stonewall* (New York: McGraw-Hill, 1957), J. W. Thomason, Jr., *Jeb Stuart* (New York: Charles Scribner's Sons, 1930), J. P. Dyer, *The Gallant Hood* (Indianapolis: Bobbs-Merrill, 1950), T. Harry Williams, *P. G. T. Beauregard: Napoleon in Gray* (Baton Rouge: Louisiana State University Press, 1955), and Grady McWhiney, *Braxton Bragg: Field Command* (New York: Columbia University Press, 1969) are leading biographies of Confederate generals; and Bell I. Wiley's *Life of Johnny Reb* (Indianapolis: Bobbs-Merrill, 1943) depicts the routine life of the Confederate soldier. John Bakeless, *Spies of the Confederacy* (Philadelphia: J. B. Lippincott, 1970) is a general study of Confederate undercover operations; Nash K. Burger, *Confederate Spy* (New York: Franklin Watts, 1967) tells the fascinating story of Rose O'Neale Greenhow; and James D. Horan, *Confederate Agent* (New York: Crown Publishers, 1954) describes an elaborate effort by Confederate agents to undermine Union military operations in the late stages of the War.

BEHIND THE LINES

Charles Ramsdell, *Behind the Lines in the Southern Confederacy* (New York: Greenwood Press, 1969) is a general account of life on the home front; and H. H. Cunningham, *Doctors in Gray* (Baton Rouge: Louisiana State University Press, 1958) is a valuable study of the Confederate medical service. R. C. Todd, *Confederate Finance* (Athens: University of Georgia Press, 1954) describes the difficulties of the Confederate government in financing the war; Robert C. Black, *Railroads of the Confederacy* (Chapel Hill: University of North Carolina Press, 1952) gives a good account of transportation difficulties in the South; and Frank Vandiver, *Ploughshares into Swords* (Austin: University of Texas Press, 1952) describes the efforts of Josiah Gorgas, chief of ordnance, in providing the Confederacy with the tools of war. Albert Moore, *Conscription and Conflict in the Confederacy* (New York: Macmillan, 1924) focuses upon the difficulties of manpower in the South; and J. Cutler Andrews, *The South Reports the Civil War* (Princeton, N. J.: Princeton University Press, 1970) studies Southern journalism during the war years. Mary E. Massey's *Ersatz in the Confederacy* (Columbia: University of South Carolina Press, 1952), and *Refugee Life in the Confederacy* (Baton Rouge: Louisiana State University Press, 1964) are extremely valuable for their material on hardships on the home front; and her *Bonnet Brigades* (New York: Alfred A. Knopf, 1966) updates earlier works by Matthew P. Andrews, *The Women of the South in Wartime* (Baltimore: Norman, Remington, 1923) and Katherine M. Jones, *Heroines of Dixie* (Indianapolis: Bobbs-Merrill, 1955) on the contribution of Southern women to the Confederate war effort. Bell I. Wiley's *Plain People of the Confederacy* (Baton Rouge: Louisiana State University Press, 1944) and his *Southern Negroes, 1861–65* ° (New Haven: Yale University Press, 1938) are indispensable for a complete understanding of life behind the lines.

THE DIPLOMACY OF THE CIVIL WAR

Despite the passage of more than a hundred years, there is still no satisfactory, comprehensive history of the diplomacy of the Civil War. Ephraim D. Adams, *Great Britain and the American Civil War* (2 vols., London: Longmans, Green, 1925) is still the best source for Union diplomacy, while Frank L. Owsley, *King Cotton Diplomacy* (Chicago: University of Chicago Press, 1931; 1959) and James M. Callahan, *Diplomatic History of the Southern Confederacy* (New York: Greenwood Press, 1968) supply the background for Southern relations with Europe. Jay Monaghan, *Diplomat in Carpet Slippers* (Indianapolis: Bobbs-Merrill, 1945) is a useful study of Lincoln's involvement in foreign affairs; and Philip Van Doren Stern, *When the Guns Roared* (Garden City, N. Y.: Doubleday, 1965) is a readable but superficial account of Union diplomacy. D. Jordan and E. Pratt, *Europe and the American Civil War* (New York: Columbia University Press, 1926) describes the reaction of various European countries to the American conflict; and B. Sideman and L. Friedman, eds., *Europe Looks at the Civil War* ° (New York: Orion Press, 1960) supplies contemporary European sources regarding the American Civil War.

In addition to Adams's study, relations between Great Britain and the United States are treated by H. C. Allen, *Great Britain and the United States* (New York: St. Martin's Press, 1955). Thomas L. Harris, *The Trent Affair* (Indianapolis: Bobbs-Merrill, 1896) is an older account of the crisis between the two nations, and Evan John, *Atlantic Impact, 1861* (New York: G. P. Putnam's Sons, 1952) is a more recent study of the *Trent* affair. Martin Duberman's excellent biography of *Charles Francis Adams* ° (Boston: Houghton Mifflin, 1961) supplies a great deal of valuable information on America's relations with Britain during the war years; and Milledge L. Bonham, *British Consuls in the Confederacy* (New York: Columbia University Press, 1911) is an interesting source for British views on the War. Helen E. Macdonald, *Canadian Public Opinion on the American Civil War* (New York: Columbia University Press, 1926) is a general study of reaction north of the border; and Robin Winks, *Canada and the United States: The Civil War Years* (Baltimore: Johns Hopkins Press, 1960) is a scholarly treatment of relations between the two governments.

French reaction to the American Civil War has been dealt with by W. Reed West, *Contemporary French Opinion on the American Civil War* (Baltimore: Johns Hopkins Press, 1924) and Lynn Case, *French Opinion on the United States and Mexico, 1860–1867* (New York: D. Appleton, 1936); more recently Lynn Case and Warren Spencer have produced a much-needed study of American-French relations with *The United States and France: Civil War Diplomacy* (Philadelphia: University of Pennsylvania Press, 1970). Benjamin Thomas, *Russo-American Relations, 1815–1867* (Baltimore: Johns Hopkins Press, 1930) is a good general account of America's relations with the Czarist government; and Albert A. Woldman, *Lincoln and the Russians* (Cleveland: World, 1952) is a readable and valuable study of Lincoln's attitudes toward Russo-American relations.

THE AGE OF RECONSTRUCTION

TRADITIONAL VIEWS

The literature of the Reconstruction period has undergone a significant transformation in the last decade, and this is still one of the most lively periods of historical research. The first significant treatment of Reconstruction came with William Dunning's *Reconstruction: Political and Economic, 1865–1877* ° (New York: Harper & Brothers, 1907) which emphasized the evils of Black Reconstruction and applauded the return to white supremacy in the South. Dunning's thesis was influential in a number of later publications, such as Walter Fleming's *Sequel to Appomattox* (New Haven: Yale University Press, 1919), Claude Bowers's popular but heavily biased *The Tragic Era* ° (Boston: Houghton Mifflin, 1929), and even Hodding Carter's *The Angry Scar* (Garden City, N. Y.: Doubleday, 1959) shows the persuasiveness of this earlier school of history. Treatments of presidential reconstruction followed much the same pattern, with such works as George Fort Milton, *The Age of Hate: Andrew Johnson and the Radicals* (New York: Coward-McCann, 1930), Howard K. Beale, *The Critical Year: A Study of Andrew Johnson and Reconstruction* (New York: Harcourt, Brace, 1930; 1958), Lloyd P. Stryker, *Andrew Johnson: A Study in Courage* (New York: Macmillan, 1929), and Robert W. Winston, *Andrew Johnson: Plebeian and Patriot* (New York: Henry Holt, 1928), which sympathized with the efforts of Johnson to establish a just and generous reconstruction program in the face of unreasonable attacks by selfish and vindictive Radicals.

REVISIONIST STUDIES

In recent years, however, new works have taken issue with these earlier interpretations. Rembert W. Patrick's *Reconstruction of the Nation* ° (New York: Oxford University Press, 1967) is a much more balanced and objective treatment of the period; and John Hope Franklin's *Reconstruction: After the Civil War* ° (Chicago: University of Chicago Press, 1961) gives much more attention to the constructive role of the black man. W. R. Brock, *An American Crisis: Congress and Reconstruction, 1865–67* ° (New York: St. Martin's Press, 1963) and David Donald, *The Politics of Reconstruction, 1863–1867* ° (Baton Rouge: Louisiana State University Press, 1965) are much more thorough in their investigation of the complex conditions of the Reconstruction period. Eric L. McKitrick, *Andrew Johnson and Reconstruction* ° (Chicago: University of Chicago Press, 1960) is much more critical of the personal and political shortcomings of the President in formulating reconstruction policies, while John and La Wanda Cox, *Politics, Principles and Prejudices, 1865–1866* ° (New York: Free Press of Glencoe, 1963) bring out the additional factor of racism in many of Johnson's decisions. Kenneth Stampp, *The Era of Reconstruction, 1865–1877* ° (New York: Alfred A. Knopf, 1965) is a brief but brilliant synthesis of the historiography of Reconstruction; and Kenneth Stampp and Leon Litwack, eds., *Reconstruction: An Anthology of Revisionist Writings* ° (Baton Rouge: Louisiana State University Press, 1969) is a stimulating collection of recent articles dealing with Reconstruction. Harold Hyman, ed., *The Radical Republicans and Reconstruction, 1861–1870* ° (Indianapolis: Bobbs-Merrill, 1967), Richard N. Current, ed., *Reconstruction, 1865–1877* ° (Englewood Cliffs, N. J.: Prentice-Hall, 1965), Grady McWhiney, ed., *Reconstruction and the Freedmen* ° (Chicago: Rand McNally, 1963), Harvey Wish, ed., *Reconstruction in the South, 1865–1877* °

(New York: Farrar, Straus & Giroux, 1965), and Hans L. Trefousse, ed., *Background for Radical Reconstruction* * (Boston: Little, Brown, 1970) are useful editions of eyewitness accounts and contemporary documents. Edwin Rozwenc, ed., *Reconstruction in the South* * (Boston: D. C. Heath, 1952) and Seth M. Scheiner, ed., *Reconstruction: A Tragic Failure?* * (New York: Holt, Rinehart & Winston, 1968) provide interpretive readings on the Reconstruction era.

THE SOUTH AFTER THE CIVIL WAR

On conditions in the South during the postwar decades, E. Merton Coulter, *The South during Reconstruction* (Baton Rouge: Louisiana State University Press, 1947) is extremely valuable; and William B. Hesseltine, *Confederate Leaders in the New South* (Baton Rouge: Louisiana State University Press, 1950) provides a helpful study of the transition from war to peace. George Woolfolk, *The Cotton Regency* (New York: Bookman Associates, 1958) supplies a scholarly work on the interreaction of Northern merchants and the reconstruction process, while Jonathan Daniels, *Prince of Carpetbaggers: M. S. Littlefield* (Philadelphia: J. B. Lippincott, 1958) and Otto Olsen, *Carpetbagger's Crusade: The Life of Albion Winegar Tourgée* (Baltimore: Johns Hopkins Press, 1965) offer new insights into the lives and motives of leading carpetbaggers. Stanley Horn, *The Invisible Empire* (Boston: Houghton Mifflin, 1939) and Allen Trelease, *White Terror* (New York: Harper & Row, 1971) are reliable accounts of the Ku Klux Klan during the Reconstruction period. Robert Durden, *James Shepherd Pike* (Durham, N. C.: Duke University Press, 1954), Vincent P. De Santis, *Republicans Face the Southern Question* (Baltimore: Johns Hopkins Press, 1959), and Stanley P. Hirshson, *Farewell to the Bloody Shirt* * (Bloomington: Indiana University Press, 1962) are all extremely valuable studies of the relationship between the Northern Republican party and the Southern Negro. Jacobus ten Broek, *The Antislavery Origins of the Fourteenth Amendment* * (Berkeley: University of California Press, 1951) and William Gillette, *The Right to Vote: Politics and the Passage of the Fifteenth Amendment* (Baltimore: Johns Hopkins Press, 1970) contribute essential background for the constitutional aspects of the period.

THE BLACK MAN DURING RECONSTRUCTION

Robert Cruden, *The Negro in Reconstruction* * (Englewood Cliffs, N. J.: Prentice-Hall, 1969) is a sound, interpretive account of the black man during the Reconstruction era. John Eaton, *Grant, Lincoln and the Freedmen* (New York: Negro Universities Press, 1969) is a reprint of an old but still valuable study. George R. Bentley, *A History of the Freedmen's Bureau* (Philadelphia: University of Pennsylvania Press, 1955) and William McFeeley, *Yankee Stepfather: General O. O. Howard and the Freedmen* ° (New Haven: Yale University Press, 1969) provide scholarly studies of the operations of the Freedmen's Bureau; and Willie Lee Rose, *Rehearsal for Reconstruction: The Port Royal Experiment* ° (Indianapolis: Bobbs-Merrill, 1964) is a brilliant account of the attempts to establish equality on the sea islands of South Carolina. Otis Singletary, *Negro Militia and Reconstruction* ° (Austin: University of Texas Press, 1957) is an important monograph on the Negro militia movement; Samuel D. Smith, *The Negro in Congress, 1870–1901* (New York: Kennikat Press, 1966) focuses on the black man's political contributions; and Charles H. Wesley, *Negro Labor in the United States, 1850–1925* (New York: Vanguard Press, 1927) analyzes the role of the black man in the labor movement. W. E. B. Du Bois, *Black Reconstruction* ° (Philadelphia: Albert Saider, 1935) is essential reading as a pioneer work by a noted black scholar who brought to light the accomplishments of the Negro, and the reprint of his sensitive and moving *Souls of Black Folks* ° (New York: Fawcett Publications, 1961) contains material helpful to an understanding of the Reconstruction period. Francis B. Simkins and Robert H. Woody, *South Carolina During Reconstruction* (Chapel Hill: University of North Carolina Press, 1932), George B. Tindall, *South Carolina Negroes, 1877–1900* ° (Columbia: University of South Carolina Press, 1952), and Joel Williamson, *After Slavery: The Negro in South Carolina During Reconstruction* ° (Chapel Hill: University of North Carolina Press, 1965) are scholarly studies; and Hampton Jarrel, *Wade Hampton and the Negroes* (Columbia: University of South Carolina Press, 1949) views the black problem in South Carolina through the eyes of one of its white Reconstruction leaders. Joe M. Richardson, *The Negro in the Reconstruction of Florida, 1865–1877* (Tallahassee: Florida State University Press, 1965), Vernon L. Wharton, *The Negro in Mississippi, 1865–1890* ° (Chapel Hill: University of North Carolina Press, 1947), and Charles Wynes, *Race Relations in Virginia, 1870–1902* (Charlottesville: University of Virginia Press, 1961) are recent scholarly works of unusually high caliber dealing with the plight of the black man in various states. Rayford Logan, *The Negro in American Life and Thought: The Nadir: 1877–1901* °

(New York: Dial Press, 1954) is valuable for tracing the consequences of Reconstruction upon the black man in the years that followed.

PARTIES AND POLITICS IN THE POSTWAR ERA

Hans L. Trefousse, *The Radical Republicans: Lincoln's Vanguard for Racial Justice* (New York: Alfred A. Knopf, 1969) is a modern and much more sympathetic treatment of the Radical Republicans and their attempts to achieve full equality for the Negro; and David Donald's second volume, *Charles Sumner and the Rights of Man* (New York: Alfred A. Knopf, 1970) traces the important influence of the Massachusetts statesman during the postwar years. Ralph Korngold, *Thaddeus Stevens* (New York: Harcourt, Brace, 1955) and Fawn Brodie, *Thaddeus Stevens* * (New York: W. W. Norton, 1959) are sympathetic studies of the Pennsylvania Congressman, while Richard N. Current, *Old Thad Stevens* (Madison: University of Wisconsin Press, 1942) emphasizes his personal eccentricities and his political ambitions. Charles H. Coleman, *The Election of 1868* (New York: Columbia University Press, 1933) is the standard work on Grant's election; William B. Hesseltine, *Ulysses S. Grant, Politician* (New York: Dodd, Mead, 1935) is one of the few works that deal with the General's presidential years; and Stanley P. Hirshson, *Grenville M. Dodge* (Bloomington: Indiana University Press, 1967) is a helpful biography of one of the many Civil War generals who became prominent industrialists during the Age of Big Business that followed the War. Thomas C. Cochran and William Miller, *The Age of Enterprise* * (New York: Macmillan, 1942) and Edward C. Kirkland, *Industry Comes of Age* (New York: Holt, Rinehart & Winston, 1961) provide an excellent general background for the industrial transformation of the nation; David Montgomery, *Beyond Equality* (New York: Alfred A. Knopf, 1967) offers an unusual treatment of the relationship between organized labor and the Radical Republicans; and Robert V. Bruce, *1877: Year of Violence* * (Indianapolis: Bobbs-Merrill, 1959) gives an exciting account of the great railroad strikes. Recent works by Robert P. Sharkey, *Money, Class, and Party* * (Baltimore: Johns Hopkins Press, 1959), Irwin Unger, *The Greenback Era* (Princeton, N. J.: Princeton University Press, 1964), and Walter T. K. Nugent, *The Money Question During Reconstruction* * (New York: W. W. Norton, 1967) have done much to revise older views on the money question during the Reconstruction years. Glyndon Van Deusen, *Horace Greeley* * (New York: Hill & Wang, 1953) and Martin Duberman,

Charles Francis Adams * (Boston: Houghton Mifflin, 1961) are extremely helpful in understanding the Liberal Republican movement of the 1870's.

THE FINAL COMPROMISE

Paul L. Haworth, *The Hayes-Tilden Disputed Election of 1876* (Cleveland, Ohio: Burrows Brothers, 1906) is still the standard history of the disputed election; Alexander Flick, *Samuel Jones Tilden* (New York: Dodd, Mead, 1939) is a sound analysis of the New Yorker who was the Democratic candidate in 1876; and Harry Barnard, *Rutherford B. Hayes and His America* (Indianapolis: Bobbs-Merrill, 1954) is a valuable treatment of the Republican side of the picture. C. Vann Woodward, *Reunion and Reaction* * (Boston: Little, Brown, 1939) made a significant contribution to the historian's understanding of the Compromise of 1877 with the economic factors it brought to bear on the subject, and his *Origins of the New South, 1877–1913* * (Baton Rouge: Louisiana State University Press, 1951) is helpful in appreciating the last phases of Reconstruction. Paul H. Buck, *The Road to Reunion, 1865–1900* * (Boston: Little, Brown, 1937) is still a fascinating piece of social history which analyzes many of the factors that eventually led to reconciliation between the North and South by the end of the nineteenth century.

INDEX